Social Media and Election Campaigns

W0234956

This book aims to further the research in the fields of social media and political communication by moving beyond the hype and avoiding the most eye-catching and spectacular cases. It looks at stable democracies without current political turmoil, small countries as well as large continents, and minor political parties as well as major ones. Investigating emerging practices in the United States, Europe, and Australia, both on national and local levels, enables us to grasp contemporary tendencies across different regions and countries.

The book provides empirical insights into the diverse uses of different social media for political communication in different societies. Contributors look at the ways in which novel arenas connect with other channels for political communication, and how politicians as well as citizens in general use social media services. Presenting state-of-the-art methodological approaches, drawing on a combination of qualitative and quantitative analyses, the book brings together an interdisciplinary group of researchers in order to address emerging practices of the mediation of politics, campaign communication, and issues of citizenship and democracy as expressed on social media platforms.

This book was originally published as a special issue of *Information, Communication & Society*.

Gunn Enli is Professor of Media Studies and project leader for 'Social Media and Election Campaigns' (2012–2015) at the Department of Media and Communication at the University of Oslo, Norway. She has published extensively in the field of media and communication studies, with a recent focus on politics and social media, media history, Nordic media, and authenticity.

Hallvard Moe is Professor of Media Studies in the Department of Information Science and Media Studies at the University of Bergen, Norway. His research interests are public service broadcasting, online media, ICT and cultural policy, television studies, democratic theory, and media history.

Social Media and Election Campaigns

Key tendencies and ways forward

Edited by
Gunn Enli and Hallvard Moe

Routledge
Taylor & Francis Group

LONDON AND NEW YORK

First published 2015
by Routledge

2 Park Square, Milton Park, Abingdon, Oxon OX14 4RN
711 Third Avenue, New York, NY 10017, USA

Routledge is an imprint of the Taylor & Francis Group, an informa business

First issued in paperback 2017

British Library Cataloguing in Publication Data
A catalogue record for this book is available from the British Library

ISBN 13: 978-1-138-93046-9 (hbk)
ISBN 13: 978-1-138-08535-0 (pbk)

Typeset in Perpetua
by RefineCatch Limited, Bungay, Suffolk

Publisher's Note
The publisher accepts responsibility for any inconsistencies that may have
arisen during the conversion of this book from journal articles to book chapters,
namely the possible inclusion of journal terminology.

Disclaimer
Every effort has been made to contact copyright holders for their permission to
reprint material in this book. The publishers would be grateful to hear from any
copyright holder who is not here acknowledged and will undertake to rectify
any errors or omissions in future editions of this book.

Contents

CONTENTS

Citation Information

The chapters in this book were originally published in *Information, Communication & Society*, volume 16, issue 5 (June 2013). When citing this material, please use the original page numbering for each article, as follows:

Introduction

Introduction to special issue: Social media and election campaigns – key tendencies and ways forward
Gunn Enli and Hallvard Moe
Information, Communication & Society, volume 16, issue 5 (June 2013) pp. 637–645

Chapter 1

Wave-riding and hashtag-jumping: Twitter, minority 'third parties' and the 2012 US elections
Christian Christensen
Information, Communication & Society, volume 16, issue 5 (June 2013) pp. 646–666

Chapter 2

Political networks on Twitter: *Tweeting the Queensland state election*
Axel Bruns and Tim Highfield
Information, Communication & Society, volume 16, issue 5 (June 2013) pp. 667–691

Chapter 3

Between broadcasting political messages and interacting with voters: The use of Twitter during the 2010 UK general election campaign
Todd Graham, Marcel Broersma, Karin Hazelhoff and Guido van 't Haar
Information, Communication & Society, volume 16, issue 5 (June 2013) pp. 692–716

Chapter 4

Mastering the art of social media: Swiss parties, the 2011 national election and digital challenges
Ulrike Klinger
Information, Communication & Society, volume 16, issue 5 (June 2013) pp. 717–736

Chapter 5

Dodging the gatekeepers?: Social media in the campaign mix during the 2011 Danish elections
Morten Skovsgaard and Arjen Van Dalen
Information, Communication & Society, volume 16, issue 5 (June 2013) pp. 737–756

Chapter 6

Personalized campaigns in party-centred politics: Twitter and Facebook as arenas for political communication
Gunn Sara Enli and Eli Skogerbø
Information, Communication & Society, volume 16, issue 5 (June 2013) pp. 757–774

Chapter 7

Untangling a complex media system: A comparative study of Twitter-linking practices during three Scandinavian election campaigns
Hallvard Moe and Anders Olof Larsson
Information, Communication & Society, volume 16, issue 5 (June 2013) pp. 775–794

Chapter 8

An investigation of influentials and the role of sentiment in political communication on Twitter during election periods
Linh Dang-Xuan, Stefan Stieglitz, Jennifer Wladarsch and Christoph Neuberger
Information, Communication & Society, volume 16, issue 5 (June 2013) pp. 795–825

For any permission-related enquiries please visit:
http://www.tandfonline.com/page/help/permissions

Notes on Contributors

Marcel Broersma is Professor of Journalism Studies and Media, and heads the Groningen Centre for Media and Journalism Studies, University of Groningen, The Netherlands. His research interests focus on the current and historical transformation of European journalism. He currently directs research projects on the impact of digital technology on journalism, on changing role perceptions, and on the transformation of the form, style, and strategies of European Journalism between 1880 and 2005. He has published widely on both the history and current development of journalism, most recently *Rethinking Journalism: Trust and Participation in a Transformed News Landscape* (Routledge, 2013; edited with Chris Peters).

Axel Bruns is Associate Professor in the Creative Industries Faculty at Queensland University of Technology, Brisbane, Australia, and a Chief Investigator in the ARC Centre of Excellence for Creative Industries and Innovation. He is the author of *Blogs, Wikipedia, Second Life and Beyond: From Production to Produsage* (2008) and *Gatewatching: Collaborative Online News Production* (2005), and a co-editor of *A Companion to New Media Dynamics* (2012, with John Hartley and Jean Burgess) and *Uses of Blogs* (2006, with Joanne Jacobs). He is an expert on the impact of user-led content creation, or produsage, and his current work focuses on the study of user participation in social media spaces such as Twitter, especially in the context of acute events.

Christian Christensen is Professor in the Department of Media Studies at Stockholm University, Sweden.

Linh Dang-Xuan is a Ph.D. candidate in Information Systems and a Research Assistant of the Research Group for Communication and Collaboration Management in the Department of Information Systems at the University of Münster, Germany. His current research areas are computer-mediated communication, online social networks, and web data mining. His research has been presented at many conferences and he has also published in several reputable journals such as *Journal of Management Information Systems* and *Social Network Analysis and Mining*.

Gunn Enli is Professor of Media Studies and project leader for 'Social Media and Election Campaigns' (2012–2015) at the Department of Media and Communication at the University of Oslo, Norway. She has published extensively in the field of media and communication studies, with a recent focus on politics and social media, media history, Nordic media, and authenticity.

Todd Graham is an Assistant Professor in Political Communication at the Groningen Centre for Media and Journalism Studies, University of Groningen, The Netherlands. His main research interests include (new) media and democracy, popular culture, online journalism, online deliberation, public sphere theory, and deliberative democratic theory.

Karin Hazelhoff completed her Master's in Journalism at the University of Groningen, The Netherlands. She is now an independent researcher.

Tim Highfield is Research Fellow in the ARC Centre of Excellence for Creative Industries and Innovation at Queensland University of Technology, Brisbane, Australia. He was awarded his Ph.D. in 2011 from Queensland University of Technology for research into political blogging in Australia and France.

Ulrike Klinger is Senior Research and Teaching Associate in the Department of Media and Politics at the Institute for Mass Communication and Media Research at the University of Zurich, Switzerland. Her research focuses on political communication, online communication, and comparative studies.

Anders Olof Larsson is a Postdoctoral Research Fellow at the University of Oslo, Norway.

Hallvard Moe is Professor of Media Studies in the Department of Information Science and Media Studies at the University of Bergen, Norway. His research interests are public service broadcasting, online media, ICT and cultural policy, television studies, democratic theory, and media history.

Christoph Neuberger is Professor in the Department of Communication Science and Media Research at Ludwig-Maximilians-University, Munich, Germany. His research focuses on the Internet (public sphere, online journalism, activities of the press and broadcasting media on the Internet, search engines, social media), journalism, media quality, and media change. He has published several books and articles in journals such as *Journalism*, *Journalism Practice*, *European Journal of Communication*, *Publizistik*, and *Medien und Kommunikationswissenschaft*.

Eli Skogerbø is Professor in the Department of Media and Communication, University of Oslo, Norway. She participates in the networked project Social

Media and Agenda-Setting in Election Campaigns (2012–2015), financed by the Norwegian Research Council and in related projects. She has published extensively on political communications and media policy.

Morten Skovsgaard is an Assistant Professor at the Center for Journalism/ Department of Political Science at the University of Southern Denmark, Odense, Denmark. He wrote his Ph.D. dissertation on the professional norms, values, and autonomy of Danish journalists. His research interests are journalism and political communication, particularly on journalists' professional ideals, their practice, and the effects of their products on the audience. He has published in books such as *The Global Journalists in the 21st Century* and journals such as *Journalism*, *Journalism Studies*, and *Journalism Practice*.

Stefan Stieglitz is an Assistant Professor in Communication and Collaboration Management at the Department of Information Systems at the University of Münster, Germany. He is founder and academic director of the Competence Center Connected Organization at the European Research Center for Information Systems. His work is interested in investigating the usage of social media in enterprises and political context, and his research focuses on economic, social, and technological aspects of collaboration software. He has published several articles in reputable international journals such as *Journal of Management Information Systems*, *Communications of the AIS*, *MIS Quarterly Executive*, and *International Journal of Social Research Methodology*.

Arjen Van Dalen is an Assistant Professor at the Center for Journalism/Department of Political Science at the University of Southern Denmark, Odense, Denmark. He wrote his Ph.D. dissertation on Political Journalism in Comparative Perspective. His research interests are in comparative communication research, in particular the relations between journalists and politicians. He has published about these topics in *The Global Journalists in the 21st Century* and journals such as the *European Journal of Communication*, *Political Communication*, *International Journal of Press/Politics*, and *Journalism Practice*.

Guido van 't Haar is a research master student in Modern History and International Relations at the University of Groningen, The Netherlands, and worked on this project through the Academy Assistantship Programme for talented research master students, funded by the Netherlands Organisation for Scientific Research.

Jennifer Wladarsch is a Ph.D. candidate in Communication Science and Research Assistant at the Department of Communication Science and Media Research at Ludwig-Maximilians-University, Munich, Germany. Her research focuses on (online) journalism and social media. Her research has been presented at national and European conferences.

Gunn Enli & Hallvard Moe

INTRODUCTION TO SPECIAL ISSUE
Social media and election campaigns –
key tendencies and ways forward

Introduction

The field of social media and political communication is currently surrounded by hype. A shared interest between different academic branches, such as informatics, social science, humanities, and marketing/PR-studies (e.g. Woolley *et al.* 2010; Bruns *et al.* 2011; Scott 2011; Vergeer 2013), in addition to a massive public interest in mainstream media and social media, have driven the topic into the top league among researchers. The huge interest is largely a result of couplings between the 'social media and political communication'-field, and hyped phenomena such as Barrack Obama and the Arab Spring, which were widely interpreted in light of social media (Christensen 2011).

This special issue aims to bring the research in the field of 'social media and political communication' a step further, by moving beyond the hype, by avoiding the most eye-catching and spectacular cases. It looks at stable democracies without current political turmoil, small countries as well as large continents, and minor political parties as well as major ones. Investigating emerging practices in the United States, Europe, and Australia, both on national and local levels, enables us to grasp contemporary tendencies across different regions and countries, and thus avoid an over-emphasis on the most obvious cases.

Online politics have, in line with former innovations of new media technology, been expected to reduce the power of the elites, and to enable a more democratic participation. The most idealistic expectations have largely resulted in disappointment, and thus follow the pattern of previously new media technologies such as broadcast radio, cable television, and local media (Skogerbø 1996; Loader & Mercea 2012; Larsson 2013 for discussion). We aim to move beyond dichotomies such as innovation/normalization (Schweitzer 2008), optimist/pessimist (Bentivegna 2006), shift/enhancement (Jackson & Lilleker 2009). While different social media are by now routinely ascribed key roles during election campaigns by political actors as well as the mainstream media, it nevertheless remains unclear to what extent they are used – by whom and for what purposes

– and how they relate to the overall media landscape. Our ambition is to investigate how these dynamics are manifested in times when political communication is at its most strategic, pre-planned, and intense: During election campaigns in stable democracies across the world.

This special issue provides empirical insights into the diverse uses of different social media for political communication in different societies. The articles look at the ways in which novel arenas connect with other channels for political communication, and how politicians as well as citizens in general use the services. Presenting findings from studies in the United States, Switzerland, Germany, Norway, Sweden, Denmark, and Australia, based on state-of-the-art methodological approaches drawing on a combination of qualitative and quantitative analyses, the issue brings together an interdisciplinary group of researchers in order to address emerging practices of the mediation of politics, campaign communication, and issues of citizenship and democracy as expressed on social media platforms.

Social media definitions and the aim of this issue

'Social media' is, as catchphrases tend to be, not easy to pin down. A widespread approach is to list specific existing services (such as MySpace, Facebook, YouTube, Twitter, Tumblr, Sina Weibo, and Cyworld), or more or less established web genres (e.g. blogs or microblogs) (e.g. Hansen *et al.* 2011; Nah & Saxton 2013 for discussion). Such an approach gives an impression of some of the instances we are dealing with. Another approach is to link social media to earlier buzzwords like Web 2.0 or user-generated content (UGC). In some instances, this approach leads to quite sophisticated definitions. Within the field of management studies, Kaplan and Haenlein (2010, p. 61) describe social media as 'a group of Internet-based applications that build on the ideological and technological foundations of Web 2.0, and that allow the creation and exchange of User Generated Content', which they further classify according to the richness of the medium and what degree of social presence the medium allows for. The challenge with such an approach lies in its fundament, since Web 2.0 and UGC are no less amorphous and difficult to define than social media.

Yet other definitory attempts start from social network sites, often building on boyd and Ellison's (2007) definition of the latter. Social media is sometimes used interchangeably with social network sites (e.g. Aalen 2013; Curran *et al.* 2012). Others describe social media as one step further from social network sites, as technological advances made audio-visual content more important, and the sites got connected to traditional media actors – e.g. in the case of News Corp. acquiring MySpace (Mjøs 2012). This approach seems hard to apply as a general definition, as it depicts a historical movement found in some cases, but far from all. In other takes on social media, it is 'an umbrella term that refers to the set of tools, services, and applications that allow people to interact with others using network technologies' (boyd 2008, p. 92). This means social media not only predates social network sites, but also the internet itself, and include email and other systems that facilitate one-to-one communication.

Focusing on the perception of the users, Bechmann and Lomborg (2012) highlight three characteristics to define social media. First, the ability each user has to make, contribute, filter and share content means 'communication is de-institutionalized' (Bechmann & Lomborg 2012, p. 3). Second, the user is seen as producer and participant. Third, 'interaction and networked' describe the communication between users and their shifting roles (Bechmann & Lomborg 2012, p. 3). For Bechmann and Lomborg, these characteristics open up a double-sidedness in media studies approaches, since the user is empowered or exploited, depending on whether one takes a user-centric perspective or an industry-centric one.

The contributions in this issue address this tension. All the articles assess the degree to which different practices adhere to the characteristics of social media. They ask to what degree communication on these new platforms is de-institutionalized, who the users, producers and participants are, and to what extent they employ the potential to contribute, filter and share, and in which ways this leads to interactive and networked communication. Some of the analyses concentrate on specific services, like Twitter and Facebook, while others look at bouquets of services, some of which would be included in definitions of social media, and some that would not. In these instances, the connections between new platforms and established ones are scrutinized. A shared aim of all the contributions is to analyze emerging practices to get a better grasp of how social the media are: to what extent the uses of these novel platforms for communication adhere to their potential, and how they fit in a wider media ecology.

The articles: three key tendencies

Individually, the contributions provide insights into varied practices. The articles include studies of individual countries with quite different political system and media landscapes: the United States, Australia, United Kingdom, Germany, and Switzerland. In addition, the contributions present results from studies of regions such as the Scandinavian, with a comparative approach to recent election campaigns in Sweden, Norway, and Denmark. In the era of 'big data', the articles show how a mix of methodological approaches and data sets – ranging from qualitative interviews and qualitative content analysis, via quantitative survey data to large-scale computer-assisted quantitative analysis of massive data sets – are needed to yield a comprehensive picture of the emerging practices (see also boyd & Crawford 2012).

Together, then, the articles point to some tendencies in the emerging practices of social media and election campaigns:

Personalized campaigning

The studies discussed in this issue identify a tendency in which the personalized
relationship with the voters have been strengthened as a result of social media.
This tendency is identified in several contribution to this issue, including Enli and
Skogerbø's study of Norwegian campaigning which pinpoint that social media
have strengthened the tendency of an increased personalization of the political
campaigning, meaning that sharing of private images and messages containing
non-political information have become more common in tandem with the
spread of social media. Moreover, in their study of Danish politics, Van Dalen
and Skovsgaard find that the politicians used Twitter and Facebook to strengthen
their position in intra-party competition, and that communication directly with
the voters were among the key motivations for being active on social media.

Still, the increasingly personalized campaigning did not result in an extensive
amount of dialogue between voters and politicians. The politicians' use of social
media might be motivated by a wish to establish a dialogue with voters, but in
practice, this form of communication is limited. As a result, broadcasting of political messages is a more common tendency than to engage in dialogue with the
public. In the study from United Kingdom, Graham, Broersma, Hazelhoff, and
Van't Haar found that even though the large majority of the tweets were defined
as broadcasting, a quarter of all tweets were reciprocal. Comparably higher, reciprocal elements were found among the tweets in the analyzed Norwegian election campaign. These numbers are explained by the fact that the active Twitter
users in the sample were fairly few, but nevertheless very engaged and com-
mitted to take advantage of the interactive potential of the new media technology, and as such avoid the professional distance or the strictly political messaging.
This again implies that the sample of tweets included a share of fairly private
tweets, reporting on interests such as the politicians' favorite football team,
and dialogue with users about other subjects than politics. As a result, we see
a strengthened position of the semi-private politician, which we also know
from television talk shows and other behind-the-scenes genres such as the political biography and the interview with the gossip magazines. Still, election campaigns in social media nevertheless has increased personalization, and enabled
a more individualistic and private, and less mass media-drive and gatekeeper-
influenced, political communication.

Beyond the hype

A second tendency demonstrated by the articles concerns what is beneath the
surface. Political communication is not revolutionized, and the degree of

change is limited and modest. New digital communication technology has imposed changes on political campaigns, but not to an extent that contradicts traditional media campaign strategies. The hype surrounding social media in election campaigns is largely a result of the media-friendly success story of President Barrack Obama's use of Twitter and Facebook to communicate with young people and hard-to-reach user groups. In this volume, Christensen moves beyond the Obama case, and rather studies US minority political parties, and how they include social media in their campaign strategy in a climate where the two main parties dominate media coverage of politics in mainstream media outlets. Elsewhere, the hype is contrasted by findings in the studies of less obvious cases than the United States. Analyses of social media use during election campaigns in small countries, such as Scandinavia and Switzerland, and during regional and local campaigns in Norway, Germany, and Australia, enable investigations on a small-scale, yielding new kinds of insights.

Nielsen (2011, p. 759), in a US-based study, found that '[...] campaigns depend on a wide range of internet tools in their relations with their surroundings, and most of these tools are increasingly mundane, not developed specifically for political purposes, and equally available to staffers and volunteers'. Email is Nielsen's main example, and he contrasts such mundane services to emerging and specialized ones. The articles in this issue show how new services grow mundane. Twitter and Facebook are by no means lumped into the same category as mass emails. Still, the insights offered across the contributions presented here illustrate how the use of social media to a certain extent has moved beyond the unstable, pioneering phase. As a consequence, the practices found and discussed in the contributions describe a nuanced everyday-like use among diverse groups.

Context matters

As social scientists, we know, of course, that social, cultural, and political context matters. Still, studies from various cultural and political setting bring to light how social media use for political communication is not an isolated phenomenon with a set of internal and deterministic rules. Rather, the impact of social media on election campaigns is fairly diverse across different regions and countries, depending on media environments, cultural practices, and political systems. Even measures such as the size of the country, and the number of inhabitants which the politicians relate to as (potential) voters, matter for political communication, and its forms and intensity across platforms. This issue illuminates the variety of uses in countries of different size, but this is also inseparable from other cultural and political factors, such as the political system.

As an emerging field, social media and political communication clearly benefits from a combined social science and humanities approach, alongside approaches from informatics and computer science. Indeed, studies paying due attention to local contexts and cultural factors such as social divides, standards of living, educational level, and language and linguistics, should provide a more fruitful and rich understanding of the phenomena at hand.

Because social media, as demonstrated in several of the studies presented here, are part of the total campaign mix, discussions of media systems and theoretical insights from the field of media studies have come across as a valuable strength in this issue. The articles each in their own way illuminate how the surrounding media structures and systems impose on how the use of social media. One example is how a media situation where a large share of the politicians only has limited access to mainstream media will increase the emphasis on social media. The extreme cases are often found in regimes with restricted or even censured media, but we should not ignore differences in media systems also within the stable democracies, which are under scrutiny in this issue. For example, commercial and often large companies dominate the US media landscape, while a mix of public and private media companies characterizes the British and the Scandinavian media cultures. These opposites point to the importance of including social, cultural, political contexts in analyzes of social media's impact on election campaigns. This issue demonstrates the importance of analysing smaller and less obvious countries than the United States, in order to pinpoint how social media practices emerge differently in various contexts.

Ways forward

Building on the individual articles and the overarching tendencies discussed here, we can highlight three aspects, which will be of importance as the research on social media and political communication move forward.

First, the articles pinpoint a potentially powerful dynamic between mainstream media and social media, which, uncovers a research gap in the field of social media and political communication. A mutual influence between user-generated content and mass communication has evolved over time, and is not exclusive for political media (Enli 2009). Still, inter-media dynamics has become an increasingly important factor in political campaigning, which should be addressed in research. One step in the right direction is *inter-media agenda-setting* studies, which seeks to identify how new outlets such as social media work with mainstream media as a communicative power in relation to the political arena (Lee *et al.* 2005; Lim 2006; Wallsten 2007; Sweetser *et al.* 2008). Further, with such a framework, one seeks to identify key patterns in a new, hybrid media ecology, and to examine to what degree traditional power-hierarchies are challenged. We will suggest that classic insights and theories from the field of agenda-setting studies are implemented and revitalized in the field of 'social media and political communication', because the fast-paced dynamics requires an updated, and theoretically grounded, methodological framework.

A second consequence of the findings in the present contributions is that the research on social media and political communication would benefit from more studies of Facebook. As of now, the analytical focus on Twitter risks to overshadow Facebook studies, not least because the methods for tracking and downloading Twitter data have made it the preferred social medium to study. Such pragmatic reasons do not make Twitter data any less sound or rich, and the need to continue Twitter studies seems evident. Nevertheless, we want to make a point about the mismatch between the widespread uses of Facebook both by publics/voters, and by politicians, and the limited research devoted to Facebook as a tool for political communication.

This points to a third issue for the field, which has to do with methods and data. There is a continued need to strengthen efforts of methodological innovations, for quantitative as well as qualitative analyses, and across specific emerging and fading services. An important part of this effort should be to increase the sharing of data and tools for data gathering. We should strive to avoid situations where replications of previous studies are made difficult for technical reasons, or where technical issues hinder the fruitful combination of different data sets (e.g. Bruns & Liang 2012; Moe & Larsson 2012). Such endeavors will also make key ethical issues with studying internet use all the more evident.

References

Aalen, I. (2013) *En kort bok om sosiale medier.* Fagbokforlaget, Bergen.

Bechmann, A. & Lomborg, S. (2012) 'Mapping actor roles in social media: different perspectives on value creation in theories of user participation', *New Media & Society*, pp. 1–18. Published online 26 November 2012. doi:10.1177/1461444812462853.

Bentivegna, S. (2006) 'Rethinking politics in the world of ICTs', *European Journal of Communication*, vol. 21, no. 3, pp. 331–343.

boyd, d. (2008) *Taken out of context: American teen sociality in networked publics*, Doctoral Thesis, University of California, Berkeley, CA. Available at: http://www.zephoria.org/thoughts/archives/2009/01/18/taken_out_of_co.html

boyd, d. & Crawford, K. (2012) 'Critical questions for big data', *Information, Communication & Society*, vol. 15, no. 5, pp. 662–679.

boyd, d. & Ellison, N. B. (2007) 'Social network sites: definition, history, and scholarship', *Journal of Computer-Mediated Communication*, vol. 13, no. 1, Available at: http://jcmc.indiana.edu/vol13/issue1/boyd.ellison.html (8 April 2013).

Bruns, A. & Liang, X. E. (2012) 'Tools and methods for capturing Twitter data during natural disasters', *First Monday*, vol. 17, no. 4.

Bruns, A., Burgess, J., Highfield, T., Kirchhoff, L. & Nicolai, T. (2011) 'Mapping the Australian networked public sphere', *Social Science Computer Review*, vol. 29, no. 3, pp. 277–287.

Christensen, C. (2011) 'Discourses of technology and liberation: state aid to net activists in an era of "Twitter revolutions"', *The Communication Review*, vol. 14, no. 3, pp. 233–253.

Curran, J., Freedman, D. & Fenton, N. (2012) *Misunderstanding the Internet*, Routledge, London.

Enli, G. S. (2009) 'Mass communication tapping into participatory culture. Exploring *strictly come dancing* and *Britain's got talent*', *European Journal of Communication*, vol. 24, no. 4, pp. 481–493.

Hansen, D. L., Shneiderman, B. & Smith, M. A. (2011) *Analyzing Social Media Networks with NodeXL: Insights from a Connected World*, Elsevier, New York.

Jackson, N. A. & Lilleker, D. G. (2009) 'Building an architecture of participation? Political parties and web. 2.0, in Britain', *Journal of Information Technology and Politics*, vol. 6, no. 3, pp. 232–250.

Kaplan, A. M. & Haenlein, M. (2010) 'Users of the world, unite! The challenges and opportunities of Social Media', *Business Horizons*, vol. 53, no. 1, pp. 59–68.

Larsson, Anders (2013) '"Rejected bits of program code": why notions of "politics 2.0. Remain (Mostly) unfulfilled"', *Journal of Information Technology & Politics*, vol. 10, no. 1, pp. 72–85.

Lee, B., Lancendorfer, K. M. & Lee, K. J. (2005) 'Agenda-setting and the internet: the intermedia influence of internet bulletin boards on newspaper coverage of the 2000 general election in South Korea', *Asian Journal of Communication*, vol. 15, no. 1, pp. 57–71.

Lim, J. (2006) 'A cross-lagged analysis of agenda setting among online news media', *Journalism & Mass Communication Quarterly*, vol. 83, no. 2, pp. 298–312.

Loader, B. D. & Mercea, D. (2012) 'Networking democracy? Social media innovations in participatory politics', in *Social Media and Democracy: Innovations in Partcipatory Politics*, eds B. D. Loader & D. Merca, Routledge, New York, pp. 1–10.

Mjøs, O. J. (2012) *Music, Social Media and Global Mobility: MySpace, Facebook, YouTube*, Routledge, New York.

Moe, H. & Larsson, A. O. (2012) 'Methodological and ethical challenges with large-scale analyses of online political communication', *Nordicom Review*, vol. 33, no. 1, pp. 117–125.

Nah, S. & Saxton, G. D. (2013) 'Modeling the adoption and use of social media by nonprofit organizations', *New Media & Society*, vol. 15, no. 2, pp. 294–313.

Nielsen, R. K. (2011) 'Mundane internet tools, mobilizing practices, and the coproduction of citizenship in political campaigns', *New Media & Society*, vol. 13, no. 5, pp. 755–771.

Schweitzer, E. J. (2008) 'Innovation or normalization in e-campaigning? A longitudinal content and structural analysis of German party Websites in the 2002 and 2005 national elections', *European Journal of Communication*, vol. 23, no. 4, pp. 449–470.

Scott, D. M. (2011) *The New Rules of Marketing & PR: How to Use Social Media, Online Video, Mobile Applications, Blogs, News Releases, and Viral marketing to Reach Buyers Directly*, Wiley, Horboken, NJ.

Skogerbø, E. (1996) *Privatising the Public Interest: Conflicts and Compromises in Norwegian Media Politics 1980–1993*, Doctoral Dissertation, University of Oslo, Oslo.

Sweetser, K. D., Golan, G. J. & Wanta, W. (2008) 'Intermedia agenda setting in television, advertising, and blogs during the 2004 election', *Mass Communication and Society*, vol. 11, no. 2, pp. 197–216.

Vergeer, M. (February 2013) 'Politics, elections and online campaigning: past, present. . . and a peek into the future', *New Media & Society*, vol. 15, pp. 9–17.

Wallsten, K. (2007) 'Agenda setting and the blogosphere: an analys of the relationship between mainsteam media and political blogs', *Review of Policy Research*, vol. 24, no. 6.

Woolley, J. K., Limperos, A. M. & Oliver, M. B. (2010) 'The 2008 presidential election, 2.0: a content analysis of user- generated political facebook groups', *Mass Communication and Society*, vol. 13, no. 13, pp. 631–652.

Christian Christensen

WAVE-RIDING AND HASHTAG-JUMPING
Twitter, minority 'third parties' and the 2012 US elections

With the description of the 2012 election as the 'most tweeted' political event in US history in mind, considering the relative media invisibility of the so-called 'third-party' presidential candidates in the US election process, and utilizing the understanding of retweeting as conversational practice, the purpose of this paper is to examine the use of Twitter by the four main 'third-party' US presidential candidates in the run-up to the 2012 presidential election in order to better understand (1) the volume of tweets produced by the candidates; (2) the level of interaction by followers in the form of retweeting candidate/party tweets; and, (3), the subject and content of the tweets most retweeted by followers of the respective parties. The ultimate goal of the paper is to generate a broader picture of how Twitter was utilized by minority party candidates, as well as identifying the issues which led followers (and their respective followers) to engage in the 'conversational' act of retweeting.

Introduction

In the early hours of 7 November 2012, and upon receiving confirmation that he had been re-elected President of the United States, Barack Obama sent out what has come to be the most retweeted message in the short-but-hyped history of Twitter. Within a matter of hours the simple message 'Four more years', together with a picture of Obama embracing his wife, Michelle, generated over 400,000 retweets. At the time of the writing of this article – in early January 2013 – the tweet has reached over 817,000 retweets, and just over

304,000 'Favorites'. Such was Obama's dominance in the Twittersphere that the most retweeted message (by far) during the *Republican* National Convention was Obama's humorous response to actor Clint Eastwood's convention speech in which Eastwood engaged in mock conversation with an empty chair (meant to signify Obama). Obama's response – containing a picture of the president taken from behind his chair in the Oval Office – was brief: 'This seat's taken'. Within three days the tweet received over 50,000 retweets, compared to a rather thin 4,800 retweets for Republican nominee Mitt Romney's most retweeted message during his own convention: 'Our economy runs on freedom, not government. It's time we put our faith back in the American people'.

As was widely reported by the United States and international media, the 2012 election was the 'most tweeted event' in US political history, with 10 million tweets during the first presidential debate, and over 20 million tweets sent on 6 November regarding the battle between Obama and Romney. At the point at which the election results began to come in on the US east coast, Twitter reported that 327,000 tweets were being sent per minute. Of course, with 19 million (Obama) and one million (Romney) Twitter followers respectively, high levels of retweeting were to be expected, yet Democrats and Republicans were not the only parties taking part in the 2012 elections. For example, Libertarian Party candidate Gary Johnson also sent out a message of thanks to his voters in the early hours of 7 November 2012, in which he wrote: 'Nobody who votes their conscience wastes a vote. Thank you for making history today'. The tweet generated over 1,700 retweets and 700 favorites: nowhere near the half-million obtained by Obama, but impressive considering Johnson's relatively modest Twitter following of 100,000 (and not insignificant in comparison to the 12,000 retweets of Mitt Romney's 10 November message of thanks to his one million followers).

With the description of the 2012 election as the 'most tweeted' political event in US history in mind, considering the relative media invisibility of the so-called 'third-party' presidential candidates in the US election process, and utilizing the boyd *et al.* (2010) understanding of retweeting as conversational practice, the purpose of this paper is to examine the use of Twitter by the four main 'third-party' US presidential candidates in the run-up to the 2012 presidential election in order to better understand (1) the volume of tweets produced by the candidates, (2) the level of interaction by followers in the form of retweeting candidate/party tweets, and (3) the subject and content of the tweets most retweeted by followers of the respective parties. The ultimate goal of the paper is to generate a broader picture of how Twitter was utilized by minority party candidates, as well as identifying the issues which led followers (and their respective followers) to engage in the 'conversational' act of retweeting.

Third-party candidates

There are a wide range of minority parties in the United States, ranging from the neo-Nazi National Socialist Movement Party to the Communist Party of the United States. The majority of the smaller parties have some form of presence on social media, yet, for the purposes of this study, four so-called 'third parties' were selected: The Libertarian Party, Green Party, Constitution Party and Justice Party. The selection was based upon one clear criterion: that the party had either ballot access or 'write-in access' to at least 270 electoral votes: the minimum required to win the Presidency in the Electoral College system (whereby candidates are awarded 'electoral college votes' when winning the popular vote in a given state). Two of the four parties – Libertarian (515 possible votes) and Green (457 possible votes) – had more than the minimum number of votes available via ballot access alone (i.e. the name of the party candidate was already listed on the state voting ballot); the name of the Constitution Party candidate appeared on state ballots totaling 257 possible votes, thus meaning that the party had to secure at least 23 more electoral vote states via write-in ballots, which it did. Finally, the Justice Party had only secured the candidate name on ballots totaling 145 electoral votes, but, impressively, managed to make up the difference via write-in ballots. The Libertarians were eligible to win 531 of 538 possible votes, the Greens 458, the Constitution Party 390 and the Justice Party 305.

Libertarian Party (@GovGaryJohnson)

The Libertarian Party candidate was the former Republican governor of New Mexico, Gary Johnson (Johnson switched political parties in 2011). The Libertarian Party is the third largest party in the United States, and is marked by a firm belief in the reduction of state influence in and over socio-economic life. Although difficult to define, the party is marked by a combination of fiscal conservatism (e.g. the deregulation of markets, consumer competition) social liberalism (e.g. the legalization of marijuana and support for same-sex marriage) and geo-political isolationism (e.g. withdrawal from the United Nations). Johnson received 1,276,000 popular votes (0.99 percent).

Green Party (@jillstein2012)

The Green Party candidate was Jill Stein, a physician from the state of Massachusetts. The Green Party was founded in 1991, and does not accept any donations from corporations, and operates under what are known as their 'Ten Key Values': Grassroots democracy, social justice and equal opportunity, ecological wisdom, nonviolence, decentralization, community-based economics, feminism and gender equality, respect for diversity, personal and global responsibility, future focus and sustainability. Stein received 470,000 popular votes (0.36 percent).

Constitution Party (@cnstutionprty)

The Constitution Party candidate was Virgil Goode, a member of the US House of Representatives as a Democrat (1997–2000) and Republican (2000–2008). Goode left the Republican Party and became the Constitution Party candidate in 2012. The party is considered to be Conservative Christian, with the ideological basis being a stricter adherence to the US Constitution and the Bible, and is both fiscally and socially conservative as well as internationally isolationist. Goode received 122,000 popular votes (0.09 percent).

Justice Party (@RockyAnderson)

The Justice Party candidate was former Democratic Mayor of Salt Lake City, Rocky Anderson. The primary focus of the party is on economic, social and environmental justice, and the elimination of corporate influence over US political and social life. In relative terms, the Justice Party is considered to be to the left of the Democratic Party, with candidate Anderson frequently stating his dissatisfaction with the corporate drift of the Democrats. Anderson received 43,000 popular votes (0.03 percent).

Review of literature

While the theoretical focus of this paper is on communicative elements and processes in relation to Twitter, it is important to begin this section by framing the study within the context of third-party politics in the United States. To begin, Lem and Dowling (2006) have written that scholars have attributed the very existence of third-party politics in the United States to 'ideological gaps created by major party competition' (p. 471). The 2000 elections, which saw over 15 million American voters cast ballots for candidates other than a Republican or Democrat was trumpeted as evidence that many US voters are, in fact, searching for alternatives to mainstream political fare (Lem & Dowling 2006, p. 471). The current paper is a study in the use of Twitter by smaller, more marginalized political parties such as the Greens and Libertarians – along with their smaller follower numbers and organizational infrastructure – who, importantly, bear the burden of socio-political barriers not present for Democratic and Republican candidates. Former presidential candidate for the Green Party, Ralph Nader, wrote a co-authored article in which barriers such as sparse media coverage, limited ballot access and refusals to participate in presidential debates were outlined (Nader & Amato 2001, p. 163). The issue of limited media coverage for third-party candidates discussed by the authors is salient in relation to the use of Twitter. In a wide-ranging study on the rhetoric of third-party politics in the United States, Shepard (2011) wrote that the mainstream media have traditionally marginalized third-party candidates, characterizing them as, 'the freak show in the electoral circus' (p. 9). In part due to this marginalization, and in part due to the paucity of media exposure, Shepard notes that third-party candidates have (historically) utilized a rhetorical style that is, 'polarizing, populist, rich in markers of authenticity, and aimed at producing public spectacle' (p. iii). Thus, social media such as Twitter can be seen as providing new opportunities to candidates relegated to the electoral margins.

The rise of Twitter and other forms of social media as factors in election campaigns in the United States and globally, although relatively recent phenomena, have been well-documented in academic research (e.g. Golbeck *et al.* 2010; Baxter & Marcella 2012; Dylko *et al.* 2012; Gasser & Gerlach 2012; Hong & Nadler 2012; Larsson & Moe 2012; Strandberg 2013) Grusell and Nord (2012) have noted that Twitter is a particularly interesting media form to examine in relation to political campaigns due to the relative newness of the tool, and the fact that the brevity of the messaging system (with a maximum of 140 characters) raises questions regarding both the possibilities and efficacy of Twitter as a vehicle for political mobilization and support (p. 49). The use of online media for the purposes of engaging, 'those ... marginalized from the existing political system' was the cornerstone of what was known as a 'mobilization thesis' whereby the aforementioned marginalized groups could, via online participation become 'drawn into public life and civic communities' (Norris 2001, p. 218; cited in Strandberg 2013).

The idea of using Twitter for the purposes of mobilization discussed by Norris (2001), Strandberg (2013) and others raises the question of the distinction between social media use for the purposes of political *participation* versus political *communication*. Hoffman (2012) notes that much of what passes for online political 'participation' in both academic research and popular discourse, is, in fact, political communication. In addition, in her study, the author notes that not only is the number of people engaging online relatively small, but also that:

> the activities they engage in most have little to do with what many would define as political participation in the true sense. Indeed, the most frequently reported activities were watching online video from a campaign or news organization (50 per cent), discovering on a social networking site which candidate a friend voted for (42 per cent), and communicating with others about politics via email or text messaging (33 per cent). Importantly, in the present framework, each of these activities is defined as communication, not participation. (p. 231)

The distinction between political participation and political communication discussed by Hoffman is important, as it raises the question of at which point communication might transfer into political action and/or participation? In relation to Twitter, the communicative act of retweeting is both the relaying of a given message, but also an act that could be construed as an attempt to persuade other voters to support a candidate, or other candidates to adjust or modify an existing position. As Larsson and Moe (2012) point out, however, even the 'conversational and collaborative' potential of Twitter described during its early stages by Honeycutt and Herring (2009; in Larsson & Moe 2012, p. 733) has given way to a far more one-way, top-down use of Twitter by politicians. Importantly, this hierarchical use of Twitter by politicians does not necessarily have to mean that interaction and dialog are not possible. As Ausserhofer and Maireder (2013) note, recent research has shown that citizens are increasingly using Twitter for political reasons, and doing so in and around specific events such as the 2009 Climate Change Conference in Copenhagen and Austrian student protests (and, presumably, national elections). The communication surrounding these events via tools such as Twitter expanded to include individuals who were not directly involved but were subsequently absorbed into the online conversations, thus exposing them to a more diverse range of opinions than previously available (p. 4; citing Yardi & boyd 2010).

The expansion of Twitter discussions is, of course, at the heart of this study, and the use of retweets by Twitter users is, other than the sending out of an original message, a vital component of such expansions. In their study on the practice of retweeting, boyd *et al.* (2010) wrote that:

> While retweeting can simply be seen as the act of copying and rebroadcasting, the practice contributes to a conversational ecology in which conversations are composed of a public interplay of voices that give rise to an emotional sense of shared conversational context. For this reason, some of the most visible Twitter participants retweet others and look to be retweeted. This includes users of all kinds, but notably marketers, celebrities and politicians. (p. 1)

The notion of the cultivation of a 'conversational ecology' via retweets is a particularly useful concept for understanding the lines between political participation and conversation discussed by Hoffman (2012). As boyd *et al.* (2010) note, retweeting is more than just simple information distribution, but also more complex social engagement whereby the retweet is, 'a form of information diffusion and . . . a means of participating in a diffuse conversation' as well as an act 'to validate and engage with others;' thus, 'regardless of why users embrace retweeting, through broadcasting messages, they become part of a broader conversation' (p. 10). In addition to the question of how to conceive of the retweet (in communicative and participatory terms), a final issue worth addressing is why and what people retweet. Meraz and Papacharissi (2013), citing Cha *et al.* (2010), noted that retweets are often driven by the perceived content value of the tweet (rather than, for example, the person who sent the tweet), while Hansen *et al.* (2011) have described the factors that play into the decision-making process behind retweets, noting that, 'it may depend on both the type of content and whether the communication is intended for a broader audience or for a more closed community of friends'. Ultimately, however, Hansen *et al.* discovered that, in general, negative sentiment tended to reduce the number of retweets, but not, interestingly, when in conjunction with news. Or, as the authors put it: 'if you want to be cited: Sweet talk your friends or serve bad news to the public!' (p. 12)

Methodology

In this study, tweets posted to the Twitter accounts of three of the 'third-party' US presidential candidates: Gary Johnson (Libertarian; @GovGaryJohnson), Jill Stein (Green; @JillStein2012) and Rocky Anderson (Justice; @RockyAnderson), as well as the official feed of one party (Constitution; @cnstutionprty) were harvested for two weeks leading up to the election: between 23 October and 6 November 2012 (the election day was included because candidates continued to tweet while voting took place). It is important to note that the official feed of the Constitution Party was used rather than the account of candidate Virgil Goode because Goode did not post any tweets after late October 2012. In addition, the Jonhson, Green and Anderson Twitter accounts were by far more active and popular (in terms of number of followers) than their respective official party accounts; thus, the four accounts followed represented the most popular Twitter accounts for the four presidential campaigns.

The first step was to accumulate all of the tweets. This was done by simply copying all tweets during the period of analysis and pasting them into a document. From the four accounts, a total of 559 tweets were harvested. For each candidate, tweets originating from the candidate/party were then checked for the number of Retweets. This was done by opening all candidate tweets and writing down the number of retweets for each: it was from this list that the total number of retweets, top 10 tweets, etc. were obtained. From this, a rank-order of the most 'Retweeted' and 'Favorite' tweets emerged, and, from this meta list, the most popular tweets were subsequently categorized and analyzed. It should be noted that messages not originating from the candidate/party account, but Retweeted by the candidate/party, were not included in these lists. The reason for this is that the message did not originate with the candidate/party, and, thus, it is impossible to know if the number of 'Retweets' that message ultimately received was a function of the candidate forwarding it, or of the relative popularity of the original tweeter (e.g. if a tweet from a celebrity was Retweeted by a candidate, it is likely that the Retweet number would be high regardless of the forwarding of the message by the candidate). Thus, only original tweets from the candidate/party were included in the sample.

The second step in the analysis was to look at the top 10 tweets for each candidate based on the number of Retweets, and to conduct a content analysis of those tweets to identify the topic and scope of the tweets. The purpose of this second phase of the analysis is to gage which topic generated the most interest amongst followers, with 'interest' defined as the motivation to forward the message to followers. A number of important caveats are worth mentioning at this point. Clearly, the time of day a tweet is sent can have a clear impact upon whether or not a tweet is retweeted or favorited; similarly, if a tweet is one in a long series of tweets sent out over a relatively short period of time – an intensive burst of tweets – it is also reasonable to assume that it is less likely to be retweeted: in part because it is lost in a larger flow of tweets, and in part because followers might 'switch off' after seeing a particularly heavy flow from one user.

Finally, as will be seen in the results, depending upon the person/party who sent them out, there can be a wide variation in the number of retweets and favorites that tweets generate. The number of followers that a candidate/party has is, of course, a determining factor in who has the largest *number* of retweets and favorites. However, it is important to note that this study looks at the 'popularity' of a tweet in relation to the feed itself, and not in comparison to the other three feeds (although that will be discussed in the conclusions). Were this not the case, the pure number of retweets and favorites for tweets from Libertarian candidate Gary Johnson, with well over 100,000 followers, would dwarf tweets from all other candidates as, at the time of the election, Jill Stein of the Green Party had the second most popular account with roughly 23,000 followers, Rocky Anderson of the Justice Party had 4,000 followers, and the Constitution Part account only 2,000 followers.

Results

Tweets and retweets: Volume

The most striking result to emerge from the initial examination of the tweets from the four third-party candidates was the extent to which Jill Stein of the Green Party dominated in terms of volume of tweets sent out (see Table 1). Her 23 tweet-per-day average was four times that of Libertarian Gary Johnson, and six times higher than both Rocky Anderson (Justice) and the Constitution Party. While Stein dominated in terms of activity, Johnson had the clear advantage in terms of followers, with approximately 100,000: fully four times

TABLE 1 Candidate tweets 23 October to 6 November 2012.

Candidate	No. of followers	Total no. of tweets	Tweets/ day	Heaviest day	Second heaviest day
Johnson (Lib.)	100,000	91	6	Oct 23 (17)	Nov 6 (12)
Stein (Green)	23,000	340	23	Oct 23 (58)	Nov 6 (54)
Anderson (Just.)	4,000	62	4	Nov 3 (18)	Nov 6 (10)
Constitution	2,000	66	4	Nov 5 (7)	Oct 24 (7)
Total (comb.)	129,000	559	37	Oct 23 (82)	Nov 6 (79)

that of nearest rival Stein, and dwarfing both Anderson and the Constitution Party. The meager follower levels and output of both the Anderson and the Constitution Party are, as we will see in the subsequent sections, reflected in low levels of retweeting.

While there was variation between the candidates in terms of volume of tweets and followers, there was a fair degree of consistency in relation to *when* the candidates/parties tweeted. A logical assumption would have been that candidates would tweet heaviest in the days leading up to the election, and the figures indicate that 5 November (the day before the election) and 6 November (the day of the election) were indeed active days. However, an interesting result of the study was that, for the two 'main' third-party candidates (Johnson and Stein), 23 and 24 October proved to be pivotal days in that they were the days immediately following the third presidential debate (22 October 2012) and what was known as the 'First Free and Equal Elections Foundation' debate (23 October) featuring the four main third-party candidates (Johnson Stein, Anderson & Goode). In other words – and as will be discussed – the candidates piggy-backed not only their own third-party debates (which obtained only meager media attention in the United States), thus generating significant volumes of retweets, but also the third debate between Obama and Romney.

Once the volume and frequency of the tweets had been calculated, the number of retweets obtained by the candidates/parties was then calculated. As Table 2 shows, Libertarian Gary Johnson averaged over 500 retweets for every tweet sent out. Jill Stein, with only one-quarter as many followers as Johnson, managed an average of 55 retweets per tweet (with Anderson and the Constitution Party languishing far behind). The seeming domination of Johnson, however, could be offset by a couple of factors. First, the spread of retweets must be seen in exponential terms; thus, all tweets being equal, if a person has four times as many followers as someone else, that does not necessarily mean that she/he will receive four times as many retweets. There is a

TABLE 2 Candidate followers, total re-tweets and re-tweets of top 10 tweets.

Candidate	No. of followers	Total RTs	Total RTs of top 10 tweets	Top 10 RT number as percent of all RTs	Ten tweets as percent of all tweets	Average no. of RT per tweet
Johnson (Lib.)	100,000	45,652	17,579	38	11	502
Stein (Green)	23,000	18,556	3,364	18	3	55
Anderson (Just.)	4,000	333	236	70	16	5
Constitution	2,000	137	65	47	15	2

particular economy of scale in tweeting whereby the larger the number of followers you have, the further and faster your tweets can spread. Second, Stein's average of 55 retweets per tweet should also be seen in relation to the fact that she sent out nearly four times as many tweets as Johnson.

As the second important result presented in Table 2 is the extent to which the most retweeted messages sent out by the four parties accounted for the overall number of retweets obtained. In other words: did the most 'popular' tweets dominate the overall numbers, leaving a large number of 'less popular' messages out in the cold? While it is interesting to note, for example, that the 'top 10' retweeted messages accounted for 38 percent of all of the retweets obtained by Gary Johnson, but for only 11 percent of the retweets for Jill Stein, these numbers are only relevant when considered in relation to the *total* number of tweets sent out by these individuals. In this context, while Johnson's most retweeted messages accounted for 38 percent of his retweets, those messages also represented (a relatively high) 11 percent if his total output. Stein, on the other hand, obtained nearly one-fifth of her retweets from only 3 percent of her tweets (10/340). In other words, even though they made up far less of her *overall* number of retweets, the 10 most 'popular' tweets (gaged by retweets) were far more important to Stein than they were to Johnson. Again, the large advantage held by Johnson in terms of followers could explain a lesser reliance on his part upon high-impact tweets in comparison to Stein, as Johnson was more likely to see exponential retweeting of an average, 'non-top 10' tweet than Stein. The low tweet and retweet numbers for Anderson and the Constitution Party were also reflected in the heavy importance of a low number of popular tweets upon their overall retweet volume (more so with Johnson than the Constitution Party).

The 10 most retweeted tweets: Topic and scope

Gary Johnson (libertarian). As outlined in Table 3, the tweets sent out by the Libertarian candidate Gary Johnson are marked by three clear themes: (1) a critique of current US military policy, (2) a blanket condemnation of the Republican and Democratic candidates and (3) the encouragement of supporters to break the political *status quo* in the United States by voting for the Libertarians. Interestingly, two of the top three tweets — including the most retweeted message,

TABLE 3 Top 10 tweets by RT volume: Johnson (libertarian).

Rank	# RTs and Fav.	Date	Content
1	3379/672	Oct 23	#Obama says he's worried about innocent young people in the Middle East. Perhaps he should start by not killing them with drones. #debate
2	2399/411	Oct 23	Tonight we saw two men with two very different plans…on how to increase our debt & decrease our civil liberties. #debate #johnson2012
3	2037/416	Oct 23	#Romney says he supports #Obama's use of #drones. I am the only candidate who will not use drones to murder innocent people. #debate
4	1594/283	Nov 6	Today is the day we make history. Go out and vote, and be part of the 5% that changes the future. #bethe5percent pic.twitter.com/TTm295kY
5	1579/269	Nov 5	Wasting your vote is voting for somebody that you don't believe in. #bethe5percent pic.twitter.com/j4Q8jtMh
6	1522/284	Oct 23	#Obama says #Romney is all over the map. Under Romney OR Obama, our troops would be all over the map — literally. Bring them HOME! #debate
7	1415/225	Oct 30	5% ends the two-party system & allows Libertarian candidates equal ballot access. #BeThe5percent #Johnson2012 pic.twitter.com/gwiIJDdK
8	1340/185	Oct 26	5% of the vote ends the two-party abuse & allows #Libertarian candidates equal ballot access & federal funding. pic.twitter.com/rQUyjo7Z
9	1159/177	Oct 23	#Obama & #Romney may have different plans, but both lead to an increase in military spending & debt. #debate
10	1155/263	Nov 6	Make history. Make a difference. Vote for Gary Johnson and #BeThe5Percent. #YouAreLibertarian pic.twitter.com/PsWi7aXf

which obtained nearly 1,000 more retweets than the tweet in the second place – attack the use of unmanned drones by the US military, while the sixth and ninth most retweeted tweets address troop safety and military spending. These attacks on military action and spending clearly struck a chord with Johnson's followers, rooted in the Libertarian tradition of international non-intervention and the primacy of domestic politics and economics over global.

In 5 of the 10 tweets, Johnson makes use of the #Obama, #Romney and/or #Debate hashtags to (potentially) expand exposure and retweeting beyond his core supporters (one would assume that the #johnson2012 and #Libertarian hashtags would lead to a more shallow spread). The tweets pushed the idea of the Libertarians as a viable third party, playing upon the call to reach 5 percent of the national vote (which would give ballot access and federal election funding to the party). Finally, the impact of piggy-backing both the presidential and third part debates upon Johnson's retweet numbers is worth considering, as 5 of his top 10 tweets – including all of his top three – were made on the same day: 23 October 2012.

Jill Stein (Green Party). Before discussing the general topics addressed in Jill Stein's messages, the dramatic gap between the number of retweets of her most forwarded tweet and all other tweets is worth mentioning (Table 4). Stein's most retweeted message on the topic of marijuana has more retweets (936) and Favorities (213) than the next three most popular tweets combined. The dominance of this tweet is compounded by the fact that the exact same tweet was sent out two days later, and still ranked fourth on the list with 280 retweets (giving the tweet an actual total of 1,216 retweets). None of the other candidates have such a large numerical chasm between their first and second most retweeted messages. Without a more detailed examination, it is impossible to explain why this particular tweet generated so many more retweets than any other of Stein's tweets, but a combination of post-debate interest and the use of the #marijuana hashtag may have contributed to the (relatively) dramatic numbers.

In her most retweeted tweets, Stein clearly links the Green Party to broader social movements such as Occupy Wall Street and climate change via a discussion of corporate corruption and the use of hashtags such as #Occupy, #OWS, #climatechange and #indyvote. As with Libertarian Gary Johnson, Stein also received a fair number of retweets (248) for her message regarding the use of drones (using the #drones hashtag); and, like Johnson, Stein used the main presidential debates as a springboard for her own messages: in Stein's case on marijuana legalization, corporate corruption and environmentalism.

Rocky Anderson (Justice Party). While the most prominent third-party candidates (Johnson and Stein) utilized Twitter by sending messages articulating personal and party policy, Justice Party candidate Rocky Anderson (Table 5) saw his

TABLE 4 Top 10 tweets by RT volume: Stein (Green).

Rank	# RTs and Fav.	Date	Content
1	936/213	Oct 24	'#Marijuana is dangerous on account of being illegal. It is not illegal on account of being dangerous!' #NowThatsADebate
2	347/87	Oct 24	One constitutional amendment? End corporate personhood. Money is not speech and corporations are not people! #NowThatsADebate #Occupy
3	308/16	Oct 23	PLS RT if you agree that independent party candidates deserve more media coverage! #Election2012 #POTUS #Debates
4	280/73	Oct 26	'#Marijuana is dangerous on account of being illegal. It is not illegal on account of being dangerous!' #NowThatsADebate
5	277/37	Oct 24	There are 90 million voters who don't plan on voting. Those are voters saying NO to politics as usual. They have choices! #NowThatsADebate
6	266/57	Nov 4	'To go into the voting booth and vote for either Wall-Street-backed candidate, that is the definition of throwing away your vote'
7	259/58	Oct 27	'I'd rather vote for what I want and not get it, than for what I don't want and get it' – Eugene Debs. #indyvote #election2012 #OWS
8	248/46	Oct 24	We need to put an end to the use of #drones! Dropping bombs on weddings & funerals is not a good way to win the hearts & minds of people
9	236/48	Oct 29	Neither #Obama or #Romney mentioned #climatechange during their #debates, yet random, dangerous weather affects nearly 1 in 5 tonight
10	207/33	Nov 6	The two-party system is not serving the 99%. Let's make history & get a new party in the #Whitehouse. #VoteGreen #OWS PLS RT

greatest, albeit modest, success when posting tweets giving details of interviews, rallies and magazine articles. Anderson's (by far) largest number of retweets (65) came for a message regarding the jailed whistleblower Bradley Manning, and the related pattern established by Johnson and Stein attacking Obama for drone attacks and human rights abuses was continued by Anderson in a number of

TABLE 5 Top 10 tweets by RT volume: Anderson (Justice).

Rank	# RTs and Fav.	Date	Content
1	65/16	Nov 3	I would pardon and thank Bradley Manning. http://www.voterocky.org/rocky_bradley_manning...More whistle blowers prosecuted during Obama than all others combined
2	31/5	Nov 1	When our Constitution is being shredded and the rule of law undermined, where are the lawyers? Save our Republic. http://bit.ly/SsCl69
3	25/5	Nov 6	Rocky Anderson Knows Mitt Romney Well and Thinks He Has No Integrity	VICE http://www.vice.com/read/rocky-anderson-knows-mitt-romney-well-and-thinks-he-has-no-integrity ... via @VICE
4	25/3	Oct 29	I discuss #Obama's abysmal civil/human rights record tonight on #alJazeera, 8:30 ET. Assassinations, illegal wiretapping, state secrets, etc.
5	21/7	Nov 4	Don't miss @RockyAnderson in the #ThirdParty debate tonight hosted by @Ralph_Nader! Watch online: http://busboysandpoets.com/videos/live-streaming... pic.twitter.com/pxXTVccT
6	17/3	Nov 5	Join us in front of the White House at 10 am to demand accountability for torture. Tell Obama and Holder no one is above the law. RT
7	15/1	Oct 30	#RockyAnderson blasts corporate media for its mass deception and degradation of our democracy. RT and spread the word! http://bit.ly/UeLLkO
8	13/4	Nov 3	To D.C. tomorrow for Sunday debate. Ralph Nader moderating. Watch: http://www.voterocky.org/events Other debates: http://www.voterocky.org/television
9	12/3	Oct 29	What a Difference Other Candidates Make|The Nation http://www.thenation.com/blog/170756/what-difference-other-candidates-make...
10	12/2	Nov 3	Is there anyone who doesn't think D.C. residents deserve representation in Congress? Amend Constitution now! http://www.voterocky.org (Write-in)

tweets. The remaining tweets generally adhered to the conventional practice of encouraging readers to watch the candidate take part in debates and rallies, as well as undermining the integrity of the opposition.

The Constitution Party (Virgil Goode). Unlike all of the other third-party candidates, and with the exception of one tweet urging withdrawal from the United Nations, the Constitution Party (Table 6) made no use of hashtags (e.g. #debate

TABLE 6 Top 10 tweets by RT volume: Constitutional/Goode.

	# RTs and Fav.	Date	Content
1	65/16	Nov 3	I would pardon and thank Bradley Manning. http://www.voterocky.org/rocky_bradley_manning...More whistle blowers prosecuted during Obama than all others combined
2	31/5	Nov 1	When our Constitution is being shredded and the rule of law undermined, where are the lawyers? Save our Republic. http://bit.ly/SsCl69
3	25/5	Nov 6	Rocky Anderson Knows Mitt Romney Well and Thinks He Has No Integrity|VICE http://www.vice.com/read/rocky-anderson-knows-mitt-romney-well-and-thinks-he-has-no-integrity ... via @VICE
4	25/3	Oct 29	I discuss #Obama's abysmal civil/human rights record tonight on #alJazeera, 8:30 ET. Assassinations, illegal wiretapping, state secrets, etc.
5	21/7	Nov 4	Don't miss @RockyAnderson in the #ThirdParty debate tonight hosted by @Ralph_Nader! Watch online: http://busboysandpoets.com/videos/live-streaming ... pic.twitter.com/pxXTVccT
6	17/3	Nov 5	Join us in front of the White House at 10 am to demand accountability for torture. Tell Obama and Holder no one is above the law. RT
7	15/1	Oct 30	#RockyAnderson blasts corporate media for its mass deception and degradation of our democracy. RT and spread the word! http://bit.ly/UeLLkO
8	13/4	Nov 3	To D.C. tomorrow for Sunday debate. Ralph Nader moderating. Watch: http://www.voterocky.org/events Other debates: http://www.voterocky.org/television
9	12/3	Oct 29	What a Difference Other Candidates Make|The Nation http://www.thenation.com/blog/170756/what-difference-other-candidates-make...
10	12/2	Nov 3	Is there anyone who doesn't think D.C. residents deserve representation in Congress? Amend Constitution now! http://www.voterocky.org (Write-in)

or #obama) or references to specific 'hot button' issues (such as drones or corporate corruption) in their tweets. This fact perhaps goes some way toward explaining why the party had such low retweet numbers, and for the general lack of interest in their messages. The Constitution Party stuck to general slogans and quotations, as well as reminders to watch or listen to debates and vote. In most of the tweets, the party linked to their Facebook page, where additional information was provided, yet none of the tweets managed to elevate above the meager number of 10 retweets.

Analysis and discussion

In order to analyze the material retweeted by followers (and non-followers) of the four third-party US presidential candidates, it is worth revisiting the conceptual outline on retweeting as 'conversation' provided by boyd *et al.* (2010). And, as Meraz and Papacharissi (2013; citing Cha *et al.* 2010) noted, retweets are very often driven by 'content value', thus, the retweeting of material posted by Johnson, Stein, Anderson and the Constitution Party should be seen as extended discussions and contributions to the broader political 'conversational ecology'. Three broad themes emerged in the tweets retweeted most heavily by third-party followers: (1) military, security and human rights, (2) the failure of the two-party system, and (3), corporate power. In this analysis and discussion of the results presented above, I would like to consider these themes and topics that attracted retweets from fellow Twitter users, as well as the tactics used by the candidates themselves for linking their political messages to broader themes and agendas.

Military, security and human rights

One of the striking results of this study was the way in which anti-aggression, anti-surveillance and pro-human rights tweets generated a fair number of retweets for all candidates who posted them. This is not striking because of the parties in question – the Green and Justice parties are openly against military aggression, while the Libertarians have historically been in favor of withdrawing from international conflict – but rather because the discourse is in stark contrast with that forwarded by mainstream Republican and Democrat politicians. Open critique of drone strikes, torture and the imprisonment of Bradley Manning were very much off the agenda in the presidential debates between Obama and Romney, while Johnson, Stein and Anderson followers all found the issues worthy of forwarding to their respective followers. Libertarian candidate Johnson, in particular, was firm on the issue of drones, and generated thousands of retweets (to potentially hundreds of thousands of citizens) with his opposition to the use of the technology.

What emerged from the top tweets examined was a clear pattern whereby the mention of military abuse, human rights violations and/or excessive surveillance of US citizens for the purpose of national security – particularly in conjunction with broader hashtags such as '#drones' – was a recipe for increased retweeting. Support for these tweets cut across political boundaries, with Libertarian followers (usually seen as linked to neo-conservatism) retweeting messages critical of the US exercise of military and judicial power in much the same way as their Green and Justice counterparts. The retweeting of negative opinion regarding these issues also appears to support the contention by Hansen *et al.* (2011) that, while negative sentiment does not drive retweets in general, it does when in conjunction with news and information (and these candidate opinions could be construed as a form of news/information). In other words, in these cases, broader disappointment with mainstream political engagement with issues of torture and illegal killings drove up the number of retweets.

Failure of the two-party system and corporate power

A second, broadly supported position held by the minority candidates is that the established two-party system in the United States is defective, and in need to reform. All four candidates/parties received decent levels of retweets for messages supporting the notion that a vote for a third-party candidate is a vote for your ideals, or your conscience (suggesting that a vote for a Republican or Democrat would not be a conscience or ideals decision). This is perhaps unsurprising, given the fact that the four parties in question are outside of that two-party system, yet this topic generated a fair amount of retweeting on the part of followers. The Libertarians had a clear (and popular) agenda to push the notion of gaining the 5 percent vote needed to access ballots and federal financing, while the Greens dispelled the notion that a vote for their party was a wasted vote (an angle also taken by the other parties).

Where the parties split on this issue was on the relationship between private capital, corporate power and perceived political failure. Supporters of Green candidate Jill Stein and Justice candidate Rocky Anderson promoted tweets positing clear linkages between corporate control and political decline, while Libertarian Gary Johnson and the Constitution Party's Virgil Goode merely highlighted the failure of Obama and Romney – logical, given that the Libertarians and Constitution party trumpet the primacy of the free market. Despite these differences, the 'conversation' relayed by supporters of all four parties included clear condemnations of a two-party system defined as in steep decline.

Finally, the Green and Justice party generated a significant number of retweets by addressing the general level of corruption in the United States in relation to corporate power. While issues such as campaign finance reform were not off-limits for the main presidential debate between Obama and Romney, the corrupting nature of corporate influence on US socio-political life had not been a topic for discussion.

Enhancing content value in 'conversational ecologies'? Riding waves and hashtag jumping

If we consider retweeting to be a component in a 'conversational ecology', then it would be valuable to examine the results of this study and consider the ways in which the third-party candidates encouraged the relaying of messages via retweets, thus expanding the conversational ecology and (potentially) attracting new participants. As the preliminary quantitative data from an examination of the four Twitter feeds indicated, the four candidates/parties placed a great deal of emphasis upon tweeting on and around both their own third-party debate (on 23 October), as well as the mainstream presidential debate between Obama and Romney (22 October). The strategy of riding the convention Twitter wave appears to have paid off, as Johnson (Libertarian) saw his top three tweets come on 23October; Jill Stein saw four of her top five retweet numbers on 23 and 24October; and the Constitutional Party (Goode) had two of their top three tweets on those same days. Only Rocky Anderson (Justice) had no tweets from either of those dates in his list of top 10 tweets.

As smaller political parties in the US struggle to garner even minimal mainstream media coverage, the well-documented flood of tweets surrounding the third presidential election debate (the first two were not covered in the scope of this study) provided an excellent opportunity for minority party candidates to jump on top of that tweet wave, and to weave their respective political messages into the broader political discourse. In some cases, Obama and Romney were attacked for what they said; but, interestingly, some of the highest levels of retweets came when third-party candidates played off of the main presidential debates – by, for example, using the #debate and #election2012 hashtags – by addressing a topic from those same debates, but injecting what was unsaid, as exemplified by the following messages from Gary Johnson and Jill Stein (respectively):

> #Obama says he's worried about innocent young people in the Middle East. Perhaps he should start by not killing them with drones. (23 October 2012) We need to put an end to the use of #drones! Dropping bombs on weddings & funerals is not a good way to win the hearts & minds of people. (25 October 2012)

In these cases, Johnson and Stein reminded their followers of the innocent civilians killed by drone strikes in Pakistan and Afghanistan. By hashtagging #Obama, #debate and #election2012, the candidates essentially utilized the popularity of broad Twitter conversations as a spring board for specific policy critique and suggestions. Thus, 'wave riding' already significant twitter flows proved to be successful in a number of cases.

The use of hashtags by third-party candidates with relatively low follower numbers (in relation to mainstream candidates) for the purposes of expanding exposure was also a notable tactic. Jill Stein's identical tweets on marijuana ('#Marijuana is dangerous on account of being illegal. It is not illegal on account of being dangerous!' #NowThatsADebate) which generated a total 1,216 total retweets is also a good example of maximizing exposure through selective hashtagging, as was her practice of using the widely-used #OWS ('Occupy Wall Street') and #Occupy hashtags when tweeting about corporate corruption. Of the four third-party candidates, Stein was the most creative in her use of such hashtags, while the other three tended to stick to traditional tags related to their own names, parties or the main presidential candidates (#Obama, #Romney). Stein's practice is one which we might label 'hashtag jumping' (in a non-pejorative sense), whereby pre-existing tags are incorporated into the political twitter conversation in order to deliberately expand the discussion beyond the original base of followers.

Conclusions

It was the purpose of this paper to give an overview of the use of Twitter by the main third-party presidential candidates during the 2012 US elections, and to identify a number of the topics which generated a clear interest by Twitter users, expressed in the form of retweeting messages. With a wealth of research on the use of social media by mainstream US political parties, examining the use of tools such as Twitter by much smaller parties and their followers can perhaps shed light upon issues which the mainstream media, and their mainstream political counterparts, tend to miss or willfully ignore. It is also worth considering the implications of this study upon politics, political movements and a wide array of smaller-scale grassroots organizations both inside and outside of the United States. While it is difficult to generalize beyond the parties examined in this paper, the results point to interesting new possibilities regarding the role of social media in pushing supposedly 'marginal' issues toward the political center, while, on the other hand, raising questions about the extent to which, even amongst smaller parties and organizations at the 'fringes' of mainstream politics, offline size and access to material resources drive online success.

In an era of billion-dollar political campaigns, parties such as the Libertarians and Greens can be brushed aside as political irrelevances; yet, the nearly two million votes the four minority party candidates managed to attract cannot simply be dismissed out of hand, and especially so in an electoral system where races for individual states can sometimes be decided by thousands, or even hundreds of votes. The impact of Ralph Nader upon the 2,000 general election, and the difference his votes would have made to Al Gore in the state of Florida, is a stark reminder that issues concerning third-party voters can sometimes impact mainstream politics. In more recent years, the quasi-grassroots Tea Party movement, initially labeled as a rabble of wayward ultra-conservatives, wielded a significant level of power within US politics during a short-but-intensive burst of activity.

As the use of Twitter continues to grow, and without falling prey to a techno-romantic view of the impact of social media upon political life, the material presented in this paper suggests that, while perhaps not shaping politics, Twitter can serve as a useful indicator of the topics and issues that are of interest to an increasing minority within the US political spectrum (be they conservative or leftist). This use of Twitter as a potential bellwether for gauging interest levels on given issues is all the more vital due to the fact that large-scale commercial media have anchored themselves in uncritical, *status quo* reporting, perhaps causing supporters of marginalized political parties to turn to tools such Twitter in order to participate in 'conversational ecologies' not provided via mainstream journalism or popular culture.

References

Ausserhofer, J. & Maireder, A. (2013) 'National politics on twitter: structures and topics of a networked public sphere', *Information, Communication & Society*, vol. 16, no. 3, pp. 291–314.

Baxter, G. & Marcella, R. (2012) 'Does Scotland "like" this? Social media use by political parties and candidates in Scotland during the 2010 UK general election campaign', *Libri*, vol. 62, no. 2, pp. 109–124.

boyd, d., Golder, S. & Lotan, G. (2010) 'Tweet, tweet, retweet: conversational aspects of retweeting on twitter', Proceedings of 43rd Hawaii International Conference on Systems Science (HICSS-43 2010), Kauai, Hawaii, 5–8 January, IEEE, pp. 1–10.

Cha, M., Haddadi, H., Benevenuto, F. & Gummadi, K. P. (2010, May) 'Measuring user influence in twitter: the million follower fallacy', paper presented at 4th Int'l AAAI Conference on Weblogs and Social Media, George Washington University, Washington, DC, 23–26 May, 2010 (vol. 14, no. 1, p. 8).

Dylko, I. B., Beam, M. A., Landreville, K. D. & Geidner, N. (2012) 'Filtering 2008 US presidential election news on youtube by elites and nonelites: an examination of the democratizing potential of the internet', *New Media & Society*, vol. 14, no. 5, pp. 832–849.

Gasser, U. & Gerlach, J. (2012) 'E-campaigns in old Europe: observations from Germany, Austria, and Switzerland', in *iPolitics: Citizens, Elections and Governing in the New Media Era*, eds R. L. Fox & J. M. Ramos, Cambridge University Press, Cambridge, pp. 151–182.

Golbeck, J., Grimes, J. M. & Rogers, A. (2010) 'Twitter use by the US congress', *Journal of the American Society for Information Science and Technology*, vol. 61, no. 8, pp. 1612–1621.

Grusell, M. & Nord, L. (2012) 'Three attitudes to 140 characters the use and views of twitter in political party communications in Sweden', *Public Communication Review*, vol. 2, no. 2, pp. 48–61.

Hansen, L. K., Arvidsson, A., Nielsen, F., Colleoni, E. & Etter, M. (2011) 'Good friends, bad news-affect and virality in twitter', *Future Information Technology*, vol. 185, pp. 34–43.

Hoffman, L. H. (2012) 'Participation or communication? An explication of political activity in the internet age', *Journal of Information Technology & Politics*, vol. 9, no. 3, pp. 217–233.

Honeycutt, C. & Herring, S. C. (2009). 'Beyond microblogging: Conversation and collaboration via Twitter', Proceedings of 42nd Hawaii International Conference on Systems Science (HICSS-42 2009), Big Island, Hawaii, 5–8 January, IEEE, pp. 1–10.

Hong, S. & Nadler, D. (2012) 'Which candidates do the public discuss online in an election campaign?: The use of social media by 2012 presidential candidates and its impact on candidate salience', *Government Information Quarterly*, vol. 29, pp. 455–461.

Larsson, A. O. & Moe, H. (2012) 'Studying political microblogging: twitter users in the 2010 Swedish election campaign', *New Media & Society*, vol. 14, no. 5, pp. 729–747.

Lem, S. B. & Dowling, C. M. (2006) 'Picking their spots: minor party candidates in gubernatorial elections', *Political Research Quarterly*, vol. 59, no. 3, pp. 471–480.

Meraz, S. & Papacharissi, Z. (2013) 'Networked gatekeeping and networked framing on# Egypt', *The International Journal of Press/Politics*, vol. 18, no. 2, pp. 138–166.

Nader, R. & Amato, T. (2001) 'So you want to run for president? Ha! barriers to third-party entry', *National Civic Review*, vol. 90, no. 2, pp. 163–172.

Norris, P. (2001) *The Digital Divide? Civic Engagement, Information Poverty and the Internet Worldwide*. Cambridge University Press, New York.

Shepard, R. M. (2011) *Deeds done in different words: a genre-based approach to third party presidential campaign discourse*. Unpublished doctoral dissertation, University of Kansas.

Strandberg, K. (2013) 'A social media revolution or just a case of history repeating itself? The use of social media in the 2011 Finnish parliamentary elections', *New Media & Society*, pp. 1–20, [online] Available at: http://nms.sagepub.com/content/early/2013/01/13/1461444812470612.full.pdf+html (6 February 2013).

Yardi, S. & boyd, d. (2010) 'Dynamic debates: an analysis of group polarization over time on Twitter', *Bulletin of Science, Technology & Society*, vol. 30, no. 5, pp. 316–327.

Axel Bruns & Tim Highfield

POLITICAL NETWORKS ON *TWITTER*
Tweeting the Queensland state election

This paper examines patterns of political activity and campaigning on Twitter *in the context of the 2012 election in the Australian state of Queensland. Social media have been a visible component of political campaigning in Australia at least since the 2007 federal election, with* Twitter, *in particular, rising to greater prominence in the 2010 federal election. At state level, however, they have remained comparatively less important thus far. In this paper, uses of* Twitter *in the Queensland campaign from its unofficial start in February through to the election day of 24 March 2012 are tracked. Using innovative methodologies for analysing Twitter activities, developed by the research team, this study examines the overall patterns of activity in the relevant hashtag #qldvotes, and tracks specific interactions between politicians and other users by following some 80 Twitter accounts of sitting members of parliament and alternative candidates. Such analysis provides new insights into the different approaches to social media campaigning which were embraced by specific candidates and party organizations, as well as an indication of the relative importance of social media activities, at present, for state-level election campaigns.*

Introduction

The use of social media, including *Twitter*, for political campaigning is increasingly commonplace; it has spread from the major contests of the 2008 US presidential election and other national elections to more regional and local levels (cf. Larsson & Moe 2012, forthcoming). At such lower levels, given the significantly more limited number of politically active *Twitter* users in these smaller constituencies as well as the more modest party infrastructure available to candidates, political campaigning is likely to differ notably from the well-funded, high-stakes social media campaigns of national elections. Candidates who have a social media presence may be considerably more likely to post their own messages rather than being able to rely on a well-resourced media staff. The styles of tweeting may also vary between campaign accounts, from broadcast-only models of sharing messages without responding to other comments, to attempts to foster a wider dialogue among *Twitter* users. Finally, campaign accounts may employ different strategies around *Twitter* conventions such as hashtags and @mentions or retweets of other users, and especially of other candidates (whether from the same party or contesting the same electorate).

The use of *Twitter* in elections below the national level remains under-researched at present; a focus on national elections (and national elections in well-resourced political systems such as those of the United States and UK at that) obscures the more mundane, unglamorous experience of electioneering that is shared by candidates and political staffers in the majority of elections. This paper, therefore, examines patterns of political activity and campaigning on *Twitter* in the context of the 2012 election in the Australian state of Queensland. It takes a quantitative approach to the identification and evaluation of politicians' tweeting styles, in order to investigate the strategic choices made by specific parties and individual candidates in planning and conducting their *Twitter* activities during the election campaign, and it examines the *Twitter* activities of the wider Queensland electorate, in order to explore whether candidates' activities generate any substantial resonance; in turn, this provides an insight into the Australian political establishment's current understanding of *Twitter* as a campaigning tool, and into the effectiveness of such strategies at galvanizing electoral support.

Social media have been a visible component of political campaigning and debate in Australia at least since the 2007 federal election (see, for example, Flew 2008; Kirchhoff *et al.* 2009), with *Twitter*, in particular, rising to greater prominence in the 2010 federal election (Bruns & Burgess 2011a). At the state level, on the other hand, they have remained less important; while there is still interest in, and discussion of, state political issues and elections in tweets and blog posts, such coverage represents a much smaller amount of social media activity than found for political themes of national importance. However, the steady growth of social media use in Australia is likely to lead to an increased presence of such media in political campaigning with each new election, across different levels of government. Coming two years after the previous federal election, and one year ahead of the next, the Queensland state election of 2012 demonstrates the evolving uses of *Twitter* by politicians and candidates alike, with clear implications for subsequent campaigns.

We begin this paper by outlining current uses of *Twitter* in Australian political communication in general, before describing prevalent uses of the platform by Australian politicians against the backdrop of current political and media contexts in the country. We then discuss the situation at the start of the 2012 Queensland election campaign, and trace politicians' uses of *Twitter* through the campaign, before comparing such activity overall discussion in the election-related #qldvotes hashtag. We conclude by situating the activity patterns we have observed during the campaign within the wider electoral context of the 2012 state election, in order to highlight how the specific communicative choices made by each politician and campaign office represent a range of campaigning strategies.

Australian politics and *Twitter*

Online discussions of Australian political issues are now commonplace; the pioneering work of early political bloggers and the development of opinion and commentary websites run by the mainstream media and by independent groups (Highfield & Bruns 2012) have been supplemented by the widespread use of social media platforms such as *Twitter* and *Facebook* in Australia. Indeed, commenting on politics now takes place across a multi-platform media ecology, as social media are integrated into traditional media coverage – for example, the mainstream public broadcaster, the Australian Broadcasting Corporation, has enjoyed considerable success with its integration of live tweeting into the political panel show *Q&A*, under the hashtag #qanda. Some panellists and ABC presenters actively engage with the show's *Twitter* audience before and after the show, and selected tweets are displayed on screen during the show itself. Tweeting about Australian politics is also a high-volume activity; in the first half of 2012, the umbrella hashtag for the discussion of domestic political issues, #auspol, appeared in over one million tweets, averaging over 5,000 tweets per day.

However, while discussing politics on blogs, on *Facebook*, or in tweets is a regular activity for many Australians, the place of the Internet within election campaigns themselves is less established. During the 2007 federal election, the Australian Labor Party (ALP) used sites such as *Facebook* and *MySpace* as part of their wider 'Kevin07' campaign promoting party leader Kevin Rudd as an appealing Prime Minister-in-waiting. The Internet strategy of the other major party, the Liberal Party (which at that point had been in power for 11 years), was less clear, with an attempt to use *YouTube* for policy announcements met with criticism, and the video itself overshadowed by parodies and alternative clips (Flew 2008).

By the time of the next federal election, three years later, online platforms had become more established parts of the media landscape. In particular, *Twitter*, barely established in Australia in 2007, had become an important means for breaking news as it happened. In June 2010, late-night rumours of an ALP leadership challenge between the Prime Minister, Kevin Rudd, and his deputy, Julia Gillard, were confirmed and reported first on *Twitter*, soon accompanied by the #spill hashtag to denote the upcoming vote. Tweets about the leadership spill were complemented by more in-depth analysis and commentary on other web-sites, but the ease of publishing, and spreading, short comments on *Twitter* high-lighted the role of social media in providing immediate reactions to sudden developments (Bruns 2012; Burgess & Bruns 2012).

Just over three weeks after taking over the role of Prime Minister and ALP leader, Gillard called a federal election for August 2010. During the resulting campaign, online media were used by both major parties as part of their wider strategies – but unlike 2007, neither the ALP nor the Liberal Party had a clearly distinct approach to online campaigning. Politicians and candidates from both major parties, as well as representatives of the minor parties, such as the Australian Greens, and independents, used *Twitter* as a further means to promote their, or their party's, messages, while journalists tweeted updates from the campaign trail. The discussion of the election, and the ques-tioning of candidates and journalists, was not limited to these two groups, though. Among the election tweets, a central hashtag emerged – #ausvotes – which during the five weeks of the campaign featured in over 415,000 tweets (Bruns & Burgess 2011a). Peaking at over 94,000 tweets on election day itself, the use of #ausvotes demonstrates the presence of a large group of *Twitter* users commenting on the election campaign, and also the develop-ment of a public, linked discussion around this topic; the use of a common hashtag is not a requirement for tweets about a given subject, but by including such a marker, a tweet is then automatically linked to the wider group of com-ments that use the same hashtag.

The examples of #ausvotes and, post-election, #auspol have led to deriva-tive conventions for tweeting about Australian politics at the state level, too. Publishing a comment on *Twitter* about the New South Wales state government, for example, might be accompanied by the #nswpol hashtag, while tweets con-cerning the election in the state of Victoria would include the #vicvotes hashtag. For the 2012 Queensland election, then, *Twitter* users made use of both #qldpol and #qldvotes in their tweets, although the more limited interest in state-level political events also meant that these hashtags were featured to different extents and without universal adoption during the campaign.

Of course, the examples of specific hashtags such as #auspol also show that tweeting a lot in these discussions is not necessarily the same as participating in public debate; while there are thousands of #auspol tweets per day, analysis shows that a very small group of users provide the majority of these comments (Bruns & Burgess 2012). As #auspol became established as the standard hashtag for discussing Australian politics, tweets and users employing this marker con-tributed to #auspol's transformation into an increasingly antagonistic and parti-san hashtag community rather than a space for public debate (Jericho 2012): its leading users form an in-group which is highly active at talking (and often, arguing) amongst itself, but rarely connects with wider public debate about Aus-tralian politics on *Twitter*.

The technical limits of tweeting – in particular the 140-character restrictions put on each tweet – also create difficulties for sharing considered, detailed, and nuanced thoughts on an issue. It remains to be seen what, if anything, tweeting alone can achieve within Australian politics, beyond acting as a barometer of public opinion (although it should also be noted that the population of Australian *Twitter* users is not representative of the entire Australian electorate). However, what *Twitter can* provide is a simple mechanism for citizens to invoke politicians – or journalists, sportspeople, celebrities, or anyone else with a *Twitter* account – in their comments, and for these thoughts to be public and visible in a way that emailed communication, telephone calls, letters, or electorate office visits are not.

Politicians' uses of social media

The increasing presence of individual Australian politicians on sites such as *Twitter* is a notable change in their use of online communication platforms. Although politician websites are commonplace, few active federal members of parliament started blogging, for example, as a further means of communicating with their electorate or publishing their own views on current political issues (Highfield & Bruns 2012). This has changed with the advent of more recent social media platforms: a study examining tweeting patterns by politicians at the federal, state, and local government levels in 2009 drew initially on a (not exhaustive) list of 152 *Twitter* accounts (Grant *et al.* 2010); as of July 2012, at least 146 of the 226 members of the federal Upper and Lower Houses had *Twitter* accounts.

This growing adoption of social media has the potential to increase the interactions between citizens and politicians, raising the level of participation in public debate, by putting these different voices in the same space. Prior to the advent of *Twitter*, citizens could already communicate with politicians via Internet-mediated platforms. However, in Australia, using such means as email to get in contact with politicians was an action carried out primarily by those with higher levels of engagement with both politics and the Internet (Gibson *et al.* 2008). Emailing a politician or their staff is also a private form of communication, limiting any discussion to the people sending and receiving the email. Tweeting at a politician, on the other hand, takes this initial communication (except if it is a direct message or involves 'private' *Twitter* accounts) and makes it publicly visible, potentially accessible by all *Twitter* users and by anyone else reading tweets on the *Twitter* website itself.

Politicians, both in Australia and internationally, have developed different strategies for their use of *Twitter*, given this generally public nature of tweets and replies. Grant *et al.* (2010), comparing Australian politicians with a random sample of other Australian *Twitter* users, found that the politicians were more active in terms of the number of tweets published. However, these higher numbers of tweets did not mean that politicians were in conversation on *Twitter*; their tweets were mostly broadcasting messages at their followers, rather than engaging with other users. Similar general patterns have been found in a national election context in the UK, where tweets-as-broadcast were the preferred style for politicians and candidates (Broersma & Graham 2012); however, the same study found that Dutch politicians at the national level, in contrast, were more likely to interact and engage in dialogue with other *Twitter* users.

Replying to other accounts may in turn depend on the identities of the people tweeting at politicians; in Austria, for example, a study of groups of politicians, journalists, citizens, and domain experts found that the politicians were most likely to @mention their peers within the same group (Maireder forthcoming; Maireder *et al.* 2012). The established political commentariat of professionals engaged in political debate – politicians, journalists, and experts – also formed a dense, interlinked network through their @mentions and retweets, indicating that the traditional participants in these discussions remained key figures when the conversation took place on *Twitter*. However, Maireder, Ausserhofer, and Kittenberger also note that some non-professional users are able to join these public debates; overall, to which users a politician will respond on *Twitter* is also dependent on the politician themselves, and especially on their own approach – broadcast or conversation, for example – to tweeting.

The electoral positioning of parties and their candidates is also likely to influence the social media strategies adopted by each political actor. For example, while major parties are essentially guaranteed mainstream media coverage, smaller parties may choose to adopt social media as a key tool for publicizing their messages, in order to make up for their more limited mainstream media presence. Such an approach may be particularly sensible in a highly limited media ecology as Queensland represents it: state-wide traditional news media options are limited to one daily state-oriented newspaper (the *Courier Mail*, operated by Rupert Murdoch's News Ltd.), as well as the national newspaper *The Australian*, from the same owner, to and five commercial and public service television operators, alongside a range of radio channels.

Queensland's population is dispersed across a very large geographical area, but a significant percentage of its inhabitants live in and around the state capital of Brisbane, in the state's highly urbanized south-east corner; this also generates substantial diversity in the state's electorates, which range from the large rural – agricultural and mining – areas of north and west Queensland to the suburban divisions of Brisbane itself. An associated concentration of media organizations in the south-east corner means that different electorates are unlikely to receive a comparable amount of coverage in the news media; in theory, this may mean that candidates outside of Brisbane could take to *Twitter* more readily to connect with their constituents through social media. At the same time, however, the rural nature of these electorates, and the limited communications infrastructure available outside of Australia's major cities, works against such ambitions; *Twitter* accessibility and take-up remains considerably stronger in urban than in rural areas.

Further, the styles of *Twitter* activity adopted by parties and politicians are likely also to depend on their current electoral fortunes (their likelihood of success or defeat in the election, as indicated by current opinion polls). Politicians who are all but assured of winning their local electoral contest, or even overall power in a state, may see social media equally as much as an opportunity to connect with voters as it presents a threat of making inappropriate statements which could be exploited by the political opponent, and may therefore choose to develop a minimal social media presence only. Conversely, politicians who are likely to be defeated at the ballot box may choose to utilize social media as a last-ditch means to mobilize supporters and campaign vigorously on *Twitter*. Candidates locked in a tight electoral contest may use the medium to engage and challenge their opponents, hoping to win the debate or goad the other side into tweeting in anger. Any such choices, of course, may also be negotiated between individual candidates and their party campaign offices, and may be influenced by the candidate's level of experience in using *Twitter*.

Finally, some politicians (particularly high-profile figures) are not necessarily the authors or publishers of their tweets – instead, those roles fall to their staff at least in part. Visible distinctions may be made between tweets written by staff and by the politician themselves; for example, ahead of the 2012 state election, Queensland Premier Anna Bligh's *Twitter* account @TheQldPremier featured tweets which were authored either by her staff (and signed as 'Prem_Team') or by herself (and left unsigned). For many of the minor candidates, on the other hand, dedicating staff to manage social media accounts is an unavailable luxury, and their tweets are more likely to be entirely their own work.

Candidates' approaches to *Twitter* in the 2012 Queensland state election

This article explores how these different approaches to tweeting were adopted by candidates in the 2012 Queensland state election. To identify how these accounts used *Twitter* during their campaigns, we located some 80 candidate accounts before the start of the election campaign, and tracked their activities throughout the campaign using *yourTwapperKeeper*, an open-source tool for capturing *Twitter* data. *yourTwapperKeeper* queries the *Twitter* API for defined keywords and hashtags, archiving relevant tweets containing each of these individual terms; by using the candidate accounts' *Twitter* handles as keywords, we were able to capture all public tweets which originated from or @mentioned these accounts. The 80 candidate accounts tracked here represent nearly one-fifth of the total candidates running in the election (430 candidates across 89 electorates); the majority of accounts are operated by candidates from the two major parties in Queensland politics. These numbers provide an indication of the relative take-up of *Twitter* as a communication tool in the Queensland state election: far from universal, but increasingly strong especially amongst the serious contenders for election to parliament. In addition to the candidate accounts, we also established archives for the major political party accounts, and for the election-related hashtag #qldvotes.

The collected data were then processed using a series of Gawk scripts developed for the analysis of large *Twitter* data sets (Bruns & Burgess 2011b). These scripts enable the filtering of tweets based on such factors as date, @mentions, hashtags, or other keywords, as well as the subsequent processing of the data sets in order to establish key activity metrics (cf. Bruns & Stieglitz 2012). In the discussion which follows, we examine *Twitter* activity patterns for these accounts, as well as for the overall #qldvotes hashtag, over the course of the 2012 Queensland election campaign.

The campaign itself must be seen in the wider context of Queensland and Australian politics, of course: the ALP state government in Queensland had been in power since the election of popular Premier Peter Beattie in 1998; his successor Anna Bligh had taken over as Premier in 2007 and won a subsequent state election in 2009, becoming the first popularly elected female state Premier in Australia, but had increasingly fallen out of favour with state voters during her second term as Premier. This decline was reversed briefly in response to her widely acclaimed crisis management during the January 2011 Queensland floods, but virtually all opinion polling ahead of the election still predicted a substantial landslide win for the opposition Liberal/National Party (LNP) under the former Lord Mayor of the state capital Brisbane, Campbell Newman (who was not a Member of Parliament at the time).

While the majority of elected MPs was expected to come from these two parties, a number of minor party candidates did have a realistic chance of election in individual electorates. Bob Katter, the outspoken Federal Member for Kennedy, in Queensland's north-west, had launched his own party in 2011 to promote agricultural and conservative views; Katter's Australian Party (KAP) subsequently nominated candidates for 76 of the 89 state electorates. Meanwhile, the Queensland branch of the Greens nominated a candidate for each electorate, and the conservative Family First party was represented in 38 electorates. Finally, the remnants of the right-wing One Nation party, which had a major impact in the 1998 Queensland election, nominated six candidates. Independent candidates also ran in many electorates. As in other Australian elections, voting in Queensland is compulsory; at the close of enrolments for the 2012 election, 2.7 million voters were registered with the state electoral commission, with just under 2.5 million voting in the election itself (including informal votes).

Although the results of previous elections had been relatively close between the ALP and Liberal/National coalitions (and later between the ALP and the merged LNP itself), the 2012 election was not anticipated to follow this trend, with the LNP expected to form the new government. In late January 2012, Premier Bligh announced a delay in setting the official election date in order to enable the report of a state commission of inquiry into the 2011 floods to be delivered before the election; this in itself signalled the start of a 'phony campaign' between the two major parties, however. An official Writ of Election was eventually issued by the Governor of Queensland on 19 February 2012, setting 24 March as election date. The election finally did result in the expected landslide result, with Queensland's unicameral, Westminster-style electoral system delivering a parliament dominated by 78 LNP members, compared to Labor's seven seats, two KAP members, and two independents.

Tweeting styles of the major political accounts

In the following analysis, we therefore focus on the months of February and March, taking in both the 'phony' and the official election campaign as well as its immediate aftermath. We begin by examining the tweeting styles of the key political accounts (Figure 1), including the party accounts @QLDLabor and @LNPQLD as well as the accounts of Premier Bligh (@TheQldPremier) and her opponent @Campbell_Newman and their respective deputies, Treasurer and Deputy Premier @AndrewFraserMP and Shadow Treasurer @TimNichollsMP. (This excludes the nominal pre-election Leader of the Opposition, Jeff Seeney, who occupied this parliamentary leadership role before Newman's entry into parliament and subsequently became Deputy Premier, but who was the most prominent Queensland politician *not* to operate a personal *Twitter* account during

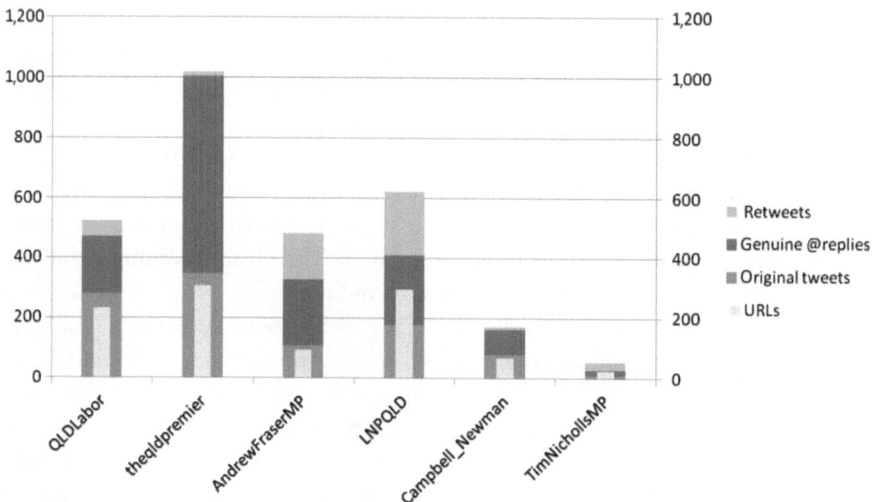

FIGURE 1 Parties' and leaders' tweeting styles, 1 February–31 March 2012.

the election. Seeney, or his staff, did eventually create a *Twitter* presence, @Jeff-Seeney, on 19 October 2012 – some seven months after the election.)

Figure 1 shows clear differences between the six accounts. Premier Bligh's account is considerably more active than the others, and indeed sent more tweets during the campaign than the three LNP-aligned accounts combined; she also sent a considerably higher percentage of genuine @replies (as opposed to retweets, or tweets which make original statements without mentioning any other users) than the other accounts. A substantial number of these @replies were not signed with the 'Prem_Team' handle, and must therefore be assumed to have been posted by Bligh herself; this points to a deliberate strategy of citizen engagement and conversation through *Twitter*.

Her deputy Andrew Fraser, on the other hand, posted substantially more retweets, but here, too, it should be noted that many such retweets contain conversational elements: they quote a previous tweet but add further commentary, agreement or rebuttal to the tweet itself. Compared to Bligh's conversational approach of focusing on @replies, such interaction through retweeting can be seen as a somewhat more combatant, debate-like style of interaction which seeks to address and where necessary correct specific political points, rather than generally establishing an image of approachability.

Both Bligh (17 tweets per day) and Fraser (8) tweeted at relatively high volumes over the two months covered in our analysis; this cannot be said for their opponents Newman (<3) and Nicholls (<1), however. On the conservative side, it is the @LNPQLD party account which provides the central pivot point for LNP-related *Twitter* activity, while its ALP counterpart @QLDLabor is largely overshadowed by the personal effort of the Premier. This is largely in keeping with the overall political landscape ahead of the election, of course: in anticipation of a landslide election result, LNP candidates did not need to go out of their way to engage the electorate by using social media, and could let the party office take care of media activities. (Many of the @Campbell_Newman updates were themselves signed by his campaign staff, indicating relatively limited genuine *Twitter* activity by the candidate himself.)

Indeed, avoiding substantial use of *Twitter* also meant minimizing the potential of making embarrassing campaign gaffes which could be exploited by Newman's opponents. This appears in keeping with an overall strategy of campaigning from a position of electoral strength: as the clear frontrunner in the campaign, the LNP and its leading candidate could afford to employ a relatively passive social media strategy, while the ALP government needed to try a considerably more aggressive approach to changing voters' views. Potential for embarrassment of the conservative challenger did arise briefly during the campaign, however, when – in addition to @Campbell_Newman – the candidate did create his 'own' account, @CD_Track (the account name apparently standing for 'Can Do' – Newman's self-appointed nickname – 'On Track'). Initiated on 5 March, and used sporadically over the following days, Newman announced its termination on 8 March, tweeting 'I am going to use the other account as it has all the followers. I will use it myself from now on' (Newman 2012), thus also implying that the official @Campbell_Newman account had at least until then been run mainly by campaign staff. While Newman denies in the same tweet that campaign pressure led to his termination of @CD_Track, we might speculate that the LNP campaign team would not have looked favourably on a potential dilution of its campaign messages across two Newman-related accounts. (On the *Twitter* website, the @CD_Track account remains accessible, but dormant, at the time of writing.)

Twitter activities by the leading politicians' accounts are relatively steady throughout the campaign period. Figure 2 shows the cumulative number of original tweets, @replies, and retweets by both the @TheQldPremier and @Campbell_Newman accounts. For both, the rate of tweeting clearly increases as the election proper is called on 19 February, and daily activity is relatively steady throughout the campaign, through to 24 March. Notably, the @Campbell_Newman account only begins to tweet substantially once the election is called, however; this points to the use of social media simply as an additional campaign tool, compared to Bligh's pre-existing use of *Twitter* as a significant means of communication, dating back at least as far as the 2011 Queensland floods (cf. Bruns *et al.* 2012). Further, both accounts virtually flatline immediately after the election, failing even to engage substantively with the messages of congratulation or commiseration, which are publicly tweeted at them. The @TheQldPremier account finally re-emerges

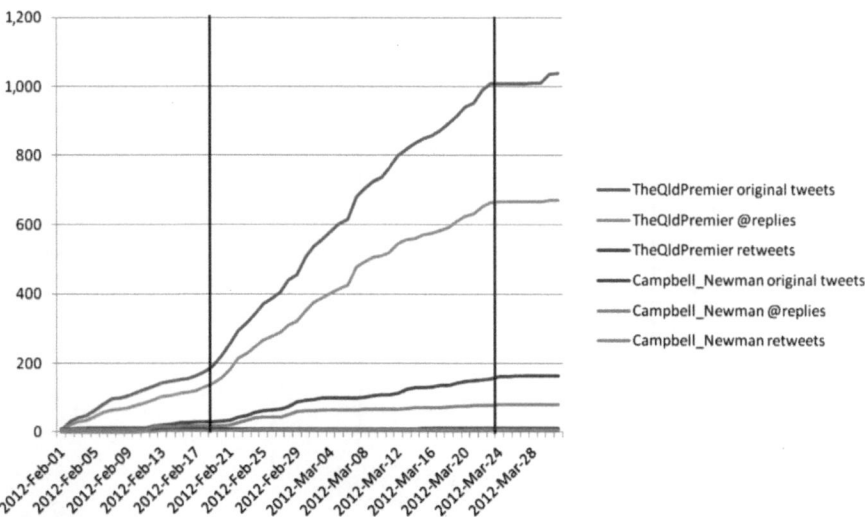

FIGURE 2 Cumulative account activity by @TheQldPremier and @Campbell_Newman over the course of the campaign.

several days after the election, following the renaming of Bligh's personal account to @annambligh, the consequent availability of the @TheQldPremier *Twitter* handle, and its re-registration by the LNP campaign team (Burgess 2012). Subsequently, the @Campbell_Newman account ceased its activities: at the time of writing, its last tweet dated to 26 March 2012. (This process may well constitute the first recorded handing over – if indirectly – of an Australian Premier's *Twitter* username following a change of government.)

The divergence in *Twitter* activity between the two parties and their respective leaders, which this analysis has shown, does not necessarily manifest in a matching divergence in responses by the general *Twitter* audience, however. In addition to the accounts' own activities, we also tracked the volume of @mentions received by either account. The corresponding cumulative volume of @mentions across the election period, shown in Figure 3, does not point to a significant divergence between the two leaders' accounts, especially over the course of the campaign proper.

During the 'phony' campaign which precedes the official start of the election campaign on 19 February, Bligh pulls ahead – most likely by virtue of her more established *Twitter* presence at the time. By the time, the election itself is called, on the other hand, @Campbell_Newman has become better known, and mentions of the account track mentions of @TheQldPremier closely; between 19 February and 24 March, Bligh receives fewer than 1,000 more mentions than Newman. It is only after the election, as the full results become known, that Bligh's account is again mentioned substantially more than Newman – with

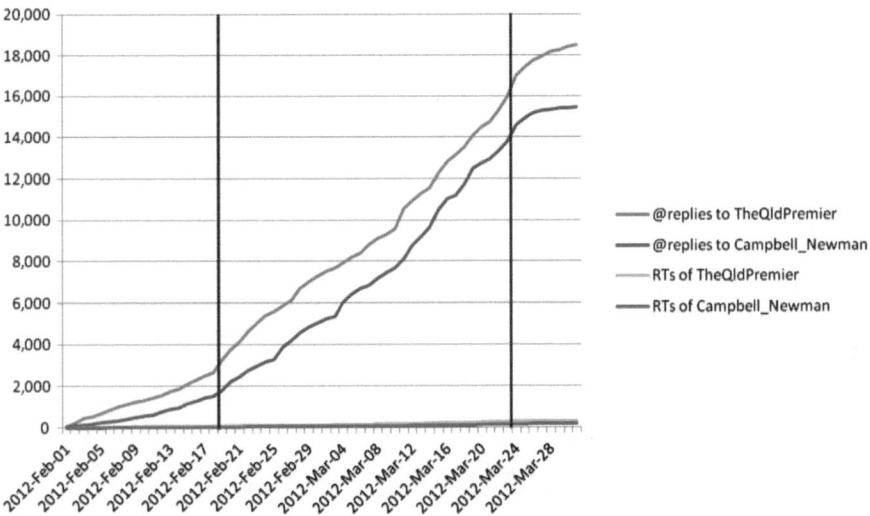

FIGURE 3 Cumulative @mentions of @TheQldPremier and @Campbell_Newman over the course of the campaign.

many @mentions sent to express both sorrow and relief at the change of government.

This clearly indicates that at least in the present case, the volume of *Twitter* activity by the leading accounts themselves is a poor predictor for their popularity as recipients of @mentions. While – as we have shown above – Bligh does considerably more work to actively engage with *Twitter* users through her @replies, the interactions generated through this conversational approach do not manifest in a substantial advantage for her as a recipient of @mentions; rather, regardless of their own endeavours, both leaders are frequently @mentioned on *Twitter* throughout the campaign period. This points to the widespread use of @mentions of relevant accounts in political discussions on *Twitter* not with the principal intention of getting in touch and striking up a conversation with these politicians; instead, account handles are used simply as a convenient shortcut for referring to the leaders which is appropriate to the platform of conversation.

This interpretation of user activities around the leaders' accounts is also borne out by the comparatively low rates of retweeting which are experienced by both. The retweeting of messages originating from the leaders' accounts implies that conscious attention is being paid to their *Twitter* activities, but this appears to be the case only for a small minority of the total number of users who @mention the accounts; by contrast, many of the users who do @mention the leaders may not even actively follow these accounts, but simply tweet about them rather than seeking to engage with them.

Such observations must again be understood against the specific context of the 2012 Queensland state election, however: a tighter electoral contest may well see markedly different activity patterns and a more significant engagement with the tweets posted by leading political accounts, as partisan supporters of either side seek to promote their leader's statements and activities. During the 2012 election, LNP supporters largely did not need, and ALP supporters may have lacked the enthusiasm, to help promote their respective leaders on *Twitter*.

This part of our analysis clearly points to different *Twitter* campaigning strategies for the two leaders. Bligh had already been an active *Twitter* user through much of her Premiership, and (with her staff) further stepped up activities once the campaign officially commenced; this can be read as a clear attempt to use all available media channels to avert electoral defeat. By contrast, Newman and his team – already well ahead in the opinion polls – did not need to expend substantial energy on social media campaigning, and engaged only minimally; indeed, they used the @Campbell_Newman account almost precisely from the official election announcement on 19 February to election day on 24 March, ceasing activities as soon as the election was won. Neither strategy, however, affected how ordinary *Twitter* users tweeted *about* the candidates, however.

Networks of interaction

These observations also raise further questions about the overall patterns of *Twitter* users' interactions with the political accounts we tracked during the 2012 Queensland state elections. In their seminal analysis of interlinkage patterns amongst US political blogs during the 2004 presidential election campaign, Adamic and Glance (2005) discovered substantial network divisions along partisan lines, with progressive blogs linking to other progressive blogs and conservative blogs linking to fellow conservative blogs, but not frequently connecting across the ideological divide. This has been seen as an indication of 'echo chamber' structures in the US political blogosphere, where supporters of either side are exposed only to their own side's views, but may never encounter the arguments of their opponents in their original form.

Even though political divisions between the two major party organizations in Australia have been pronounced in recent years, however, our analysis and visualization of the patterns of @mentions of political *Twitter* accounts by everyday *Twitter* users during the Queensland election does not produce similar results. In Figure 4, we show the core network of @mentions of the political accounts we tracked during the election, visualized using the Force Atlas 2 algorithm provided by the open-source network visualization software *Gephi* (Gephi.org 2012) which places close to one another those accounts which are frequently connected with each other. Nodes in the graph represent individual users, and are coloured – for the political accounts along party lines: red for Labor, blue for the LNP, green for the Australian Greens, and brown for KAP; grey nodes – the majority – represent the everyday *Twitter* users who mention these accounts. To simplify the graph, we limited it to nodes which sent or received at least 10 @mentions during the election period.

Connections between accounts – representing @mentions – are coloured according to the party affiliation of the recipient political account. What results from this visualization is a clear indication of the relative interest in candidates of different political colours; that interest is centred mainly on Labor and LNP politicians, with minor clusters of interest around Greens and KAP candidates. Most notably, however, there is virtually no substantial separation between the two major parties: while both do have a range of followers who mention only 'their' side of politics, the graph overwhelmingly shows a thorough mixture of blue and red, indicating that *Twitter* users are generally as likely to @mention LNP candidates as they are to @mention ALP representatives. Indeed, the two major nodes for the two parties, representing @TheQldPremier and @Campbell_Newman, are located at the centre of the graph and in close proximity to one another, indicating that they were both @mentioned frequently by the same *Twitter* users, sometimes even in the same tweet.

This divergence of our results from the patterns established by Adamic and Glance (2005) and similar studies is not necessarily surprising, given the different

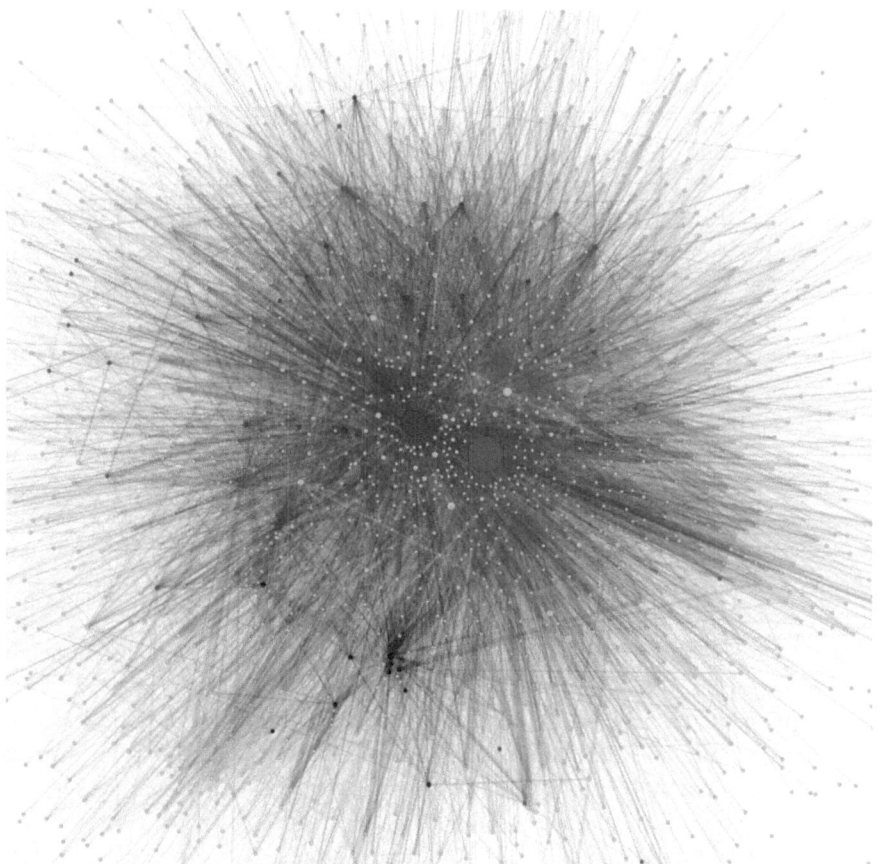

FIGURE 4 Network of accounts @mentioning the political candidates during the election period, coloured by party affiliation of the @mentioned accounts.

communicative affordances of blogs and *Twitter*. Hyperlinks in political blogs can reference additional information (when embedded in blog posts) or signal ideological affiliation (when included in blogrolls) (Highfield 2011). They are rarely used simply to reference other blog authors or commenters, nor is it common practice to include links to the websites or other Web presences of all public figures mentioned in a post. Hyperlinks in blogs, therefore, constitute a more rarefied commodity which is activated only where, especially relevant – to the extent that blog research and common blogging etiquette consider them to be part of a gift economy of mutual linking (Schmidt 2007; Francoli & Ward 2008). This can lead logically to a more partisan use of hyperlinks to support only political fellow travellers.

By contrast, @mentioning on *Twitter* is a substantially more everyday practice which includes political friends and enemies alike; indeed, some @mentions may well stem from messages which retweet or @mention political opponents only in order to criticize their statements or general views. Such critical @mentioning of political opponents may even be undertaken deliberately in order to evoke an (angry) response which may then be further exploited for political gain. Beyond such intentionally combative activities, too, @mentions of their accounts simply provide a convenient shortcut for referring to public figures in any domain, and are used on *Twitter* as a matter of course. This explains the lack of overwhelming partisanship in how @mentions were mobilized by the general *Twitter* public in the present case, then: few users, for example, would have referred to @TheQldPremier by her *Twitter* username, but then avoided doing the same for @Campbell_Newman in order to deprive him of *Twitter* exposure, it seems.

However, if the network of *Twitter* interactions through @mentioning is narrowed to display interactions only between the candidate and party accounts themselves a different pattern emerges. Figure 5 shows the political *Twitter* accounts which we tracked during the Queensland election, coloured by party affiliation, and indicates the strength of interaction between the accounts through the size of the lines connecting them; connections are coloured here according to the originating account. First, it is immediately obvious again that the Greens and KAP accounts form their own clusters which are connected to the rest of the network only through a small number of interactions with political opponents (usually at a local level, where opposing candidates in the same electorate @mention one another). Mainly, candidates of both parties group around their party leaders or prominent local candidates, supporting each other through mutual @mentions and retweets. To the extent that such activity is orchestrated by each party's campaign headquarters, it also represents a dedicated multi-account political promotion strategy, of course.

There is also strong interaction between the accounts affiliated with each of the two major parties; most centrally, in each case, between the respective general party accounts and the party leaders. Minor candidates also @mention the party and leadership accounts with some degree of frequency. But a considerable amount of @mentioning also takes place across party lines between the two party organizations – and here, especially directed by Labor candidates at their LNP opponents. Of the party leadership teams, Labor's Deputy Premier @AndrewFraserMP is the most prominent combatant: he frequently @mentions his opposite number @TimNichollsMP as well as @Campbell_Newman, while – in spite of her otherwise frequent @replies to other *Twitter* accounts – Premier Anna Bligh remains relatively subdued in her interactions with the other side. This is likely to point to a deliberate campaign strategy which positions Fraser as leading the attack while Bligh remains in a more presidential role above the fray.

Newman's direct opponent in the Brisbane city electorate of Ashgrove, @katejonesmp, also appears as a prominent account in this analysis,

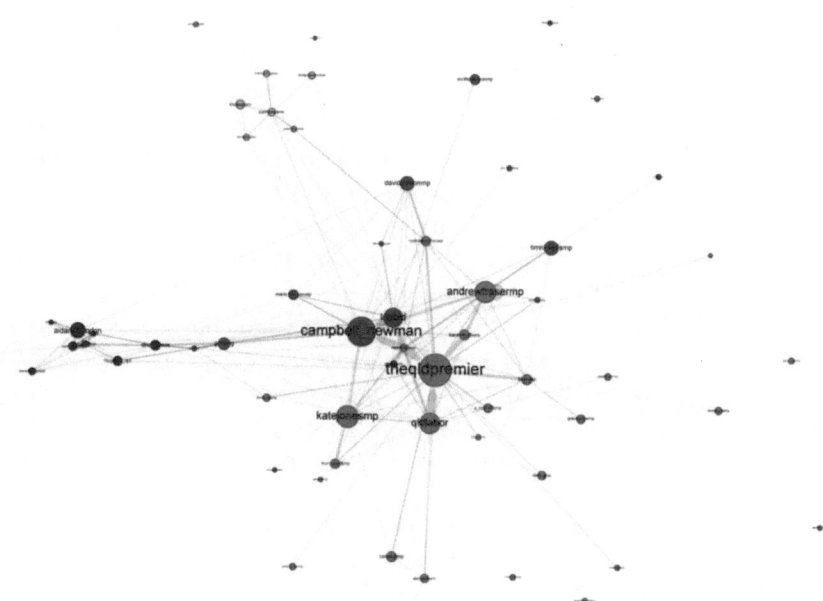

FIGURE 5 Network of @mention interactions between the political candidates during the election period, coloured by party affiliation of the @mentioned accounts.

@mentioning @Campbell_Newman with some frequency; she played a pivotal role in Labor's election strategy as a strong performance by her would have raised doubts about Newman's ability to enter parliament in order to take up the Premiership in the first place. However, her @mentions towards Newman remain comparatively muted, as the development of a perception of her as too aggressive in style would have hindered rather than helped her public image. Finally, local Surfers Paradise candidate @matt4surfersalp appears to have taken on a similar attacking role, possibly on his own initiative: his is the ALP-affiliated account which most frequently mentions @LNPQLD and @Campbell_Newman, alongside @TheQldPremier.

In keeping with their electoral positioning ahead of the election, LNP accounts largely refrain from responding in kind; again, this 'small target' strategy also serves to minimize any possible *Twitter* missteps which could be exploited by their Labor opponents. Some of @TimNichollsMP's few tweets do @mention Andrew Fraser, and the accounts of shadow minister @JPLangbroek and local candidate @ScottDriscollAu do engage with @QLDLabor as well as @AndrewFraserMP and @TheQldPremier, respectively, but generally fail to make a substantial impact on the political discussion on *Twitter*.

Hashtagged activity

The activities of *Twitter* users around the key political accounts in the 2012 Queensland state election must also be understood against the background of general activities in the #qldvotes hashtag. As it is impossible to reliably identify and analyse every last tweet which comments, however peripherally, on the Queensland election, the stream of tweets which have deliberately been marked with the #qldvotes hashtag must stand in as a reasonable approximation of overall tweeting activity; however, the self-selecting nature of this sample must be noted and understood in this context. Constituted of tweets whose authors consciously chose to contribute them to a continuing public discussion of the election, #qldvotes represents a temporary, *ad hoc* public (Bruns & Burgess 2012) – but does not contain the less visible, at least notionally private messages intended by *Twitter* users only for their networks of followers. #qldvotes may also be seen as a deliberate performance of public election discussion, therefore.

This also accords with Larsson and Moe's observation that election-related tweeting 'appears to be largely dependent on other mediated events' (2012, p. 13) – a pattern which Bruns and Burgess (2011a) found in their study of the use of *Twitter* in the 2010 Australian federal election, too. Public discussion of political events through shared hashtags will be most inclusive and effective if it discusses shared texts (newspaper reports, TV programmes, major campaign events) that are accessible to all participants; spikes in *Twitter* activity around events such as televised leaders' debates, policy announcements, or election day coverage are a common occurrence, therefore.

This is evident in our #qldvotes data as well (Figure 6). Unsurprisingly, the major spike in *Twitter* activity (at close to 10,000 hashtagged tweets that day) occurs on election day, 24 March 2012. Substantial activity begins only with the official commencement of the campaign on 19 February, with a series of minor spikes evident, especially during the second half of the election period.

After a quiet first third of the campaigning period, 4 March sees a first minor spike as the LNP celebrates its official campaign launch. A further period of heightened activity on 10 March is triggered by an opinion poll which sees Labor's Kate Jones ahead of Campbell Newman in the Ashgrove electorate, raising the possibility that the LNP might win the election, but that its declared candidate for Premier could fail to enter parliament; Labor's own official campaign launch follows on 11 March. 15 March sees a combination of major events, from a visit of former Liberal Party Prime Minister John Howard to the Ashgrove electorate in support of Newman through the escalation of a Labor campaign alleging inappropriate business dealings by Newman and his wife to a televised 'People's Forum' with the leaders. A final leaders' debate in the evening of 19 March accounts for the spike on that day.

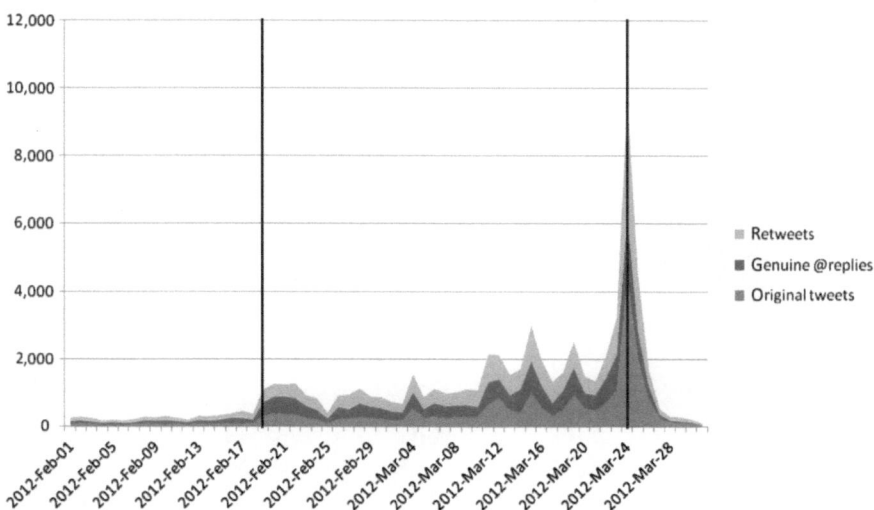

FIGURE 6 #qldvotes activity during February and March 2012.

To determine whether such user activity in the #qldvotes hashtag points to the presence of engaged *Twitter*-based followers of the campaign, or merely to a barrage of random tweets which do not engage with one another, it is also useful to explore the patterns of interaction between #qldvotes contributors. In doing so, we follow Tedjamulia *et al.* (2005) in distinguishing three groups of participants amongst the 8973 unique contributors to #qldvotes whom we observed over the course of February and March 2012: the least active 90 per cent of participants, the next 9 per cent of highly active users, and a final 1 per cent of most active contributors. For each of these groups, and for the overall hashtag data set, we may then calculate their activity patterns (see Bruns & Stieglitz 2012, for a detailed discussion of this approach).

This analysis points to the presence of a dominant core of #qldvotes participants: in combination, lead and highly active users account for more than three quarters of all #qldvotes tweets. While this points to a comparatively small base of dedicated contributors to the hashtag, it also points to the possibility of forms of close interaction – indeed, to the potential to generate a shared sense of community – which it would not be possible to develop amongst a much larger user-base (for example, in the context of a major national election attracting tens or hundreds of thousands of users to the hashtag). Further, Figure 7 shows the presence of a substantially larger percentage of @replies in the tweets of these leading user groups, as compared to those of the least active 90 per cent of contributors; this, too, supports the view that greater community interaction is taking place amongst these leading groups than with the least active group, whose activities consist predominantly of making original statements and retweeting the messages of others. (It is further notable that the percentage of

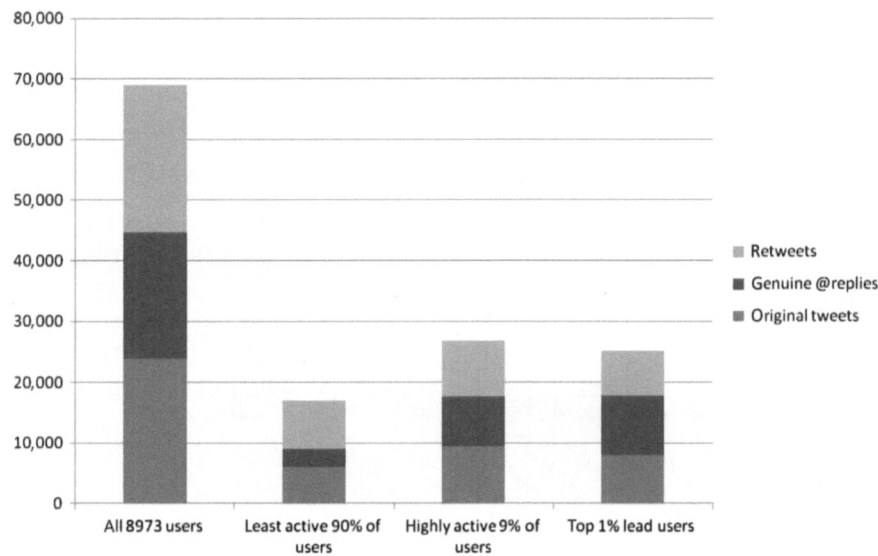

FIGURE 7 Contribution patterns to the #qldvotes hashtag, February/March 2012.

@replies for the top 1 per cent of lead users is greater yet again than that for the next 9 per cent of highly active users.)

Further outlook

The longer term impact of such temporary communion around a shared election hashtag has yet to be fully explored. It is unlikely that all of the leading #qldvotes participants will make the transition to the continuing day-by-day discussion of Queensland politics in #qldpol, for example; a post-election decline in political interest and participation is documented well beyond the specific confines of *Twitter* (Kirchhoff *et al.* 2009; Macnamara 2011).

The same is true also for the *Twitter* activities of the political accounts we have studied in this article, of course – especially in the context of a decisive election delivering a change of government. In the LNP's landslide victory, 48 seats changed their hands from one party to another; in particular, 44 seats changed from the ALP to either the LNP or KAP. Prior to the election, many of the sitting politicians on *Twitter* included their role in their user names, such as @katejonesmp or @TheQldPremier. Including 'MP' after their own name helps to authenticate the user as a politician, even if they have not sought an official verification of their account from *Twitter*.

However, the result of the election meant that many of these accounts were now no longer appropriately named, since the users in question had not been reelected or – like Anna Bligh – had lost their government functions. In addition to the changes around the Bligh and Newman accounts noted previously, other accounts were rebranded in response to the election result; Kate Jones's account, for example, changed to @katejonesqld. Further, those successful and – especially – unsuccessful candidates who had only begun to use *Twitter* at the start of the campaign, possibly at the behest of their campaign headquarters, now also had to decide whether they wanted to continue their *Twitter* activities post-election. At the time of writing in late November 2012, @katejonesqld had posted one tweet since the election day in March, while @andrewfraserqld had remained generally active, for example. As noted above, @Campbell_Newman had ceased tweeting altogether, too, in favour of the newly acquired @TheQldPremier account, whose tweets now consist almost exclusively of media releases. These post-election changes have clear implications for research which tracks the tweets by, and mentions of, specific *Twitter* accounts beyond the election campaigns themselves; regular checks of the accounts tracked are required to ensure that the project is capturing the intended data. More generally, they also indicate for each candidate whether they understand *Twitter* predominantly as a campaigning tool, or have incorporated social media fully into their everyday political activities.

Conclusion

Overall, the findings of our study must be understood against the backdrop of an election which had always been predicted to result in a landslide win for the LNP opposition. This electoral starting-point appears to have resulted in the adoption of some highly divergent social media strategies by the two major parties: on the one hand, the highly active use of *Twitter* by the ALP, with a clear distribution of roles across its leading accounts, a campaign of strong personal activity by the Premier and an at times aggressive approach to engaging with LNP opponents by Treasurer Andrew Fraser and other candidates; on the other, the 'small target' strategy of the LNP, which did institute 'personal' accounts for some of its leaders but (as it seems from the @CD_Track episode) closely policed those accounts and otherwise positioned its generic @LNPQLD party account as the central, staid *Twitter* presence. Beyond this, the smaller parties developed their own social media strategies, and mainly used *Twitter* to generate interactions between their own accounts.

We have also documented that the respective levels of active *Twitter* usage by the various candidates are generally not reflected in their prominence and visibility in the total number of @mentions made of them by everyday *Twitter* users, however; rather, the *Twitter* handles of specific politicians appear simply to stand in as substitutes for their full names, and are used by supporters and opponents alike without such use conferring any notable approval or disapproval. At least in the specific context of the 2012 Queensland election, this raises significant doubts about the ability of *Twitter* (and perhaps of overall social media) campaigning to affect electoral outcomes in any direct way; ordinary *Twitter* users appeared to be substantially more likely to use the politicians' *Twitter* handles to talk *about* them than strike up a conversation *with* them, even in spite of the considerable outreach efforts of Anna Bligh's @TheQldPremier account and those of a handful of other candidates. In the end, Bligh's highly active and Newman's largely passive accounts were @mentioned with similar frequency.

This also highlights the limited utility of any simplistic electoral sentiment schemes which merely measure the relative visibility through @mentions of political accounts without investigating in much greater depth the context in which such account names are mentioned. Even apart from the fact that *Twitter* demographics – in Australia or elsewhere – are rarely representative of the general population, any attempts to forecast election outcomes from the relative *Twitter* activity around the major candidates' accounts should be approached with great caution, therefore.

The same is true for studies which focus only on election-related hashtags, however. As our analysis of #qldvotes has shown, that hashtag was ultimately dominated by a small community of fewer than 1,000 *Twitter* users, whose interactions amongst one another may be of interest in their own right, but whose high levels of engagement with the election campaign designate them as 'political junkies' (Coleman 2003) and therefore far from representative of the wider electorate. There are few opportunities to overcome such sampling bias, short of tracking every conceivable keyword which may be used in conjunction with political discussion on *Twitter* – and on balance, a focus on the @mentions of politicians and other relevant accounts may provide a better and more diverse cross-section through election-related political discussion on that platform than is provided by a focus on hashtags alone, as it does not base itself on an already self-selected group of highly engaged political discussants in the way that a hashtag data set does.

What is necessary as a next step beyond the more limited analysis which we have been able to present in this article, then, is the comprehensive semantic analysis – including a focus on the key terms, concepts, and attitudes expressed in the tweets – of @mention data sets as we have analysed them here. In addition to tracking the relative prominence of the various political accounts, such an analysis might be able to identify the key themes and sentiments associated with such accounts, and explore how these may affect the electoral fortunes of the account holders.

Overall, our analysis here demonstrates the use of diverse *Twitter* campaigning strategies which match the divergent electoral fortunes of the various parties and candidates in the 2012 Queensland election; it also appears to show the relative inability of such strategic choices to affect the overall political debate on *Twitter* about the election, however. Further, similar analysis of comparable election campaigns must show whether these observations are unique to this election, whose outcomes were rarely in doubt, and whether a closer electoral contest, for example, may generate considerably more active use of social media by all parties, not least also in order to directly engage with the opposition and its supporters.

References

Adamic, L. A. & Glance, N. (2005) 'The political blogosphere and the 2004 U.S. election: divided they blog', [Online] paper presented at 2nd Annual Workshop on the Weblogging Ecosystem: Aggregation, Analysis and Dynamics, Chiba, Japan, 10 May 2005. Available at: http://www.blogpulse.com/papers/2005/AdamicGlanceBlogWWW.pdf (12 May 2010).

Broersma, M. & Graham, T. (2012) 'Social media as beat: tweets as a news source during the 2010 British and Dutch elections', *Journalism Practice*, vol. 6, no. 3, pp. 403–419, doi:10.1080/17512786.2012.663626.

Bruns, A. (2012) 'How long is a tweet? Mapping dynamic conversation networks on Twitter using Gawk and Gephi', *Information, Communication & Society*, vol. 15, no. 9, pp. 1323–1351, doi:10.1080/1369118X.2011.635214.

Bruns, A. & Burgess, J. (2011a) '#ausvotes: how Twitter covered the 2010 Australian federal election', *Communication, Politics & Culture*, vol. 44, no. 2, pp. 37–56.

Bruns, A. & Burgess, J. (2011b) 'Gawk scripts for Twitter processing', *Mapping Online Publics*, [Online] Available at: http://mappingonlinepublics.net/resources/ (14 March 2013).

Bruns, A. & Burgess, J. (2012) 'Notes towards the scientific study of public communication on Twitter', [Online] keynote presented at the Conference on Science and the Internet, Düsseldorf, 4 August 2012, Available at: http://snurb.info/files/2012/Notes%20towards%20the%20Scientific%20Study%20of%20Public%20Communication%20on%20Twitter.pdf (14 March 2013).

Bruns, A. & Stieglitz, S. (2012) 'Quantitative approaches to comparing communication patterns on Twitter', *Journal of Technology in Human Services*, vol. 30, nos 3–4, pp. 160–185, doi:10.1080/15228835.2012.744249.

Bruns, A., Burgess, J., Crawford, K. & Shaw, F. (2012) '#qldfloods and @ QPSMedia: crisis communication on Twitter in the 2011 South East Queensland floods', [Online], Brisbane, Available at: http://cci.edu.au/floodsreport.pdf (14 March 2013).

Burgess, J. (2012) 'Who's @TheQldPremier?', *Creativity/Machine*, [Online] 26 March, Available at: http://creativitymachine.net/2012/03/26/whos-theqldpremier/ (14 March 2013).

Burgess, J. & Bruns, A. (2012) '(Not) the Twitter election: the dynamics of the #ausvotes conversation in relation to the Australian media ecology', *Journalism Practice*, vol. 6, no. 3, pp. 384–402, doi:10.1080/17512786.2012.663610.

Coleman, S. (2003) 'A tale of two houses: the House of Commons, the Big Brother house and the people at home', *Parliamentary Affairs*, vol. 56, no. 4, pp. 733–758.

Flew, T. (2008) 'Not yet the Internet election: online media, political commentary and the 2007 Australian federal election', *Media International Australia Incorporating Culture and Policy*, vol. 126, pp. 5–13.

Francoli, M. & Ward, S. (2008) '21st century soapboxes? MPs and their blogs', *Information Polity: The International Journal of Government & Democracy in the Information Age*, vol. 13, pp. 21–39.

Gephi.org (2012) 'Gephi, an open source graph visualization and manipulation software', [Online] Available at: http://gephi.org/ (29 November 2012).

Gibson, R., Lusoli, W. & Ward, S. (2008) 'The Australian public and politics online: reinforcing or reinventing representation?' *Australian Journal of Political Science*, vol. 43, no. 1, pp. 111–131.

Grant, W. J., Moon, B. & Busby Grant, J. (2010) 'Digital dialogue? Australian politicians' use of the social network tool Twitter', *Australian Journal of Political Science*, vol. 45, no. 4, pp. 579–604, doi:10.1080/10361146.2010.517176.

Highfield, T. (2011) *Mapping Intermedia News Flows: Topical Discussions in the Australian and French Political Blogospheres*, [Online] Doctoral dissertation, Queensland University of Technology, Brisbane. Available at: http://eprints.qut.edu.au/48115/ (14 March 2013).

Highfield, T. & Bruns, A. (2012) 'Confrontation and cooptation: a brief history of Australian political blogs', *Media International Australia*, vol. 143, pp. 89–98.

Jericho, G. (2012) *The Rise of the Fifth Estate: Social Media and Blogging in Australian Politics*, Scribe, Melbourne.

Kirchhoff, L., Nicolai, T., Bruns, A. & Highfield, T. (2009) 'Monitoring the Australian blogosphere through the 2007 Australian Federal Election', in *Communication, Creativity and Global Citizenship: Refereed Proceedings of the Australian and New Zealand Communications Association Annual Conference*, [Online] Brisbane, 8–10 July, ed. T. Flew, pp. 982–1005. Available at: http://www.proceedings.anzca09.org (12 May 2010).

Larsson, A. O. & Moe, H. (2012) 'Studying political microblogging: Twitter users in the 2010 Swedish election campaign', *New Media & Society*, vol. 14, no. 5, pp. 729–747, doi:10.1177/1461444811422894.

Larsson, A. O. & Moe, H. (forthcoming) 'Twitter in politics and elections: insights from Scandinavia', in *Twitter and Society*, eds K. Weller, A. Bruns, J. Burgess, M. Mahrt & C. Puschmann, Peter Lang, New York.

Macnamara, J. (2011) 'Pre and post-election 2010 online: what happened to the conversation?' *Communication, Politics & Culture*, vol. 44, no. 2, pp. 18–36.

Maireder, A. (forthcoming) 'Political discourses on Twitter: networking topics, objects and people', in *Twitter and Society*, eds K. Weller, A. Bruns, J. Burgess, M. Mahrt & C. Puschmann, Peter Lang, New York.

Maireder, A., Ausserhofer, J. & Kittenberger, A. (2012) 'Mapping the Austrian political Twittersphere: how politicians, journalists and political strategists (inter)act on Twitter', *Proceedings of CeDem12 Conference for E-Democracy and Open Government*, [Online] eds P. Parycek & N. Edelmann, Danube University,

Krems, Austria, pp. 151–164 Available at: http://phaidra.univie.ac.at/o:154914 (14 March 2013).

Newman, C. (2012) 'Tweet', Available at: https://twitter.com/CD_Track/status/177702564224176129 (14 March 2013).

Schmidt, J. (2007) 'Blogging practices: an analytical framework', *Journal of Computer-Mediated Communication*, vol. 12, no. 4, pp. 1409–1427.

Tedjamulia, S. J. J., Dean, D. L., Olsen, D. R. & Albrecht, C. C. (2005) 'Motivating content contributions to online communities: toward a more comprehensive theory', in *Proceedings of the 38th Annual Hawaii International Conference on System Science*, Hawai'i, 3–6 January 2005. Washington, DC: IEEE, 193b.

Todd Graham, Marcel Broersma, Karin Hazelhoff & Guido van 't Haar

BETWEEN BROADCASTING POLITICAL MESSAGES AND INTERACTING WITH VOTERS
The use of Twitter during the 2010 UK general election campaign

Politicians across Western democracies are increasingly adopting and experimenting with Twitter, particularly during election time. The purpose of this article is to investigate how candidates are using it during an election campaign. The aim is to create a typology of the various ways in which candidates behaved on Twitter. Our research, which included a content analysis of tweets (n = 26,282) from all twittering Conservative, Labour and Liberal Democrat candidates (n = 416) during the 2010 UK General Election campaign, focused on four aspects of tweets: type, interaction, function and topic. By examining candidates' twittering behaviour, the authors show that British politicians mainly used Twitter as a unidirectional form of communication. However, there were a group of candidates who used it to interact with voters by, for example, mobilizing, helping and consulting them, thus tapping into the potential Twitter offers for facilitating a closer relationship with citizens.

Introduction

Twitter, with its estimated 140 million active users generating 340 million tweets a day, has become one of the most popular sites on the Internet (Twitter 2012). More than any other social network, it has been successful in connecting ordinary people to the popular, powerful and influential. Politicians across Western democracies, their careers dependent on reaching as wide an audience as possible, are therefore increasingly embracing Twitter, especially during election time. For example, in the United States, usage by candidates (from the two main parties) during the 2010 mid-term election campaign was almost universal (Wallsten, in press). In the UK, the 2010 General Election saw Twitter make its place as one of the core communication tools amongst political and media elites as Newman (2010, p. 3) maintains: 'It reached critical mass during this campaign and became an essential source of real-time information for journalists and politicians alike'. The number of British MPs using Twitter has spiked over the past several years from just under eight per cent active in 2009 (Jackson & Lilleker 2011) to nearly two-thirds of MPs with an account in 2013 (Tweetminister 2013). So, how exactly are politicians using Twitter?

Early research into how British parties and politicians adopted the Internet for campaign purposes has revealed that online campaigning tended to replicate traditional one-way, top-down communication flows (Coleman 2001; Jackson 2007). However, some scholars have argued that social media and its participatory culture and practices may help bridge the gap between politicians and citizens, fostering a mode of representation that is centred on interactive communication between the two (Coleman & Blumler 2009). Twitter is of particular interest given its popularity and defining characteristics, which offer an opportunity for developing a closer and more direct relationship between voters and politicians. The question then is how politicians are behaving on Twitter. Are they simply broadcasting their messages or are they beginning to tap into this participatory potential by engaging and interacting with the public?

This paper aims to address these questions by exploring the use of Twitter by British candidates during the 2010 General Election campaign, the ultimate aim being to establish a typology of twittering behaviour. In order to achieve this, a content analysis of 26,282 tweets produced by 416 candidates during the two weeks prior to the election was conducted. The findings reveal that, in some ways, it was indeed business as usual; candidates mainly used Twitter to broadcast their messages, as a platform for partisan attacks and as a means of acknowledging and thanking their supporters. However, given the nature of Twitter, such traditional behaviours potentially take on altered and even new meanings. Furthermore, there were a group of candidates who tapped into Twitter's potential for facilitating closer and more connected relationships with citizens.

Politicians' use of social media

In 1999, Blumler and Kavanagh mused on the possibilities the Internet potentially offers for political communication. At the time, they found the use of online tools by political parties for communicative purposes to be embryonic;

their impact was minimal (1999, p. 222). Research from the 2001 and 2005 UK General Election campaigns showed that online campaigns tended to replicate the one-way communicative patterns that we have become familiar with in offline campaigning (Coleman 2001; Jackson 2007). However, with the rise of social media, scholars have once again envisioned its potential as a possible 'equalizer' for democracy, from levelling the playing field between established and new political parties (Small 2008) to bridging the gap between politics and the public (Coleman 2005b; Coleman & Blumler 2009).

Regarding the latter, one of the major challenges is that traditional politics in many Western democracies increasingly suffers from a decline in interest and participation (Flickinger & Studlar 2007). Though voting turnout increased slightly in both the 2005 and 2010 UK General Elections from a historically low turnout in 2001 (McGuinness et al. 2012), many other indicators reveal that citizens are increasingly turning away from national politics. According to Hansard Society's (2012) *Audit of Political Engagement*, indicators such as political interest, knowledge and satisfaction are on a downward trend. Coleman (2005a) convincingly argues that this is partly a result of a breakdown in the sense of feeling represented by elected officials. He empirically shows via a national survey that politicians in the UK are failing to build meaningful connections with citizens. They felt their MPs were too distant, invisible, alien, arrogant and too partisan (see also Hansard Society 2012).

Based on these findings, Coleman (2005a, pp. 10–12) developed the concept of 'direct representation' that consists of three essential conditions. First, communication between representatives and citizens needs to be a two-way process. It requires a conversation, not just a consultation. Representatives need to find ways of tapping into the everyday political talk that takes place among the public (see also Graham 2011). This requires the development of shared and trusted spaces where collaborative interaction between representatives and citizens can unfold and develop. Second, this conversation has to be of an on-going and permanent nature. Representation should be a continuous process rather than an aggregation of preferences during election time. Finally, elected representatives should start to 'account for themselves'. This is more than simply justifying, for example, their actions when challenged by the media, but rather it is a form of accountability whereby politicians pro-actively hold *themselves* accountable by regularly justifying their decisions to the public.

Given the interactive and participatory nature of social media and politicians' need to connect, it is no surprise that they are increasingly adopting these new communicative spaces. Twitter is of particular interest. Not only is it popular, but its key features make it a potentially fruitful space for developing a more direct relationship, as Coleman describes, between politicians and citizens (see also Graham et al., in press). Twitter's open and immediate structure can facilitate closeness and visibility. Indeed, Lee and Shin's (2012, p. 15) experimental research suggests that exposure to a politician's Twitter page heightens 'a sense of direct, face-to-face conversation with him among those prone to get immersed in a mediated experience of others'. Politicians who use Twitter regularly may be able to tap into the intimacy Twitter fosters. Additionally, Twitter is a social network site, which could allow a politician to develop a reciprocal relationship with citizens by, for example, interacting, sharing information and requesting public input. Twitter too can allow a candidate to engage in a conversation; candidates can listen to and engage in political talk with citizens in this mutually shared space. To what degree are politicians actually using Twitter to support this kind of relationship with citizens?

The empirical evidence (within various contexts) does not yet indicate a shift towards such a relationship. One of the most common findings is that politicians tend to use Twitter primarily to broadcast their messages, as opposed to interacting with the public (Glassman *et al.* 2010; Grant *et al.* 2010; Small 2010, 2011; Larsson & Moe 2011; Sæbø 2011; Burgess & Bruns 2012). Golbeck's *et al.* (2010) analysis, for example, of over 6,000 tweets revealed that US national legislators primarily used Twitter to broadcast information and activities, representing more than three-quarters of their sample. Similarly, Jackson and Lilleker (2011) found that British MPs used Twitter predominately as a tool for self-promotion – broadcasting events attended and achievements in parliament. These studies suggest that social media is not yet significantly changing traditional political relationships, but there is still ample *terra incognita* left unexplored. In particular, what is needed is a more detailed and comprehensive account of how politicians behave on Twitter.

Much of the empirical research focuses on the networks and patterns of interaction that emerge via an analysis of specific hashtags in which politicians are just one of the many actors (Larsson & Moe 2011; Small 2011; Burgess & Bruns 2012). Studies that investigate politicians' twittering behaviour specifically are based on a network analysis (Vergeer *et al.* 2011) or focus on party leaders or sitting MPs/legislators (Glassman *et al.* 2010; Golbeck *et al.* 2010; Grant *et al.* 2010; Small 2010; Jackson & Lilleker 2011; Sæbø 2011). However, there are remarkably few studies of how political candidates (both incumbents and challengers) are behaving on Twitter during election time. Furthermore, studies that have focused specifically on politicians' behaviour have been limited in size and/or scope, or analytical categories were not always particular. To take two examples from previous studies: Sæbø (2011) conceptualizes seven distinct and detailed 'genres' of tweets covering form, content and purpose, but his typology is based on a small dataset. Conversely, Golbeck's *et al.* (2010) typology lacks nuance; the category 'information' encompasses a variety of behaviours. Moreover, the coding scheme mixes content with form. The authors consider interacting with another user and providing information to be mutually exclusive types of tweets while the latter can be the content of the former. There are also very few studies that investigate with whom politicians are interacting. Those that do examine this typically focus on the interaction of the *central* political actors in the Twittersphere (Larsson & Moe 2011; Ausserhofer & Maireder 2013). It is unclear if politicians use Twitter to interact with the public or are simply talking amongst themselves. Finally, there is little research on what topics politicians are twittering about, which is particularly relevant during an election campaign. Are they using Twitter to discuss and present their positions on key political issues?

Research focus and methodology

To improve our understanding of Twitter as a tool for political communication in general, and the manner in which politicians use it specifically, it is necessary to extend the analytical depth of research into the subject. This research aims to do this by investigating how British candidates from the three main parties behave on Twitter during election time and seeks to answer four research questions:

RQ1: To what extent are British candidates using Twitter to interact with others?
RQ2: With whom are they interacting?
RQ3: About which societal/political topics are they twittering?
RQ4: What functions do their tweets serve?

By addressing these questions, we aim to construct a typology of twittering behaviour. In order to provide more depth to the analysis presented below, the quantitative findings will be supplemented by qualitative examples to demonstrate tendencies among candidates.

The case

The 2010 General Election was a historical occasion. It saw the removal of the longstanding Labour government and resulted in the first coalition government since the Second World War. It was the first real competitive general election in nearly two decades with the third biggest party, the Liberal Democrats, entering the scene as possible contenders. The campaign itself consisted of several noteworthy moments and gaffes (see Newman 2010 for the campaign timeline). However, the most important by far was the arrival of the first ever televised Prime Ministerial Debates. This consisted of three debates between the main party leaders (Gordon Brown, Labour; David Cameron, Conservatives; Nick Clegg, Liberal Democrats), which were aired on ITV (15 April), Sky (22 April) and the BBC (29 April). The debates were seen by millions, reached more voters than any other episodic televised campaign coverage and dominated the election campaign, particularly news media coverage (see, e.g. Coleman *et al.* 2011).[1]

Population and sample

The population consisted of all twittering candidates from the three main parties. First, a list of all candidates who had a Twitter account was compiled. This was carried out initially on 21 April 2010 and subsequently re-checked on 29 April and 6 May to ensure that any new accounts were included. The list was gathered by consulting the party websites. For candidates where an account was not listed, two additional searches were conducted via the website www.election-tweets.co.uk/ (a site that supposedly followed all candidates) and the Twitter search function. Of the 454 candidates with an account, those who posted one or more tweets during the two weeks of the campaign ($n = 416$) were included in the analysis.

The start of the election campaign began on 6 April and ended on polling day 6 May 2010. In order to make the study more manageable while maintaining the meaningfulness of the data, the sample of tweets was based on a 15-day period. All tweets posted from 22 April to 6 May ($n = 26,282$) were included in the analysis. The final two weeks were selected as these are typically the most active weeks during a campaign.

Coding categories

A content analysis was employed as the primary instrument for examination. The coding scheme was developed as a means of identifying and describing politicians' posting behaviour. The unit of analysis was the individual tweet. The context unit of analysis was the thread in which it was situated. The context played an integral role in the coding process because tweets are often posted in the form of interaction, which range from a single pair of tweets to a string of tweets. Thus, in order to maintain the social integrity of these interactions, coders coded politicians' tweets in chronological order.

The coding scheme focused on four aspects of each tweet. First, the type of tweet was identified. Four tweet types were distinguished: normal post, @-reply, retweet (the symbols used are, e.g. ▣, 'RT' or 'via') and retweet with comment (e.g. 'That's ridicules [*sic*]! RT @nigel4selby Our party has always been big on the environment!').

Second, all those tweets coded as @-replies were subsequently coded for with whom they were interacting. Tweets were coded as one of the following categories: (1) public/citizen, (2) journalist/media, (3) lobbyist, (4) expert, (5) industry, (6) authority (e.g. police, campaign regulators), (7) celebrity, (8–11) politician (Conservative, Labour, LibDem, other party) and (12) party activist (e.g. campaign team, volunteers). In order to make the classification, coders first consulted the user's Twitter profile; then, if needed, the hyperlink provided in a user's description.[2] All Twitter IDs were then cross-referenced with a comprehensive list of twittering candidates from all seat-holding parties in the UK. These two steps along with the context in which the tweet was posted allowed a coder to classify the user.

Third, all tweets were coded for their function: (1) (update from the) campaign trail, (2) campaign promotion, (3) campaign action, (4) call to vote, (5) political news/report, (6) other news/report, (7) position taking/own stance, (8) party stance, (9) critiquing/arguing, (10) requesting public input, (11) advice giving/helping, (12) acknowledgement, (13) personal and (14) other. In those cases where a tweet had multiple functions, coders were trained to use a set of rules and procedures for identifying the dominant function (e.g. the function comprising the most characters).

Finally, in order to identify the topic, coders categorized the *primary* topic of each tweet. Tweets were coded as one of the following categories: (1) animal rights, (2) civil and human rights, (3) crime and judicial proceedings, (4) business and economy, (5) education, (6) environment, (7) EU, (8) government, (9) health and social welfare, (10) immigration, (11) military and defence, (12) religion, (13) science and technology, (14) war and conflicts, (15) world events, (16) national events and heritage, (17) infrastructure, (18) campaign and party affairs and (19) norms and values.

Reliability

The coding was carried out by a team of six coders.[3] In addition to the two coding trainers (Peter & Lauf 2002), four additional coders were trained over two training sessions and assigned to code approximately a sixth of the sample each. In order to compensate for the context unit of analysis, a form of cluster sampling was utilized. The intercoder reliability test was based on a set of tweets taken from a random sample of 10 per cent of the twittering candidates. For each candidate, 10 tweets in sequential order were randomly selected. Cohen's kappa was used to estimate intercoder reliability. It was chosen because it is a conservative measure; it does not give credit for chance agreement. The reliability scores for the average pairwise Cohen's kappa were as follows: type 0.97, interaction with 0.76, function 0.66, topic 0.67.

The twittering candidate

In this section, we will first provide an overview of the volume and frequency of twittering candidates and tweets posted. As Table 1 indicates, 22 per cent of candidates posted at least one tweet during the two weeks of the election campaign. Not only were there more Liberal Democrat candidates using Twitter, they also posted substantially more tweets (as Table 2 shows), accounting for nearly half of total tweets posted and averaging 78 tweets per candidate in comparison to 63 and 44 tweets for Labour and the Conservatives,

TABLE 1 Twittering candidates by party.

	No. of twittering candidates	Per cent of twittering candidates
Conservatives	118	18.7
Labour	136	21.6
LibDems	162	25.7
Total	416	22.0

TABLE 2 Frequency of tweets by party.

	No. of tweets	Per cent of total tweets	Mean per candidate	Median
Conservatives	5,168	19.7	43.80	22.00
Labour	8,469	32.2	62.27	30.50
LibDems	12,645	48.1	78.06	36.00
Total	26,282		63.18	30.00

TABLE 3 Rate and distribution of tweets.

	Tweet rate			Tweet distribution		
Tweets	No. of participants	Per cent	Cumulative per cent	No. of postings	Per cent	Cumulative per cent
1	16	3.8	3.8	16	0.0	0.0
2–9	77	18.5	22.4	426	1.6	1.7
10–49	175	42.1	64.4	4,422	16.8	18.5
50–99	74	17.8	82.2	5,319	20.2	38.7
100–199	50	12.0	94.2	6,820	25.9	64.7
200–400	16	3.8	98.1	4,151	15.8	80.5
>400	8	1.9	100	5,128	19.5	100
Total	416	100		26,282	100	

respectively. However, averages are slightly misleading given the divergence in posting rates among candidates.

As a means of providing more nuances, Table 3 reveals the rate and distribution of tweets. As is shown, the distribution was far from egalitarian: 64 per cent of candidates posted less than 50 tweets, accounting for only 19 per cent of the total tweets while 18 per cent (candidates posting a 100 or more tweets) were responsible for close to two-thirds of tweets posted. The Liberal Democrats and Labour had the most prolific twittering candidates; 62 of the 74

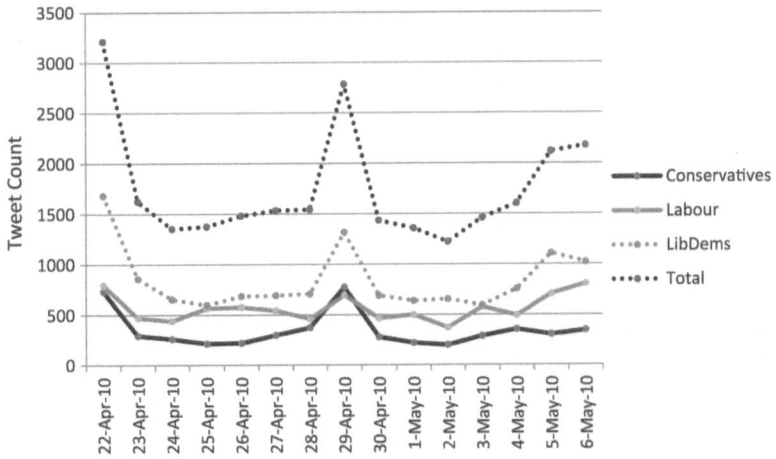

FIGURE 1 Tweet count over 15 days of the campaign.

candidates posting 100 plus tweets were from the Liberal Democrats (37) and Labour (25). Their active use of Twitter is consistent with the campaign strategies of both parties. Unlike the Conservatives, they actively encouraged and facilitated the use of Twitter during the campaign (Newman 2010; Fisher *et al.* 2011), which is reflected in our findings.[4]

When we examine the tweet count per day, we find a common pattern among all three parties. As Figure 1 shows, there were four peak days of posting activity; 39 per cent of the total tweets were posted during these days. April 22 and 29 were the most active twittering days. This activity corresponds with the final two televised Prime Ministerial Debates. Many of the tweets posted were in direct response to these debates, particularly among Conservative candidates. April 22 also marked a string of attacks by the Tory press on party leader Nick Clegg. A substantial portion of tweets from the Liberal Democrat candidates was in response to this news coverage. Indeed, the attacks provoked the Twitter community to blame the world's problems on Clegg, known as '#NickCleggsFault'; many of the Liberal Democrat candidates participated in this development, which in turn received considerable news coverage. The final two days of the campaign also hosted a sizeable amount of twittering activity, particularly among the Liberal Democrats and Labour. Much of this consisted of promoting their parties, and acknowledging and thanking their supporters.

There seems to be a reciprocal relationship between the political Twittersphere on one hand and offline events and media coverage on the other. The debates that dominated the 2010 General Election campaign and its news coverage (Coleman *et al.* 2011; Gaber 2011; Deacon & Wring 2011) also played a substantial role in shaping candidates' twittering behaviour. The effect of these debates was not confined to political insiders and the media. As Scullion's *et al.* (in press) research shows, election talk among British voters was also dominated by the debates. The interplay between Twitter and traditional mass media is in line with studies of the 2010 Australian and Swedish elections (Larsson & Moe 2011; Burgess & Bruns 2012).

Twittering behaviour

Regarding the type of tweet, as Table 4 shows, 32 per cent of all tweets were in the form of @-replies. There was a clear difference between the three parties. Conservative candidates used Twitter mainly as a form of unidirectional communication; 81 per cent of their tweets represented either a normal post, retweet or retweet with comment.[5] Labour and the Liberal Democrats, on the other hand, used Twitter substantially more often to interact with others, representing 47 and 42 per cent respectively. This can partly be explained by two factors. Unlike the Conservatives, the other two parties not only had campaign strategies that fostered Twitter use, but they also had a history of encouraging such practices (Newman 2010; Fisher *et al.* 2011; Jackson & Lilleker 2011). Consequently, many of their candidates were early adopters, affording them time to develop their twittering practices.

With whom were candidates interacting? As Table 5 shows, it was largely with members of the public (59 per cent) followed by politicians (16 per cent), journalists (10 per cent) and party activists (8 per cent). Interaction with the public typically came in the form of acknowledgments (e.g. thanking), debating and taking a position on an issue. Candidates interacted with politicians and journalists in a similar fashion, however, focusing more on attacking and debating. There were two noteworthy differences between the parties. First, Labour and Liberal Democrats used Twitter more often to interact with party activists, mostly to organize campaign activities or to thank them for their

TABLE 4 Type of tweet posted.

	Frequency and percentage of tweets per party			
	Conservatives	Labour	LibDems	Total
Normal post	3,307	4,012	5,361	12,680
	64.0	47.4	42.4	48.2
@-Replies	960	3,205	4,184	8,349
	18.6	37.8	33.1	31.8
Retweet	855	1,023	2,896	4,774
	16.5	12.1	22.9	18.2
Retweet with comment	46	229	204	479
	0.9	2.7	1.6	1.8

TABLE 5 With whom were candidates interacting?

	Frequency and percentage of (interactive) tweets per party			
	Conservatives	Labour	LibDems	Total
Public	615	1,723	2,596	4,934
	64.1	53.8	62.0	59.1
Politician/candidate	160	567	591	1,318
	16.7	17.7	14.1	15.8
Journalist/media	113	376	329	818
	11.8	11.7	7.9	9.8
Party activist	23	237	394	654
	2.4	7.4	9.4	7.8
Lobbyist	24	191	99	314
	2.5	6.0	2.4	3.8
Expert	8	48	65	121
	0.8	1.5	1.6	1.4
Celebrity	5	32	61	98
	0.5	1.0	1.5	1.2
Industry	11	27	44	82
	1.1	0.8	1.1	1.0
Authority	1	4	5	10
	0.1	0.1	0.1	0.1
Total	960	3,205	4,184	8,349
	100	100	100	100

support. This is no surprise as both parties had online campaign strategies that emphasized using the Internet (Twitter in particular) to mobilize their base (Newman 2010; Straw 2010; Fisher *et al.* 2011). Second, Liberal Democrats interacted less with journalists. This may have something to do with the fact that they were the smallest party; therefore, in some constituencies, their candidates attracted less media attention.

About which topics were candidates twittering? Eighty per cent of (valid) tweets were about campaign and party affairs.[6] This included campaigning activities (e.g. events, strategies, promotion, polling, media coverage) and party affairs (e.g. coalition partners, leadership, personalities). The level of policy talk, on the other hand, was minimal. For all three parties, business and economy was the next most common topic, accounting for only four per cent of tweets. Only two other topics (government and health & social welfare) were above two per cent. This finding mirrors studies of 2010 Election news coverage, which found that there was very little real policy discussion; it largely focused on personalities, and campaign strategies and tactics (Deacon & Wring 2011, Gaber, in press). This partly has to do with the impact of the debates on the campaign. Not only did news coverage tend to focus upon the debates as 'strategic performances' (Coleman *et al.* 2011), candidates' reactions to them too, as will be discussed below, typically focused on style and performance.

From broadcasting political messages to interacting with the public

To refine the principal difference between broadcasting and interacting and to provide more depth to our understanding of politicians' twittering behaviour, the functions of tweets were coded. The results for all 14 functions are presented in Appendix 1. Based upon these empirical findings, along with the findings from the categories discussed above, we present and discuss below our typology of candidates' twittering behaviour. Broadcasting is a form of unidirectional communication and the behaviours listed under it are primarily used in this manner. Interaction consists of behaviours that are based on reciprocity and are typically about engaging others.[7]

As Table 6 shows, 68 per cent of all tweets represented one of the five broadcasting behaviours. The most frequent behaviour was *updating* accounting for slightly less than a quarter of all tweets. This included tweets where candidates posted an update from the campaign trail such as status or location updates and reports on campaign events. Updating was slightly more common among Conservative candidates, particularly among infrequent posters (posting less than 50 tweets). Labour too promoted the use of the hashtag '#labourdoorstep' as a means of sharing positive experiences on the campaign trail.

It might not seem like it at first, but in some ways, updating from the campaign trail is a new type of behaviour. Twitter conveniently allows candidates to post real-time updates in a virtual public space, which is difficult to do via traditional media outlets. Updating potentially creates visibility for a candidate and

TABLE 6 Candidates' twittering behaviour in percentages.

| | | | Broadcasting | | | |
| | | | Percentage of tweets per party | | | |
	Updating	Promoting	Critiquing	Information disseminating	Own/party stance	Total
Conservatives	30.0	15.8	26.1	2.5	2.9	77.2
Labour	24.9	17.7	15.2	3.5	2.8	64.1
LibDems	19.0	25.0	14.4	5.1	3.8	67.3
Total	23.1	20.9	17.0	4.1	3.3	68.3

might foster a sense of closeness between them and the public. It may cultivate a sense of inclusion among active followers,[8] particularly candidates that use it in combination with other behaviours, making them feel part of the campaign, as though they are out there canvassing with them.

Promoting was the second most common behaviour representing 21 per cent of tweets. This included tweets in which a candidate promoted him/herself, a fellow politician, the party or another organization. In addition to the typical 'party poster promotion', candidates frequently promoted the ability, skills or performance of themselves or their party/party leader:

> And there you go...David Cameron, performs at his best under the greatest pressure. Resounding victory #leadersdebate
> (@louisebagshawe, April 29, 23:04)

As the tweet from Conservative Louise Mensch illustrates, promoting was commonly used in connection with the televised debates.

Liberal Democrat candidates used Twitter for promoting substantially more often than the other two parties did. This might be the result of them being a smaller party; thus, they felt the need to promote more. Some Liberal Democrat candidates were creative when it came to promoting:

> I'm looking for some non-celeb endorsements today:)
> (@CllrDaisyBenson, April 29, 16:30)

Liberal Democrat Daisy Benson on occasions solicited endorsements from voters in her constituency. The tweet above received several praises from voters. Candidates too would post a tweet about conversations they had with constituents, which were typically compliments regarding their ability, dedication and/or performance.

Campaign promotion is a traditional broadcasting behaviour used during election time, and Twitter provides candidates with another communicative platform to promote themselves and their party. However, as the example above shows, candidates, particularly the Liberal Democrats, used Twitter to tap into their followers as a means of self-promotion. Moreover, unlike traditional media outlets, promotion via Twitter is free and direct.

Critiquing accounted for 17 per cent of tweets. This typically included tweets in which a candidate criticized, challenged or contradicted another politician, party or another organization in a political context. Much of this consisted of (superficial) partisan attacks:

> Clegg on the ropes – I need to look away #leadersdebate
> (@EricPickles, April 29, 22:32)

As Conservative Eric Pickles's tweet above indicates, the debates attracted this type of behaviour, much of which focused on style and performance. More than a third of critiquing tweets were posted in response to the debates. This was particularly true for the Conservatives. Critiquing was more prevalent among their candidates, and much of this was directed at the two debates, representing nearly half of these tweets. Ironically, the debates were meant to promote public deliberation and discussion on the important issues, but the outcome was that voters (Scullion *et al.*, in press) and candidates alike tended to debate about performance and style.

For both Labour and the Liberal Democrats, these types of attacks were also directed at the news media. For Labour, this is no surprise given that, with the exception of the *Daily Mirror*, they faced a hostile press. For some candidates, especially Tom Watson, Twitter became a platform to take on the press. For the Liberal Democrats, much of this was in response to the Tory press attacks on their party leader Nick Clegg.

Overall, this type of behaviour, the 'Punch and Judy' style of politics, offers little in terms of facilitating a closer relationship with voters. The two debates in particular seemed to foster a polarized Twittersphere. As Coleman's (2005a) study suggests, citizens are tired of such partisan politics. Furthermore, Jackson's (2011, in press) research has shown that this style of politics demobilizes voters; it turns them away from politics. Indeed, the public on numerous occasions called candidates out for such behaviour. Many of the candidates too complained about this type of behaviour, yet they were doing it themselves. It seems Twitter's 140-character limit is more conducive to superficial attacks as opposed to substantial critical arguments on the issues, which is in line with Pew Research Center's (2011) findings.

Information disseminating, which accounted for four per cent of tweets, included posts where a candidate provided news (typically by dropping links) or other factual information (e.g. government reports). One of the appealing characteristics of Twitter is that it allows a candidate to disseminate information directly (unmediated) to citizens. The Liberal Democrat candidates took advantage of this by frequently posting links to research reports from various sources. However, for the other two parties, candidates dropped links mostly to the BBC and British press.

Finally, *position taking* accounted for only three per cent of tweets. This included tweets in which a candidate posted his/her opinion, argument or the party position on a political issue as the example below illustrates:

I'm against i.d. cards, tuition fees, & inequality. I'm in favour of civil liberties, free education & asset taxes. #voteld #gonick
(@clwppc, April 29, 12:16)

As the tweet from Liberal Democrat Naomi Smith shows, many of these tweets acted more as campaign sound bites. This has to do partly with Twitter's 140-characters limit. Given this constraint, some candidates would drop a link to

TABLE 7 Candidates' twittering behaviour in percentages.

	Interaction					
	Percentage of tweets per party					
	Debating/ position taking	*Acknowl- edging*	*Organizing /mobilizing*	*Advice giving/ helping*	*Consulting*	*Total*
Conservatives	7.5	7.1	1.7	0.5	0.4	17.2
Labour	12.1	11.0	2.8	2.6	1.8	30.3
LibDems	9.5	10.0	5.1	2.5	0.5	27.6
Total	9.9	9.7	3.7	2.1	0.9	26.3

their blog/website/Facebook account where a more detailed position was available.

As Table 7 reveals, interaction, which account for 26 per cent of all tweets, consisted of five behaviours. The most common type of interaction was *attacking/debating* representing 10 per cent of tweets. Many of the tweets were attack style orientated as the example below demonstrates:

> @jerryhayes1 We obviously will not agree, but Cameron most lightweight Con leader I have ever seen. At least you knew where you stood in past (Andrew Lewin (@Alewin7), LibDem, April 29, 22:58)

Most of these exchanges lacked continuity; i.e. they were typically one-off interactions. Moreover, they tended to be highly partisan (often *ad hominem* attacks as the example above) and focused mostly on party and campaign affairs. Extended debates on substantial issues were rare.

Acknowledging, which accounted for 10 per cent of tweets, included tweets in which a candidate thanked, complimented or provided words of encouragement to another person or organization. Thanking voters and party activists for their support along with wishing other politicians success accounted for more than three-fourths of these tweets. Much of this took place on the final two days of the campaign, totalling more than a third of acknowledgements.

Another type of behaviour under interacting was *mobilizing and organizing*, which accounted for four per cent of tweets. This included tweets where a candidate called for direct action, typically to sign a petition or to join the campaign team. Regarding the latter, unlike the Conservatives, the Liberal Democrats and Labour used Twitter to mobilize their base, mainly to recruit volunteers and organize their campaign activities. This finding is consistent with the parties' online campaign strategies (Newman 2010; Straw 2010; Fisher *et al.* 2011). Evan Harris, who posted an astonishing 1,342 tweets, frequently used Twitter to recruit volunteers, particularly after meeting new followers.

Overall, Twitter seemed to be a useful communicative tool for mobilizing and organizing the party base. Moreover, similar to updating, such behaviour via Twitter may create a sense of closeness with the public. For example, citizens who actively follow candidates are able to get a glimpse of 'behind the scene' of campaign activities.

Advice giving and helping, which represented two per cent of tweets, was another behaviour identified. Much of the advice and help was concerning the election (e.g. postal ballots and voting districts). There were occasions when helping moved beyond issues concerning the election. Labour candidate Stella Creasy and Liberal Democrat Daisy Benson were active helping people in their constituencies:

> @Leanne_Online there are support services – what sort of cv is it? Email me and will put you in touch with them?
> (@stellacreasy, April 22, 11:42)

The final and least frequent behaviour was *consulting*, accounting for only one per cent of tweets. This included tweets where a candidate requested public input on a specific political issue or simply when a candidate was trying to find out what mattered to his/her constituents as the example below exemplifies:

> Tell me!!!.... What is the key local issue that will influence the way local people will vote in Bournemouth East?
> (Lisa Northover, LibDem, April 26, 21:18)

Only a handful of candidates employed this type of behaviour regularly including Stella Creasy and David Kidney (Labour); and Layla Moran, Evan Harris and Lisa Northover (LibDems).

Constituency work such as advice giving, helping and consulting is something that candidates have always done. However, Twitter makes these personal exchanges between candidates and voters public. It allows candidates to create a sense of accessibility, thereby facilitating what Coleman and Blumler (2009) call 'mutuality'. It feels as though they are in touch and just one tweet away. Moreover, using social media like Twitter as a means of facilitating a locally focused campaign seems to be effective, for example, Stella Creasy contributed her electoral success to her use of Twitter and other social media in this manner (Creasy in Williamson 2010). However, given the infrequency of such behaviour, the potential benefits were largely missed.

Conclusion

Allistair Campbell, the notorious spin-doctor of Tony Blair, once said that communication is not something that should be 'tagged on the end' of politics.

Instead, it should be part and parcel of what politicians do on a daily basis (quoted in Gaber 2000, p. 507). A continuous cycle of testing the waters, developing ideas and policy, and 'selling' these to citizens has indeed become one of the key mechanisms in the business of politics. The rise of social media has provided the toolkit of political communication with an invaluable add-on to establish ongoing communication. It allows politicians to reach a growing group of citizens while especially Twitter has also become a beat that facilitates the professional exchange between journalists, lobbyists and opinion makers (Broersma & Graham 2012). As we have shown, 22 per cent of the candidates during the 2010 UK Election recognized the opportunities Twitter provides to convey their messages to the public. Especially the Liberal Democrats, who were responsible for about half of the candidate's tweets, were passionate communicators in 140-characters. Labour (32 per cent) and the Conservatives (20 per cent) had a relatively smaller share in the 26,282 tweets, but also actively incorporated Twitter in their communication strategies.

Social media provide politicians with, on one hand, private channels for unidirectional communication, and, on the other, they enable multi-directional communication within a network of citizens. While, in scholarship, the first is usually (dis)regarded as transposing traditional communicative patterns to an online environment, the latter is seen as an opportunity for politicians to engage with citizens in conversations leading to more direct or connected forms of representation (Coleman 2005a; Graham et al., in press). In this paper, we developed a typology of five broadcasting and five interactive behaviours on Twitter. We argue that both broadcasting and interaction results in meaningful differences with traditional one-way political communication through mass media, party material and traditional campaign activities.

Our research shows that slightly more than two-thirds of the candidates' tweets were used to broadcast particular information. Giving updates from the campaign trail, promoting themselves or party members and critiquing opponents are central to the 'hoopla' and 'horse race' element of election campaigns. While this made up 61 per cent of the total number of tweets, only seven per cent focused on conveying political issues, either in the form of disseminating information or putting across a political stance. This pattern is reflected in the topics that were discussed. The candidates twittered mostly (80 per cent) about campaign and party affairs and seldom about political issues. The election campaign on Twitter replicated offline one, focusing on political strategies, campaigning tactics and personal squabble. This kind of behaviour discourages citizens instead of engaging them with politics (see e.g. Jackson, in press).

However, at the broadcasting level, the most important difference with traditional campaigning is that it gives politicians more control over the content of their message as well as over its pace and time of distribution. Candidates now have the opportunity to communicate directly, continuously and unrestrictedly with the audience and are not dependent on either processes of selection, framing and interpretation by journalists or party funding and activities. The option to get every message out whenever they want and how they want it could give, theoretically, politicians more freedom to communicate spontaneously with citizens and to focus their campaign at the constituency level. Interestingly, the percentage of challenging candidates who twittered was much higher than that of the sitting Conservative and Labour MPs (15 vs. 21 per cent and 16 vs. 29 per cent, respectively). This seems to be in line with earlier research (Fisher *et al.* 2011) that found that social media, due to their relatively low costs, were particularly applied by challengers in campaigns for 'hopeless' seats, and to a lesser extent 'target' seats. However, more research into this possible causal connection would be welcomed.

Moreover, the importance of Twitter for campaigning might be for a large part in its interaction with mass media and the opportunities it offers to spin campaign topics. On one hand, many tweets were in response to television and newspaper coverage. On the other hand, politicians are well aware of the fact that the effect of a tweet multiplies when its message is picked up by traditional media. Dropping a few lines in a tweet might change the angle of news stories and consequently public debate. Because journalists are using Twitter as an 'awareness system' that informs them about the course and heat of political and societal discussions, a well-placed string of tweets can have a decisive influence on the political climate (Hermida 2010; Broersma & Graham 2012).

Even if the large majority of tweets fell under broadcasting, still 26 per cent of all tweets were reciprocal. Although we did not account for the 'followers' of politicians, it turned out that candidates were mostly engaging with members of the public (59 per cent) while in almost 10 per cent of the cases journalists were at the other end. When candidates were talking with other politicians, they mainly belonged to the same party while party activists took part in eight per cent of the interactions. A similar trend was found when taking the nature of interaction into account. Mobilizing constituents to help with the campaign, acknowledging voters and requesting information were the most prominent categories while getting into a debate – or argument – with others on political issues took part only in 10 per cent of tweets. Even in this category, however, interaction took mainly the form of one-off attacks on other politicians. Lengthier debates on political issues were much scarcer. This is also due to the 140-character limit of tweets. Candidates often requested to move these types of exchanges elsewhere (e.g. via email).

Twitter thus mainly functioned as a tool to involve the party base in the election campaign and to maintain social relations by acknowledging others or giving them advice. As a channel to discuss political issues and exchange arguments, Twitter was less important. However, our sample of two weeks before the general election might obscure the situation. It could be possible that the number of twittering politicians and tweets (temporarily) rises before the ballot and these 'newcomers' might only use Twitter in a traditional broadcasting manner as opposed to politicians that have been active for a while and have developed a network. Moreover, it might be that an election campaign triggers broadcasting of political messages and campaign updates while politicians on Twitter might be more responsive to their followers and interacting with them in 'off peak' periods. More longitudinal and internationally comparative research of the content of politician's tweets is thus necessary. Analysis of variables such as incumbency might provide more nuance just like multivariate analysis. Further issues that could be interesting to explore revolve around questions of gender, and to what extent socially constructed expectations of politicians' gender roles impact tweets or, more intriguingly, the way followers interact with the tweets of candidates.

Our findings indicate that Twitter could indeed involve people in the political process by either broadcasting information on the campaign or providing a platform for interaction and mobilization. Tapping into the potential Twitter offers for creating a closer and more connected relationship with citizens might increase democratic engagement. Most twittering candidates, however, turned out to be quite conservative. Not only did they replicate the offline campaign's focus on style, performance and strategy, the use of Twitter was also partly dependent on interaction with traditional mass media. Nevertheless, 19 per cent of the candidates' tweets interacted in one way or another with voters. On first sight this might not seem such a large percentage, but as Wright (2012, p. 249) correctly argues, 'in the face of all the hyping of technology, there is a danger that an implicitly pessimistic mindset is adopted' by researchers. Compared to other forms of political communication during the election campaign, we argue that this level of interaction with voters is quite substantial. An open question is if politicians will seize the opportunities for connectivity that social media offer even more than they do already and if future use will thus stimulate an even more engaged and more permanent relationship between politicians and citizens.

Notes

1   See Wring *et al.* (2011) for a comprehensive analysis of the campaign.
2   Google searches were permitted if necessary.
3   This study is part of a larger comparative study between British and Dutch twittering candidates during the 2010 Elections.
4   This finding is in line with previous studies, which suggest that progressive parties are more likely to adopt new social media (Vergeer *et al.* 2011; Lilleker & Koc-Michalska 2012; Ausserhofer & Maireder 2013). One possible explanation is that these parties tend to be smaller (minor parties) and younger and thus more open to new

communicative practices. However, such speculation goes beyond our analysis and would require, e.g. interviews with politicians, campaign strategists, etc.

5   We treated retweets as a form of unidirectional communication; candidates primarily retweeted tweets that were campaign promotion and partisan attacks.

6   For 1,988 tweets, the topic was not applicable.

7   The categories for each group are not mutually exclusive. For example, on occasions, updates from the campaign trail were conveyed via interaction with another person. However, updating tended to be communicated via broadcasting rather than through interaction.

8   The number of followers at the time of archiving ranged from 8 for Mark Reckless (Conservative) to 35,406 for party leader Nick Clegg. The mean was 825 with a median of 314 followers. However, the number of followers is a bit misleading. It says nothing about *active* followers (those followers who actually read a candidates tweets) and it ignores those people who visit a candidate's Twitter page or use websites such as Election-tweets and Tweetminister to actively follow candidates. See also Ausserhofer and Maireder (2013) critique. See also Gibson et al. (2010) for the level of citizen participation via social media during the 2010 Election.

References

Ausserhofer, J. & Maireder, A. (2013) 'National politics on Twitter', *Information, Communication & Society*, vol. 16, no. 3, pp. 291–314.

Blumler, J. & Kavanagh, D. (1999) 'The third age of political communication: influences and features', *Political Communication*, vol. 16, no. 3, pp. 209–230.

Broersma, M. & Graham, T. (2012) 'Social media as beat: tweets as a news source during the 2010 British and Dutch elections', *Journalism Practice*, vol. 6, no. 3, pp. 403–419.

Burgess, J. & Bruns, A. (2012) '(Not) the Twitter election: the dynamics of the #ausvotes conversation in relation to the Australian media ecology', *Journalism Practice*, vol. 6, no. 3, pp. 384–402.

Coleman, S. (2001) 'Online campaigning', in *Britain Votes 2001*, ed. P. Norris, Oxford University Press, Oxford, pp. 115–124.

Coleman, S. (2005a) *Direct Representation: Towards a Conversational Democracy*, IPPR Exchange, [Online] Available at: http://www.ippr.org/ecomm/files/Stephen_Coleman_Pamphlet.pdf (6 December 2012)

Coleman, S. (2005b) 'New mediation and direct representation: reconceptualizing representation in the digital age', *New Media & Society*, vol. 7, no. 2, pp. 177–198.

Coleman, S. & Blumler, J. G. (2009) *The Internet and Democratic Citizenship: Theory, Practice and Policy*, Cambridge University Press, Cambridge.

Coleman, S., Steibel, F. & Blumler, J. G. (2011) 'Media coverage of the prime ministerial debates', in *Political Communication in Britain: The Leader Debates, the Campaign and the Media in the 2010 General Election*, eds D. Wring, R. Mortimore & S. Atkinson, Palgrave Macmillan, Basingstoke, pp. 37–55.

Deacon, D. & Wring, D. (2011) 'Reporting the 2010 general election: old media, new media – old politics, new politics', in *Political Communication in Britain: The Leader Debates, the Campaign and the Media in the 2010 General Election*, eds D. Wring, R. Mortimore & S. Atkinson, Palgrave Macmillan, Basingstoke, pp. 281–303.

Fisher, J., Cutts, D. & Fieldhouse, E. (2011) 'Constituency campaigning 2010', in *Political Communication in Britain: The Leader Debates, the Campaign and the Media in the 2010 General Election*, eds D. Wring, R. Mortimore & S. Atkinson, Palgrave Macmillan, Basingstoke, pp. 198–217.

Flickinger, R. S. & Studlar, D. T. (2007) 'One Europe, many electorates? Models of turnout in European parliament elections after 2004', *Comparative Political Studies*, vol. 40, no. 4, pp. 383–404.

Gaber, I. (2000) 'Government by spin: an analysis of the process', *Media, Culture & Society*, vol. 22, no. 4, pp. 507–518.

Gaber, I. (2011) 'The transformation of campaign reporting: the 2010 UK general election, revolution or evolution?' in *Political Communication in Britain: The Leader Debates, the Campaign and the Media in the 2010 General Election*, eds D. Wring, R. Mortimore & S. Atkinson, Palgrave Macmillan, Basingstoke, pp. 261–280.

Gaber, I. (in press) 'The 'hollowed-out election' or where did all the policy go?' *Journal of Political Marketing*.

Gibson, R. K., Cantijoch, M. & Ward, S. (2010) 'Citizen participation in the e-campaign', in *The Internet and the 2010 Election: Putting the Small 'p' Back in Politics?* eds R. K. Gibson, A. Williamson & S. Ward, Hansard Society, London, pp. 5–16.

Glassman, M. E., Straus, J. R. & Shogan, C. J. (2010) 'Social networking and constituent communications: member use of Twitter during a two-month period in the 111th congress', *Journal of Communication Research*, vol. 2, nos. 2–3, pp. 219–233.

Golbeck, J., Grimes, J. M. & Rogers, A. (2010) 'Twitter use by the U.S. congress', *Journal of the American Society for Information Science and Technology*, vol. 61, no. 8, pp. 1612–1621.

Graham, T. (2011). 'What's reality television got to do with it? Talking politics in the net-based public sphere', in *Political Communication in Postmodern Democracy: Challenging the Primacy of Politics*, eds K. Brants & K. Voltmer, Palgrave Macmillan, Basingstoke, pp. 248–264.

Graham, T., Broersma, M. & Hazelhoff, K. (in press) 'Closing the gap? Twitter as an instrument for connected representation', in *The Media, Political Participation and Empowerment*, eds R. Scullion, R. Gerodimos, D. Jackson, & D. Lilleker, Routledge, London.

Grant, W. J., Moon, B. & Grant, J. B. (2010) 'Digital dialogue? Australian politicians' use of the social network tool Twitter', *Australian Journal of Political Science*, vol. 45, no. 4, pp. 579–604.

Hansard Society. (2012) *Audit of Political Engagement 9. The 2012 Report: Part One*, [Online] Available at: http://www.hansardsociety.org.uk/blogs/press_releases/archive/2012/04/25/audit-of-political-engagement-9-part-one.aspx (10 February 2013)

Hermida, A. (2010) 'Twittering the news. The emergence of ambient journalism', *Journalism Practice*, vol. 4, no. 3, pp. 297–308.

Jackson, N. (2007) 'Political parties, the Internet and the 2005 general election: third time lucky?' *Internet Research*, vol. 17, no. 3, pp. 249–271.

Jackson, D. (2011) 'Strategic media, cynical public? Examining the contingent effects of strategic news frames on political cynicism in the United Kingdom', *The International Journal of Press/Politics*, vol. 16, no. 1, pp. 75–101.

Jackson, D. (in press) 'Time to get serious? Process news and British politics', in *Retelling Journalism. Conveying Stories in a Digital Age*, eds M. Broersma & C. Peters, Peeters Publishers, Leuven/Paris.

Jackson, N. & Lilleker, D. G. (2011) 'Microblogging, constituency service and impression management: UK MPs and the use of Twitter', *The Journal of Legislative Studies*, vol. 17, no. 1, pp. 86–105.

Larsson, A. O. & Moe, H. (2011) 'Studying political microblogging: Twitter users in the 2010 Swedish election campaign', *New Media & Society*, vol. 15, no. 5, pp. 729–747.

Lee, E. & Shin, S. Y. (2012) 'When the medium is the message: how transportability moderates the effects of politicians' Twitter communication', *Communication Research*, published online, DOI:10.1177/0093650212466407.

Lilleker, D. G. & Koc-Michalska, K. (2012) 'Online political communication strategies: MEPs, e-representation and self-representation', *Journal of Information Technology & Politics*, published online, DOI: 10.1080/19331681.2012.758071.

McGuinness, F., Cracknell, R., Davies, M. & Taylor, M. (2012) 'UK election statistics: 1918–2012', Research Paper 12/43, House of Commons Library, [Online] Available at: http://www.parliament.uk/briefing-papers/rp12-43 (10 February 2012).

Newman, N. (2010) *#UKelection2010, Mainstream Media and the Role of the Internet: How Social and Digital Media Affected the Business of Politics and Journalism*, Reuters Institute for the Study of Journalism, University of Oxford, Oxford.

Peter, J. & Lauf, E. (2002) 'Reliability in cross-national content analysis', *J&MC Quarterly*, vol. 79, no. 4, pp. 815–832.

Pew Research Center. (2011) *Twitter and the Campaign: How the Discussion on Twitter Varies from Blogs and News Coverage and Ron Paul's Twitter Triumph*, [Online] Available at: http://www.journalism.org/analysis_report/twitter_and_campaign (6 December 2012)

Sæbø, Ø. (2011) 'Understanding Twitter™ use among parliament representatives: a genre analysis', in *Proceedings of the Third IFIP WG 8.5 International Conference on Electronic Participation*, eds E. Tambouris, A. Macintosh & H. de Bruijn, Springer, Berlin, pp. 1–12.

Scullion, R., Jackson, D. & Moleseworth, M. (in press) 'Performance, politics and media: how the 2010 British general election leadership debates generated 'talk' amongst the electorate', *Journal of Political Marketing.*

Small, T. A. (2008) 'Equal access, unequal success – major and minor Canadian parties on the Net', *Party Politics*, vol. 14, no. 1, pp. 51–70.

Small, T. A. (2010) 'Canadian politics in 140 characters: party politics in the Twitterverse', *Canadian Parliamentary Review*, vol. 33, no. 3, pp. 39–45.

Small, T. A. (2011) 'What the hashtag? A content analysis of Canadian politics on Twitter', *Information, Communication & Society*, vol. 14, no. 6, pp. 872–895.

Straw, W. (2010) 'Yes we did? What labour learned from Obama', in *The Internet and the 2010 Election: Putting the Small 'p' Back in Politics?* eds R. K. Gibson, A. Williamson & S. Ward, Hansard Society, London, pp. 43–49.

Tweetminister. (2013) 'MPs', [Online] Available at: http://www.tweetminster.co. uk/mps (13 February 2013).

Twitter. (2012) 'Twitter turns six', Twitter, [Online] Available at: http://blog. twitter.com/2012/03/twitter-turns-six.html (6 December 2012).

Vergeer, M., Hermans, L. & Sams, S. (2011) 'Online social networks and microblogging in political campaigning: the exploration of a new campaign tool and a new campaign style', *Party Politics*, published online, DOI:10.1177/1354068811407580.

Wallsten, K. (in press) 'Microblogging and the news: political elites and the ultimate retweet', in *Politics and Policy in the Information Age*, eds J. Bishop & A. M. G. Solo, Springer, Berlin.

Williamson, A. (2010) 'Inside the digital campaign', in *The Internet and the 2010 Election: Putting the Small 'p' Back in Politics?* eds R. K. Gibson, A. Williamson & S. Ward, Hansard Society, London, pp. 17–26.

Wright, S. (2012) 'Politics as usual? Revolution, normalization and a new agenda for online deliberation', *New Media & Society*, vol. 14, no. 2, pp. 244–261.

Wring, D., Mortimore, R. & Atkinson, S. (2011) *Political Communication in Britain: The Leader Debates, the Campaign and the Media in the 2010 General Election*, Palgrave Macmillan, Basingstoke.

Appendix 1. The function of candidates tweets.

	Frequency of tweets within political party			
	Conservatives	Labour	LibDems	Total
Campaign trail (update)	1,552	2,112	2,407	6,071
	30.0	24.9	19.0	23.1
Campaign promotion	814	1,503	3,167	5,484
	15.8	17.7	25.0	20.9
Campaign action	52	218	584	854
	1.0	2.6	4.6	3.2
Call to vote	36	15	57	108
	0.7	0.2	0.5	0.4
Political news/report	108	259	585	952
	2.1	3.1	4.6	3.6
Other news/report	20	41	64	125
	0.4	0.5	0.5	0.5
Own stance/position	172	519	776	1,467
	3.3	6.1	6.1	5.6
Party stance/position	94	69	280	443
	1.8	0.8	2.2	1.7
Criticism/arguing	1,617	1,959	2,446	6,022
	31.3	23.1	19.3	22.9
Requesting public input	20	149	61	230
	0.4	1.8	0.5	0.9
Advice giving/helping	28	224	310	562
	0.5	2.6	2.5	2.1
Acknowledgements	367	932	1,263	2,562
	7.1	11.0	10.0	9.7
Other	288	469	645	1,402
	5.6	5.5	5.1	5.3
Total	5,168	8,469	12,645	26,282
	100.0	100.0	100.0	100.0

Note: Tweets coded as personal and other are collapsed under the function *other*.

Ulrike Klinger

MASTERING THE ART OF SOCIAL MEDIA
Swiss parties, the 2011 national election and digital challenges

Online communication has become a central part in the communication repertoires of political actors in Western mass democracies. In Switzerland, where broadband, internet use, and media literacy are amongst the highest in the world, all major political parties run their own website and are active on social media. This article seeks to show how Swiss political parties deal with social media, how they implement it and how they use social media. The study builds on empirical data from a structural analysis of party websites, the official Facebook sites, and Twitter feeds. These social media sites were analysed for their resonance, update frequency, and thematic clusters focusing on information, mobilization, and participation. A weekly assessment of the user numbers illustrates the development of user resonance throughout the 2011 election year. While political parties claim to appreciate the dialogue and mobilization potentials of social media, they mainly use social media as an additional channel to spread information and electoral propaganda. The overall resonance is still on a very low level. The data seem to sustain the normalization hypothesis, as larger parties with more resources and voters are better able to generate effective communication and to mobilize online than small and marginal parties.

1. Introduction

Social media pose a variety of new opportunities and challenges to political parties. While parties and other political actors have long adapted to the traditional mass media logic, they currently face different functional logics (such as virality, interactivity, etc.) in the new digital intermediation channels. At the same time, online communication has become a central part of the communication repertoires of political actors in Western mass democracies (and beyond). All Swiss parties represented in Parliament run their own website and most of them have also begun to experiment with microblogging and social network sites. The latter are defined as

> web-based services that allow individuals to (1) construct a public or semi-public profile within a bounded system, (2) articulate a list of other users with whom they share connections, and (3) view and traverse their list of connections and those made by others within the system. (Boyd & Ellison 2008, p. 2)

This article refers to the broader term 'social media', including social network sites, blogs, photo and video platforms, and other forms of online communication that are de-institutionalized, interactive, networked and where the user is regarded as the producer (Bechmann & Lomborg 2012, p. 3).

This article seeks to show how Swiss political parties deal with social media, how they implement it, and how they use social media as campaign tools. The study presents empirical data generated by a structural analysis of party websites, the official Facebook sites, and Twitter feeds. These social media sites were analysed for their user resonance, update frequency, and thematic clusters focusing on information, mobilization, and participation (quantitative content analysis). A weekly assessment of the user numbers (group members, 'likers', and followers) from March to December 2011 illustrates the development of the user resonance over the year that culminated in the national elections on 23 October 2011.

It will be shown that although Swiss political parties took up the challenge of social media and the user numbers are increasing slowly, the overall resonance is still on a very low level. The data seem to sustain the normalization hypothesis that 'the use of any technology within politics reflects existing power relationships' (Lilleker et al. 2011, p. 197), as larger parties with more resources and voters are better able to generate effective communication and to mobilize online than small and marginal parties. In addition, the thematic clustering of Facebook postings suggests that the parties use social media as an additional channel to spread information rather than for rallying grassroots participation, fundraising, and localized mobilization. Although the Swiss political system was not expected to provide online campaigning comparable to the 2008 Obama campaign, Swiss political parties are still struggling to master social media and their new media logic.

2. Theoretical background: political parties and digital campaigning

The internet and online communication have become common and widely used information channels for citizens. According to the United Nations' e-Government Survey, Switzerland has the highest infrastructural development (Telecommunication Infrastructure Index 2010, see UN DESA 2010, p. 118). The use of social networks and interactive online applications is widespread. According to data from the Swiss Federal Statistical Office, the share of citizens with an own profile on a social network site reached 36 per cent in 2011, although only nine per cent claim that they express political opinions online. All parties represented in the Swiss Parliament have websites, as do most parliamentarians. More than half of Swiss parliamentarians have Facebook profiles. Although sending/receiving e-mails and searching for information are still the highest ranked daily internet routines, interactive and participative applications are growing fast. In July 2011, the top five internet pages visited by Swiss users were Google.ch, Facebook, Google.com, YouTube, and Wikipedia. The most frequented daily newspaper portals ('20 Minuten' and 'Blick') ranked 11th and 15th after Twitter (10th).

A panel survey in Germany (2000–2008) showed that citizens tend to follow their established communication routines and very few actively post political contents online. However, social media are becoming more important and particularly younger cohorts ('convenient modernists') satisfy their above-average political interests via the internet (Emmer *et al.* 2011, p. 302ff.) Political online communication is no longer a marginal phenomenon among young, urban, and high-income cohorts, but a widely known and regularly practised channel of interpersonal and impersonal intermediation. The question is, therefore, no longer whether political parties use social media in campaigns, but how they use them during campaigns and in regular public communication situations.

The theoretical approach used here to evaluate how political parties make use of social media is the equalization vs. normalization hypotheses debate, centring on the question whether online communication compensates for smaller parties' structural disadvantages, or just supports the dominant parties' advantages during electoral campaigns.

2.1 Equalization vs. normalization

Discussions about the effects that the internet and, even more so, social media have on political communication, on the exchanges between political representatives, intermediary actors and citizens have centred around the question of who will profit: Will the potentials of direct and unintermediated online communication strengthen small parties and political (grassroots) groups with very limited resources and allow them to compete with more dominant parties and groups? Or will the dominant political actors also dominate political online communication while marginal parties and groups remain marginal despite the participatory potentials that the Web offers? Can technology 'level out' the social and political playing field?

Proponents of the first assumption (the 'equalization hypothesis') have argued that the internet offers an alternative access point to the public agenda, through which marginal actors may gain the public attention they cannot otherwise obtain through the traditional mass media bottleneck. These authors see the internet as an 'inherently democratizing technology' (Colemann & Blumler 2009, p. 166), and point to the empowering potentials of mass self-communication:

> (T)he public mind is captured in programmed communication networks, limiting the impact of autonomous expressions outside the networks. But in a world marked by the rise of mass self-communication, social movements and insurgent politics have the chance to enter the public space from multiple sources. By using both horizontal communication networks and mainstream media to convey their images and messages, they increase their chances of enacting social and political change – even if they start from a subordinate position in institutional power, financial resources, or symbolic legitimacy. (Castells 2009, p. 302)

Equalization was the most important paradigm in the early and mid-1990 (going beyond simple utopian expectations of 'electronic polities'), and empirical research proved that small parties tended to profit from online communication during campaigns (e.g. Gibson & Ward, 1998). Strandberg's (2008) meta-analysis has shown that equalization is not free from conditions and its environment: the 'campaign web sphere' was more likely to be equalized when the online environment was more favourable for minor parties than the offline campaign environment (p. 238).

However, researchers, who claimed that political communication on the internet just reflected political communication offline, because it was still part of real-world power structures and resource allocation, challenged this finding. Margolis et al. (1999) called this counter-position the 'normalization hypothesis', arguing that 'just as the major parties dominate the sphere of everyday domestic politics, so they come to dominate cyberspace' (p. 26). In the interim, a variety of studies have found that marginal political parties do not in fact gain sufficient resonance via online communication to justify the use of the term equalization, i.e. compensating for their structural disadvantages:

> The access larger political parties have to the traditional media offline drive (sic) more traffic to their online presences, while their greater resources

mean that websites will be more innovative (. . .), more engaging and inter-active. (Lilleker *et al.* 2011, p. 197)

According to Ward and Gibson (2009), this approach is built on four con-straints that limit the significance and action repertoires of alternative (non-dominant) political actors: commercialization, fragmentation, new skills, and increasing regulatory control of digital media. But it is not only size that matters: Vaccari (2011) has shown that incumbency is also a relevant factor, as effective internet campaigns were 'clearly no place for outsiders' (p. 15), because they required a degree of professionalization, experience and organiz-ational resources that are easier available to those in office. In a study on Spain and Catalonia, Cardenal (2011) has argued that parties that are large, in opposition, non-programmatic and non-bureaucratic are more likely to use the internet for political mobilization.

This study takes on this discussion and seeks to find equalization and/or nor-malization tendencies among Swiss parties before and during the 2011 electoral campaign. As stated above, the internet and social media have become standard intermediation channels for political communication, and political parties are currently far more experienced in using them than they were a decade ago. Fur-thermore, internet usage has only recently reached a level of near ubiquity; in 2011, 83.9 per cent of the Swiss population claimed to be regular users (once every six months), while 77.4 per cent were frequent users (several times each week). The Swiss party system also offers better conditions to find equal-ization/normalization patterns than majoritarian two-party systems – such as in the United States – do, because there is a larger variety of smaller parties. The Swiss party system is one of the most fragmented party systems worldwide (Ladner 2004), with a government consisting of five parties (the Social Demo-cratic Party (SP), Swiss People's Party (SVP), Christian-Democratic People's Party (CVP), Liberal Party (FDP), and Conservative Democratic Party (BDP)) and 11 parties represented in parliament. Thus, the first research ques-tion is: Does the size of the parties have an effect on their political online com-munication and on the user resonance on their websites and platforms?

2.2   Challenges of political online communication

Among scholars of online participation, there is widespread consent that the internet and social media provide new opportunities and new forms of campaign-ing and engaging citizens, that it reduces costs and offers new ways to mobilize voters (e.g. Anduiza *et al.* 2009, p. 872). Today, political parties are expected to extend their campaign strategies to the online world and adapt to the new media logic that characterizes interactive and participatory media, such as social network sites and blogs. Online communication encompasses interperso-nal (e-mail) and mediated communication (online newspapers), one-to-many (blogs), many-to-one (online consultations with politicians), and many-to-many communication (discussion fora). The mass media logic does not apply to all of them, due to the shift from push to pull media, interactivity, and a 'communicative abundance' (Castells 2009) instead of limited space and time. In contrast to traditional 'push' media, which provide information to mass audiences, online communication needs to 'pull' audiences, to create public spheres, and compete with countless other information choices. Therefore, offline and online communication follow quite different logics – and not necessarily a common 'media logic'.

While news values are central to the online outposts of traditional media outlets, such as online newspapers, e-magazines or internet TV and radio channels, social network sites are built on the logic of virality, which can be defined as 'network-enhanced word of mouth' or 'the process which gives any information item the maximum exposure, relative to the potential audience, over a short duration, distributed by many nodes' (Montgomery 2001; Nahon et al. 2011). Gaining relevant resonance within social media depends on the ability to publish information and campaigns that users will forward within their networks, comment on, and recommend to other users. If information posted in social media networks does not have a specific viral quality that provokes users to spread it, it will not reach beyond a very limited circle of supporters.

As research has to date tended to focus on the correlations of viral reach and effects, we still do not know much about what drives virality and why some contents are more frequently distributed among users than others. A study by Berger and Milkman (2010) analysed 6,956 articles from the *New York Times* Online with the objective of finding indicators that explain why some articles make the paper's 'most emailed'-list and others do not. They found a strong link between evoking emotions and becoming viral – and that users prefer to share positive rather than negative content. Although articles that evoke anger or anxiety are highly shared, the authors show that 'positive content is more likely to be highly shared even controlling for how frequently it occurs' (Berger & Milkman 2010, p. 22). This finding is surprising, and underlines the different logics at work in the online and offline realms. News value theories have reliably argued that negative content is more likely to become news, raising concerns about its effects on democratic support and participation (video malaise theories). Hansen et al. (2011) tested virality on Twitter and also found that positive content is more likely to be 'retweeted', while negativity supported virality in news content (23 per cent tweets in their sample). However, virality does not always occur spontaneously, but can be stimulated by online intermediaries, such as highly frequented blogs (Nahon et al. 2011). The question that arises (and should be addressed in further research) is, therefore, whether such 'top-general' and 'elite' blogs choose content in keeping with to traditional news values.

As several studies have pointed out before, it makes sense for political parties to adapt to the new media logic, as online participatory platform offer great possibilities: The constant need to reinforce their ties with increasingly volatile voters by keeping them involved and mobilized can be met without relying exclusively on traditional mass media (Vergeer *et al.* 2011). Although effective social media sites are not without cost, indirect mobilization through party members and supporters' social networks is cheaper and can be more effective than impersonal direct mobilization (Haynes & Pitts 2009). The second research question is therefore: Do political parties use social media for mobilization and participation, or are they just another one-way information channel? Do the parties understand the new media logic of social networks?

3. Methods

The study to analyse how Swiss parties make use of social media followed four steps: (1) a structural analysis of the party home pages and their links to social media, (2) sampling data on the user numbers of Facebook and Twitter sites, and (3) Facebook and Twitter updates posted by Swiss parties. A quantitative content analysis (4) was used to identify the relevance of four thematic clusters within the parties' Facebook postings.

(1) The homepages of 11 political Swiss parties represented in the Parliament during the legislative period 2007–2011 were searched for links to social media. This study only took into account those social media applications to which the party homepages were linked on a national level. Regional and local party websites were not included. Social media sites were only considered 'official' if the party homepages were linked to them. The main reason for this (beside the practical aspects) was that we frequently found party sites and fan groups whose institutional connection to the party was unclear, i.e. individual party members, politicians or sympathizers who started Facebook groups in the name of political parties without official consent. At one point, the Green Party changed her official Facebook group to another, formally unofficial group. This latter group had accumulated more members, which is why the user number in the monitoring seems to rise suddenly, but this is only due to the methodological approach to count only the official group that was linked from the party website.

(2) From March 2011 to December 2011, a weekly assessment was conducted of the Swiss political parties' user resonance on official Facebook groups and official Twitter sites. This allowed for surveying the development of resonance, instead of only capturing the number of users at a single point in time. We then assessed the number of group members, fans or people on Facebook who 'liked' the respective group or became members or fans; with regard to Twitter, we assessed the number of followers. The numbers were assessed on

different week days at random times during the day. The study was started in March 2011 to avoid a focus on just the electoral campaign period leading to the Swiss National Election on 23 October 2011. We believed we would gain a better 'map' of the party communication in normal situations and in campaign periods.

(3) The update frequency of the political parties' Facebook fan groups and Twitter feeds was assessed from January 2011 to December 2011 by identifying and counting their original monthly postings (excluding comments and posting from other users, fans or group members). In most cases, official postings were clearly marked with a profile picture. However, in some cases, a number of administrators were responsible for official postings. In these cases, all postings by those administrators were included.

(4) For a quantitative content analysis of all Facebook postings from January 2011 to December 2011 ($N = 1274$), a codebook operationalized four thematic clusters: information, mobilization, participation, and 'other'. Information was further divided into three sub-clusters: Information, mass media references, and transparency.

1. The first cluster, information, entailed three sub-clusters. (1) Information presents information pieces about the party programme, propaganda, political positions, information about statistic/surveys, the candidates and photos (e.g. 'The Green Liberals welcome the decision of the National Council on "too-big-to-fail,"' 20 September 2011). (2) Mass media references contain all postings that link to and/or comment on articles in newspapers or broadcasted features (e.g. shared links to mass media online portals). (3) Transparency contains all postings that aim to facilitate information about internal processes and decisions that fosters democracy within the party: Information from party conventions, discussions about internal party matters, party documents or advanced training for members/laymen campaigners (e.g. 'Our campaign budget can be reviewed on our website' or 'Today at 6 pm: Online Campaign Training in Liestal', SP)

2. The second cluster, mobilization, encompasses all postings 'that enable a one-way support of the party through symbolic or material resources' (Schweitzer 2011, p. 315). This means that the users are unilaterally activated, but do not yet engage in interactive participation: They are asked to donate, to share video links; they are invited to events or games, or are offered campaign material/souvenirs (e.g. 'Send a free election reminder and win: Coffee and Cake with SP-National Council member Jaqueline Fehr in the Bundeshaus, or cinema vouchers', SP 1 October 2011)

3. Participation, our third cluster, is more demanding. It includes postings that aim to activate users to participate in the real world and join the campaign, thus facilitating a 'two-way, interactive exchange between the party and

citizens' (Schweitzer 2011, p. 315). This cluster includes calls for discussion, appeals to collect signatures and mobilize other people to participate and to vote as well as general community-building (e.g. 'Who can organize a "lemon campaign" on July 2nd? (Serve lemonade and collect signatures for a minimum wage and health insurance initiatives?)'; SP, 21 June 2011).

4. All postings that did not fit within these clusters were coded as 'other'. This was the case in only 1.6 per cent of the postings ($N = 20$), all other postings could be attributed to one of the three thematic clusters above. 'Other' postings included nonpolitical information, such as holiday greetings or job offers (e.g. for interns).

The coding was conducted by one researcher and tested for intra-coder reliability (0.88, Holsti-index, 12 per cent of all 1,274 postings were re-coded ($N = 148$)).

4. Results

4.1 Used channels

By October 2011, almost all of the 11 Swiss parties represented in the Parliament and analysed in this study communicated via social media. Facebook and Twitter were the most common social media, while only few parties applied YouTube videos, Flickr, Social Bookmarking Services or other social media applications (Figure 1).

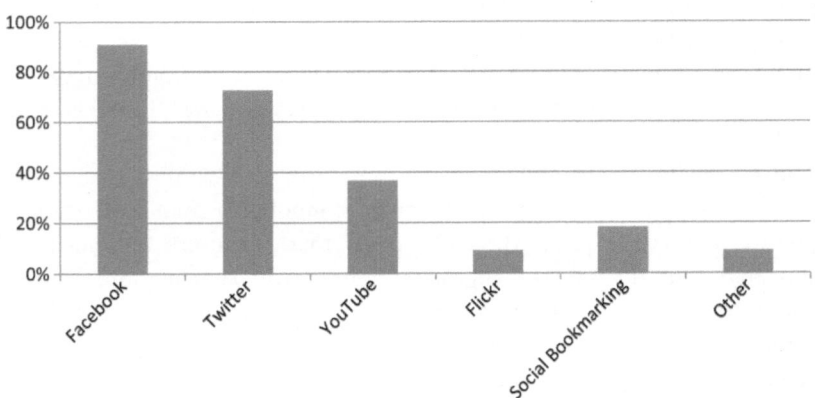

FIGURE 1 Social media channels used by Swiss political parties in per cent, 2011. Based on www.sp.ch; www.gruene.ch; www.fdp.ch; www.cvp.ch; www.evepev.ch; www.svp.ch; www.bdp.ch; www.glp.ch;www.csp-pcs.ch; www.legaticinesi.ch; http://www.mcge.ch Rev. 20.10.2011.

It is clear that social media have become established intermediation channels through which political parties communicate with their members, sympathizers, the electorate, and citizens at large. The large majority of Swiss parties specifically use Facebook and Twitter. On the other hand, the data also reflect a consolidation of the social media: Of the vast array of platforms available on the market, only a small part has been selected and applied. The above-mentioned aspects point to the question of whether there are sufficient resources to maintain these intermediation channels. Political parties (and other organizations) only add new intermediation channels to their communication repertoire if these are perceived as established channels and if sufficient resources are available to manage social media's demands (regular updates and the production of content). It is somewhat surprising that only 37 per cent use YouTube to broadcast videos and electoral spots, as Article 10 (1d) of the Federal Law on Radio and Television prohibits political advertisement for parties, political incumbents, and candidates, as well as for issues that a current referendum addresses. Thus, political parties can only show advertisements online if they do not wish to do without them. Nevertheless, only a minority of the parties has realized the potential of social networks to circumvent the legal constraints and has used them as distribution channels for audio-visual electoral propaganda.

4.2   Development of resonance

With regard to resonance, the data show that while the number of users is increasing, the general level of resonance remains very low, as can be seen in Figure 2. None of the parties reached a resonance of 5,000 users. Even the most active and frequented party sites on Facebook remained below this threshold; furthermore, between March 2011 and December 2011, the average number of users from all parties was only 1,316. The party with the highest resonance on 23 October, 2011 – the Election Day – reached an equivalent of less than 0.1 per cent of the Swiss electorate. Within social media networks, the threshold to become an informal 'member' of a party or organization is vastly lower than the one to become a formal offline member; consequently, their reach should equal or be higher than the number of formal members. However, the data show that this is not the case. The online reach remains significantly lower than the actual offline base of supports and voters, which may be due to social media's user structures (age, education, and income).

Furthermore, only a small number of Swiss parties show a noticeable growth in their reach. Most parties, particularly small parties, remain on a low level below 1,500 Facebook users, or 1,000 Twitter followers. On Facebook, only four parties show a growth in group members or 'likers', while only five parties gained a significant number of followers on Twitter over the entire period. Given that 2011 culminated in national parliamentary elections,

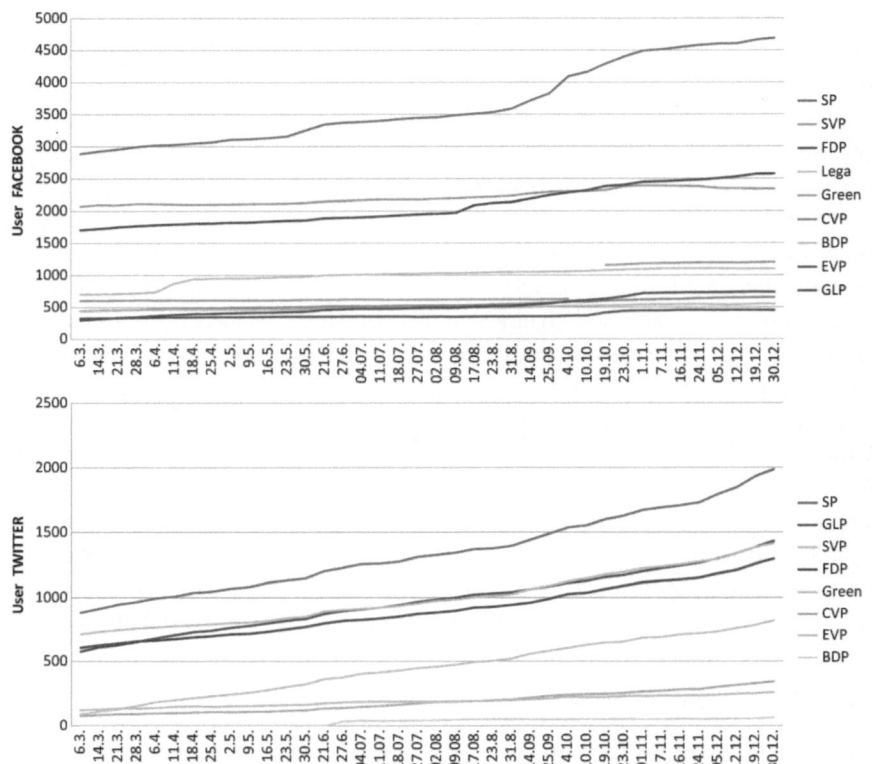

FIGURE 2 Development of users (Facebook and Twitter, March–December 2011). Weekly monitoring from March to December 2011; Lega = Ticino League; Green = Green Party. The sudden increase in users shown for the Green Party on Facebook after October 2011 is an error of measurement. The monitoring was conducted with the help of bookmarking. Between summer and October 2011, the Green Party switched from one official Facebook group to another that had gathered more users. This analysis only took into account the official Facebook groups (to which the party homepage was linked). Owing to the bookmarking, the switch of groups remained unnoticed for a few weeks.

a lack of incentives to mobilize members and voters by using social media cannot explain these low levels.

It is also particularly interesting that there seems to be no campaign effects on resonance: The user numbers were on a slow, but steady rise without any remarkable amplitude in the mobilization during the campaign. With the exception of the Social Democrats (SP) on Facebook, none of the parties improved their attraction in the weeks before the election. The resonance development on Twitter gives no sign of an election campaign, although we had expected that more citizens would follow their preferred party on Twitter in the weeks and days before the Election Day.

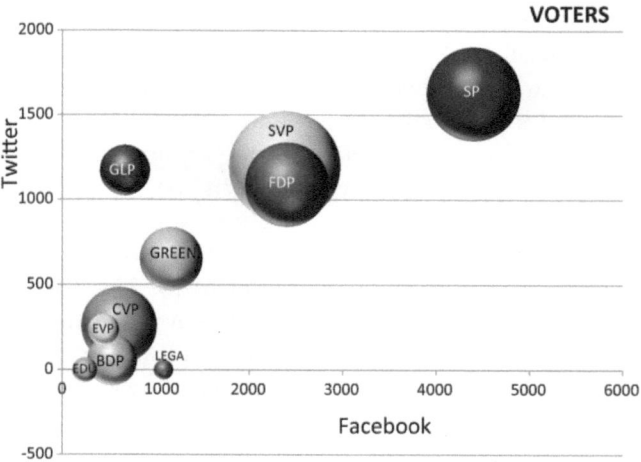

FIGURE 3 FB and Twitter users during election week (week 42): number of voters and campaign costs.

A closer look at the number of Facebook and Twitter users during the election week in October shows that especially the small parties hardly gained any resonance on social media. Figure 3 takes the relevance of the parties into account: The more votes a party received in the election on 23 October 2011, the larger its 'bubble' in the diagram. While resonance of small parties is low, it cannot be concluded that size is a guarantee of resonance: Although larger parties tend to have more users, the party with the highest share of votes (SVP) is located at the mid-level. The CVP, which has been part of the government since 1891 and gained 12.3 per cent of the votes in 2011, did not gain more resonance on Facebook and Twitter than the Evangelical People's Party (EVP), with only two per cent of the votes, did. However, the general trend is for parties with a higher share of votes to be more likely to attract users on social media platforms. It should be added that the converse argument – those parties with higher resonance on social media gain more votes – is not plausible due to the low level of online resonance: The numbers of users are too low to be considered relevant to the electoral outcome. In addition, there is no difference between the left-leaning and right-leaning parties. While previous studies have found that, in other countries, parties or candidates' ideological position makes a difference in their online activity (e.g. Åström & Karlsson 2011; Vergeer *et al.* 2011), this is not true of Switzerland.

4.3   *Update frequency*

We analysed the relationship between resonance and the update frequency and content of political parties' Facebook postings. Based on the assumption that the political parties had sufficient incentives to mobilize supporters in the months leading to the national elections, the study focused on how intense these parties tried to communicate via Facebook and Twitter. We used the number of updates, i.e. how many times the parties posted status updates, as an indicator. One assumption was that resonance is related to the amount and actuality of information offered: Parties that regularly updated and posted news were expected to generate more interest and higher resonance. However, this link could not be proved. There seems to be no connection between the average number of monthly Facebook-updates and the number of users. There is no correlation between the average number of updates and the average number of users of all parties ($r = 0.15$). Some Facebook groups with a low update frequency had many members; others, with a small number of users, updated on a daily basis, sometime several times a day. The data thus show that keeping social media sites up-to-date and providing fresh information regularly are not necessarily rewarded with a large number of users, friends or followers. It is also clear that the parties followed different social media strategies, as the variation in updates served as an indicator of a difference in resources dedicated to social media and of a divergence of attributed relevance to these new intermediation channels. In short, 'trial-and-error' is the only strategy that becomes visible.

If social media are to become a relevant intermediation channel for political parties (and there is no doubt that at least some of them will), the objective is high reciprocal activity – if not interactivity. High reciprocal activity means that both the parties offer regular, topical information via social media and that citizens, voters, and party members choose to receive them. Reciprocal activity does not yet mean interactivity, only that information providers and information receivers (who actively select this information) meet. This may seem a low expectation in light of the discourses on a participatory, deliberative or an interactive democracy aimed at the 'promotion of a communicative exchange between (established) actors of the political system and (mobilized) actors of civil society' (Leggewie & Bieber 2003, p. 143, translation by the author). However, the data show that, to date, parties have problems mastering the balance between communicative supply and demand in the field of social media. Furthermore, previous studies have shown that interactivity is not a realistic outcome when political parties go online. Baxter et al. (2011) analysed Scottish parties and candidates in the 2010 UK election and found that interactivity was mostly uncommon: 'Parties and candidates still appear reluctant to encourage online contact or to enter into any kind of visible online debate (...)' (Baxter et al. 2011, p. 479).

The axes in Figure 4 intersect at the arithmetic means of both dimensions (average users, average updates), thus forming a matrix in which we can locate parties according to their level of reciprocity. Here, we again find the SVP with a small number of updates, but a relatively large number of users, and the CVP with a high number of updates but a less-than-average number

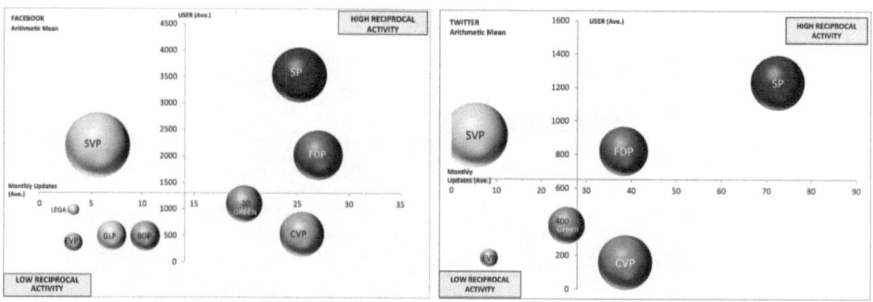

FIGURE 4 Reciprocal activity on Facebook and Twitter (January–December 2011) according to party size. Monthly updates average and user average in absolute numbers. Party size is based on the 2011 election result (calculated voters).

of users. Besides these two parties, the matrix also shows the general trend: The small parties are located in the lower left field of low reciprocal activity, while the larger parties are mainly situated in the upper right field of high reciprocal activity.

4.4 Content

Since the level of activity that the political parties had invested in their Facebook sites could not explain the degree of resonance that they gained, a quantitative content analysis was conducted to find the differences between the parties. The idea was that if mere activity could not explain resonance, then perhaps the characteristics of the content could explain it more or less. Another objective of the analysis was to test whether political parties had adopted the new media logic of social media and focused on mobilization and participation, or if they merely used Facebook as another channel to distribute one-way information.

The data presented in Figure 5 shows that three-quarters (75 per cent) of all Facebook postings of all parties consisted of simple information pieces and references to mass media. Only six per cent of the postings aimed at engaging citizens (mobilization), and 11 per cent at involving users in an interactive exchange (participation). Making internal structures and processes more transparent for citizens accounted for merely six per cent of all postings. The Swiss political parties, therefore, use Facebook predominantly as a one-way information channel, communicating political positions and sharing mass media contents that they find interesting.

There is little variation between parties with regard to the contents: 'Information' and 'mass media references' are the dominant thematic clusters of all parties. While the Social Democrats posted the highest number of

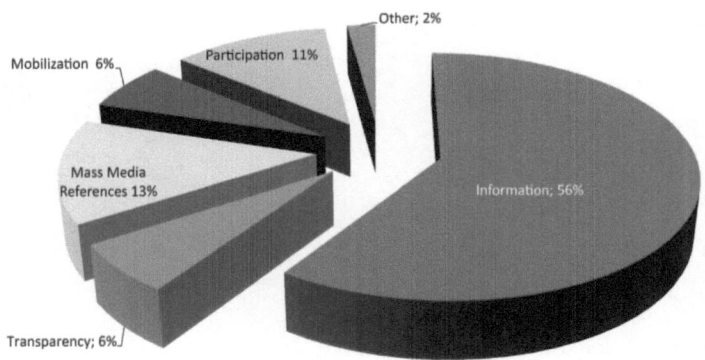

FIGURE 5 Thematic clusters of Facebook posting January–December 2011. All parties aggregated in per cent (left) and each party in absolute numbers (right); $N = 1,274$.

'mobilization'-related contents (11 per cent), the Liberals provided the most postings related to 'participation' (16 per cent). Overall, the picture is quite homogenous: Only a small number of Facebook postings over the entire 2011 aimed at mobilizing users and inviting them to participate. Again, the data provides no evidence of an ideological gap, as there are no significant differences between left-leaning and right-leaning parties.

5. Discussion

With regard to the discussion of equalization vs. normalization, the study has shown that during the 2011 Swiss election the small parties did not benefit from the potentials that social media offer. Facebook, Twitter, and other platforms did not help them compensate for their structural disadvantages. The dominant parties with larger numbers of voters also gained more resonance online and were better able to facilitate reciprocal activity on Facebook. This can be interpreted as substantiation of the normalization hypothesis.

However, there were also exceptions. Among the small parties, the Green Liberals (GLP) gained (comparatively) significant resonance on Twitter. The CVP belongs to the larger and well-established parties, was very active online with Facebook, Twitter, YouTube and Flicker, regularly published a large number of Facebook-updates in two of the official languages, and yet its resonance remained below average. Lilleker *et al.* (2011) offer an 'ebb-and-flow' thesis as a middle ground between equalization and normalization, suggesting that innovative online communication may be offered across all political parties, regardless of size. This seems to be the case in Switzerland as well, but with a very clear tendency towards normalization and the online domination of larger parties. Thus, RQ 1 (Does the size of the parties have an effect on their political online communication and on their resonance on their websites and platforms?) can be rather affirmed. Again it should be noted here that the general significance of social media remained low in the Swiss 2011 elections, and that only a marginal part of the citizens used political parties' social media sites. Strandberg (2013) stated a similar finding in the Finnish parliamentary election 2011 and raised the question of the mobilizing potential that lies within this marginal reach (p. 15). Further research should focus on this aspect and the potential target groups that political parties and candidates seek to address and mobilize via social media.

With regard to RQ 2 (Do political parties use social media for mobilization and participation, or are they just another one-way information channel? Do the parties understand the new media logic of social networks?), it can be argued that political parties in Switzerland still live predominantly in the world of traditional mass media. Instead of adopting the virality logic and its particular features, parties communicate through social media as if they were classic one-way intermediation channels such as TV or radio, or a party newsletter. The large majority of the communication items are simple information pieces and mass media references without any attempt to involve or engage the users, stipulate their participation, or to start a dialogue. By communicating in a way that does not suit the inherent logic of the medium, political parties forfeit the potentials of social media that make this new intermediation opportunity intrinsically attractive: communicative exchanges with members and supporters and building a community that might support dwindling party identifications. Thus, the answer to RQ 2 is a resounding negative: Political parties in Switzerland predominantly use social media for simple information distribution and only marginally for mobilization, participation, and greater transparency. The question that needs further investigation is whether this non-adaptation is due to a misunderstanding of the new medium (the parties do not know what to do), a lack of resources (the parties know what to do but cannot implement this), inner-party constraints (the parties know what to do but senior party officials prevent them from doing so), or for strategic reasons (the parties know what to do but choose not to).

This study has important limitations that need to be addressed. The context of the Swiss political system is a structural limitation. Compared to majoritarian political systems in which 'the winner takes all', the consociational features of democracy combined with proportional representation reduce the impact that elections have on politics and policy outcomes. The first hurdle is the stable five-party government, which has only become more dynamic since the 1990s; however, the parties are currently discussing the formalization of partisan representation in the Bundesrat. Therefore, findings such as Cardenal's (2011) conclusion that parties that are large, in opposition, non-programmatic and non-bureaucratic are more likely to use the internet for political mobilization cannot be confirmed in this context, because parties in Switzerland are generally rather small, most of them are part of the government, all are programmatic. Furthermore, another hurdle is that the extensive representation of minorities and incentives for mobilization in electoral campaigns are lower than elsewhere. In addition, the ability to launch referenda on political issues gives parties other (and sometimes more effective) policy-making instruments, while the militia system of part-time congress(wo)men reduces the lure of office-seeking. Thus, the online campaigning of political parties in Switzerland should also be tested in controversial referenda campaigns.

Another limit of this study results from methodological aspects. Only the websites and social media sites of national parties were studied, as the purpose of the study was to monitor the development of a longer period leading up to national elections. However, the Swiss political landscape is highly decentralized, with the cantonal and local parties playing an important role. It is possible that some of the parties studied here had lively and mobilizing social networks on a subnational level. Previous studies focusing on cantonal and subcantonal parties came, however, to similar findings, suggesting 'that Swiss parties rather engage in "politics as usual", not tapping the full potential ICT might offer them' (Fraefel et al. 2010, p. 1). This limitation also applies to candidates' websites and their social media sites. This analysis did not take individual candidates into account, although social media may work better for people than for organizations. Indeed, some candidates gained higher resonance on Facebook and/or Twitter than their respective parties did. This illustrates a serious limitation and may explain the low numbers and slow rise of user resonance on the parties' Facebook and Twitter sites that were found in this analysis. However, not all candidates benefit equally from social media, as their capacity, media savviness and organizational resources vary. This certainly calls for further research. For the purpose of this article, it was central to determine how parties, as organizations, adapt to social media, which meant that the level of the candidates was omitted. This study showed that Swiss political parties do not (yet) succeed in reaching relevant parts of the citizens via social media and that they hardly apply the interactive and participatory potentials that social media offer. Although the parties have adapted well to mass media logic, they still face the challenge of having to adapt to the new logic of social media as well. It will be key for them to understand and implement this new media logic if they seek to master the art of social media.

References

Anduiza, E., Cantijoch, M. & Gallego, A. (2009) 'Political participation and the internet', Information, Communication and Society, vol. 12, no. 16, pp. 860–878.
Åström, J. & Karlsson, M. (2011) 'Blogging in the shadow of parties: collectivism and individualism in the Swedish 2010 election', paper to be presented on

ECPR Joint Sessions, Workshop: After Mediatization, St. Gallen, Switzerland, 12–17 April 2011.

Baxter, G., Marcella, R. & Varfis, E. (2011) 'The use of the internet by political parties and candidates in Scotland during the 2010 UK general election campaign', *Aslib Proceedings: New Information Perspectives*, vol. 63, no. 5, pp. 464–483.

Bechmann, A. & Lomborg, S. (2012) 'Mapping actor roles in social media: different perspectives on value creation in theories of user participation', *New Media & Society*, [Online] Available at: http://nms.sagepub.com/content/early/2012/11/22/1461444812462853 (26 November 2012).

Berger, J. & Milkman, K. (2010) 'Social transmission, emotion, and the virality of online content', [Online] Wharton Research Paper, Available at: http://opim.wharton.upenn.edu/~kmilkman/Virality.pdf (23 March 2011).

Boyd, D. & Ellison, N. B. (2008) 'Social network sites: definition, history, and scholarship', *Journal of Computer-Mediated Communication*, vol. 13, no. 1, pp. 210–230.

Cardenal, A. S. (2011) 'Why mobilize support online? The paradox of party behaviour online', *Party Politics*, [Online], 11 July 2011, Available at: http://ppq.sagepub.com/content/early/2011/04/02/1354068810391287 (25 February 2012).

Castells, M. (2009) *Communication Power*, Oxford University Press, Oxford.

Colemann, S. & Blumler, J. (2009) *The Internet and Democratic Citizenship: Theory, Practice and Policy*, Cambridge University Press, Cambridge.

Emmer, M., Vowe, G. & Wolling, J. (2011) *Bürger Online. Die Entwicklung der politischen Online-Kommunikation in Deutschland*, UVK, Konstanz.

Fraefel, M., Neuroni, A., Riedl, R. & Knocks, S. (2010) 'Shake hands or join Facebook? Swiss cantonal parties' use of ICT in their communication with members and citizens during elections', Proceedings of the 2nd International Conference on eParticipation (ePart, Lausanne 2010), Trauner, Linz, pp. 326–337.

Gibson, R. & Ward, S. (1998) 'U.K. political parties and the Internet "politics as usual" in the new media?', *The International Journal of Press/Politics*, vol. 3, no. 3, pp. 14–38.

Hansen, L. K., Arvidsson, A., Aarup Nielsen, F., Colleoni, E. & Etter, M. (2011) 'Good friends, bad news. Affect and virality in Twitter', [Online], Working Paper, Available at: http://www2.imm.dtu.dk/pubdb/views/edoc_download.php/5982/pdf/imm5982.pdf (23 March 2011).

Haynes, A. A. & Pitts, B. (2009) 'Making an impression: new media in the 2008 presidential nomination campaigns?', *PS: Political Science & Politics*, vol. 42, no. 1, pp. 53–58.

Ladner, A. (2004) *Stabilität und Wandel von Parteien und Parteiensystemen: Eine vergleichende Analyse von Konfliktlinien, Parteien und Parteiensystemen in den Schweizer Kantonen*, VS, Wiesbaden.

Leggewie, C. & Bieber, C. (2003) 'Demokratie 2.0. Wie tragen neue Medien zur demokratischen Erneuerung bei?' [Democracy 2.0. How do new media contribute to democratic renovation?], in *Demokratisierung der Demokratie* [The democratization of democracy], ed. C. Offe, Campus, Frankfurt, pp. 124–151.

Lilleker, D., Koc-Michalska, K., Schweitzer, E., Jacunski, M., Jackson, N. & Vedel, T. (2011) 'Informing, engaging, mobilizing or interacting: searching for a European model of web campaigning', *European Journal of Communication*, vol. 26, no. 3, pp. 195–213.

Margolis, M., Resnick, D. & Wolfe, J. D. (1999) 'Party competition on the Internet in the United States and Britain', *The International Journal of Press/Politics*, vol. 4, no. 4, pp. 24–47.

Montgomery, A. L. (2001) 'Applying quantitative marketing techniques to the internet', *Interfaces*, vol. 31, no. 2, pp. 90–108.

Nahon, K., Hemsley, J., Walker, S. & Hussain, M. (2011) 'Fifteen minutes of fame: the power of blogs in the lifecycle of viral political information', *Policy and Internet*, vol. 3, no. 1, pp. 6–33.

Schweitzer, E. (2011) 'Normalization 2.0: A longitudinal analysis of German online campaigns in the national elections 2002–9', *European Journal of Communication*, vol. 26, no. 4, pp. 310–327.

Strandberg, K. (2008) 'Online electoral competition in different settings: a comparative meta-analysis of the research on party-websites and online electoral competition', *Party Politics*, vol. 14, no. 2, pp. 223–244.

Strandberg, K. (2013) 'A social media revolution or just a case of history repeating itself? The use of social media on the 2011 Finnish parliamentary elections', *New Media and Society*, [Online] Available at: http://nms.sagepub.com/content/early/2013/01/13/1461444812470612 (15 January 2013).

UN DESA (United Nations Department of Economic and Social Affairs) (2010) *United Nations E-Government Survey 2010, Leveraging E-Government at a Time of Financial and Economic Crisis*, New York.

Vaccari, C. (2011) 'A tale of two e-parties: candidate websites in the 2008 US presidential primaries', *Party Politics*, [Online] 4 April 2011, Available at: http://ppq.sagepub.com/content/early/2011/04/02/1354068810391287, (25 February 2012).

Vergeer M., Hermans, L. & Sams, S. (2011) 'Online social networks and micro-blogging in political campaigning: the exploration of a new campaign tool and a new campaign style', *Party Politics*, [Online] 30 June 2011, Available at: http://ppq.sagepub.com/content/early/2011/06/16/1354068811407580, (25 February 2012).

Ward, S. & Gibson, R. (2009) 'European political organizations and the internet. Mobilization, participation, and change', in *Routledge Handbook of Internet Politics*, eds A. Chadwick & P. Howard, Abingdon, Oxford, pp. 25–39.

Morten Skovsgaard & Arjen Van Dalen

DODGING THE GATEKEEPERS?
Social media in the campaign mix during the 2011 Danish elections

Although politicians, scholars and campaigners claim that social media such as Facebook and Twitter profoundly change election campaigns, still little is known about the place of social media in the overall campaign mix and its use compared to traditional campaigning channels like the mass media. Cluster analysis of a representative survey among the candidates in the 2011 parliamentary election in Denmark shows that the candidates can be divided into three groups with different campaign mixes: a group which mainly communicates through the traditional mass media, a group which emphasizes social media, and a group which puts low emphasis on media in their campaign. The place of social media in the campaign mix of Danish candidates can be explained by access to the mainstream media and incentives for individual candidates. Traditional media remain the most important communication channel in the Danish campaign, but primarily for candidates who are newsworthy due to their experience and incumbency status. These candidates use social media to generate coverage in the traditional mass media. Challengers and less experienced candidates are more likely to use social media to compensate for lack of attention from the mainstream media, in particular when they are involved in intra-party competition. It is concluded that social media are integrated into Danish campaign mix according to the incentive structure of the electoral system and the media logic which characterizes modern campaigns.

Introduction

Politicians, journalists and campaigners around the world have high expectations about the influence of social media on election campaigning, especially inspired by Barack Obama's use of social media in his successful campaign in the 2008 US presidential elections. Also in the build-up to the 2011 Danish elections, expectations about the use of Facebook were high. Reasons for the expected importance of social media as a campaign tool were the increasing use among the Danish population, the possibility to by-pass traditional media and the growing knowledge of these new media among campaign professionals (Albrecht 2011; Hoejgaard Nielsen 2011). The adaption and use of social media, such as Facebook and Twitter in election campaigns, has inspired a wave of research. Scholars have looked into the early adapters of the new technologies in their campaigns (Lassen & Brown 2011), the social media networks on politicians (Vergeer & Hermans, in press), the content of the messages they post on Facebook or Twitter (Bode *et al.* 2011) and the way journalists use these messages in their stories (Broersma & Graham 2012).

This article adds to this literature by studying the place of social media in the overall campaign mix. While previous studies have given detailed insight into the use of social media, the social media campaign is mostly studied *in isolation* of other campaign channels and we still know little about the *relative importance* of these new campaign tools in comparison to other forms of the political campaign such as mass media appearances or direct contacts with potential voters. Disregarding this campaign mix might give the false impression that social media have substituted other 'layers' of campaigning. In the words of Kleis Nielsen (2012, p. 17):

> research in political communication needs to deal with all of these different layers and to recognize that while some forms of political communication have faded away over time (...), they rarely follow one another in a neat succession of distinct epochs, as some would have it.

Thus, studying the social media in isolation and disregarding the campaign mix draws a too general picture of the use of social media. Political candidates have different interests and different access to other communication channels such as mainstream media, which might affect the significance they attach to social media and the way they use them. Or put in another way, depending on their strategic goals and access to other campaign channels, politicians may integrate social media differently in their campaign mix. This article therefore seeks to answer three research questions. First, *which campaign mixes can be distinguished and how important are social media in these mixes?* Second, *how are newsworthiness and campaign incentives related to different campaign mixes, both at the party level and at the level of individual politicians?* Third, *what is the purpose of using social media in the different campaign mixes?*

Our analysis is based on a representative survey among candidates in the 2011 parliamentary election in Denmark ($N = 375$) including questions about their campaign style in general and the use of Facebook and Twitter in particular. Denmark is among the countries with the highest internet penetration in the world. Close to 5 million people or 89 percent of the Danes have internet access (Internet World Stats 2012). Nearly 3 million Danish Facebook profiles have been created and the Facebook penetration of 55 percent is among the highest in the world and well above the mean for both North America and Europe, which are the most Facebook-active continents (Socialbakers 2012a). Similar to most other countries, the use of Twitter has grown rapidly in recent years and the hashtag #dkpol, which signals a tweet on Danish politics, is the most frequently used among Danish Twitter users (Atcore.dk 2012). In a study from Eurobarometer, 66 percent of the Danes totally agreed to the statement 'Online social media are a modern way to keep abreast of political affairs' placing Denmark high on the list of the EU countries on that question (Eurobarometer 2012).

Much of the research on the use of social media in election campaigns is conducted in the United States. However, there are good reasons to study this in other contexts, because there are important differences between the US campaigns and campaigns in many other Western democracies – as, for instance, Denmark (Plasser & Plasser 2002). First of all, though Danish campaigns have become increasingly professionalized and mediatized (Jønsson 2006), they are still not as money-driven as campaigns in the United States, and unlike the US political television commercials are prohibited during election campaigns in Denmark.[1] The low cost connected to the use of social media in the campaign can be expected to make them an attractive option for Danish candidates. Second, the US electoral system based on two dominant parties and first past the post elections differs substantially from the proportional system known in multiparty systems such as Denmark. In the United States, elections are a head-to-head race between a Republican and a Democratic candidate. In the Danish proportional system elections, parties compete against each other, while candidates at the same time compete with their colleagues within their party to win one of the seats allocated to the party. In the multiparty system, the access to traditional media and incentives of candidates taking part in the campaign vary widely, depending on party affiliation and position on the party list. This makes Denmark an interesting case to study what access to the mainstream media as well as candidates' incentives mean for the place of social media in their campaign mix. Before describing our research design and findings, we first present our argument for why we expect newsworthiness and campaign incentives to matter for the place of social media in the campaign mix of political candidates.

The place of social media in the campaign mix: Who campaigns how and why?

In election campaigns, candidates try to reach voters through a mix of campaign channels, ranging from advertisement and mass media to direct contacts and live debates (Kleis Nielsen 2012, p. 17). The widespread use of social media, in particular Facebook, among the Danish population has added yet another platform to the campaign mix of Danish politicians. The priority which candidates give to social media in the campaign mix can be expected to vary due to their access to the mainstream media, which are still the most important channel of information for the public during election campaigns in Denmark.[2] Over the last years, campaigns have become increasingly *mediatized* (Mazzoleni & Schulz 1999). Mediatized campaigns are characterized by the importance of news media as a channel to be in contact with voters. As a consequence, campaigns follow a 'media logic' which is dictated by the journalists and their news values (Strömbäck 2008). News values such as relevance, conflict and power determine whether a politician will be covered or not. Due to these news values, attention for candidates is often skewed towards politicians in power and those expected to win the elections (Hopmann *et al.* 2011; Van Dalen 2012), while it is much harder for less known candidates such as less experienced challengers at the bottom of the party list to reach potential voters through the mainstream media.

For these candidates, Facebook and Twitter offer an opportunity to compensate for the lack of attention in the mainstream media. They can by-pass the traditional mass media and communicate directly with the electorate. Incumbents and experienced candidates can of course reap some of the same benefits from social media, but since they are generally better known among the audience and have easier access to the mass media, they can prioritize social media less in their campaign mix.

These differences in newsworthiness will not only play a role for individual politicians, but also at the level of the party. Previous research has shown that the *party* is an important determinant for whether social media are adapted (Jackson & Lilleker 2011). Incumbent parties have easier access to the mainstream media than challenging parties, which means that challenging parties are more likely to give social media a prominent place in their campaign mix. Research from the United States supports this argument; belonging to the minority party was an important determinant of Twitter use among members of the US Congress (Lassen & Brown 2011).

A second reason why some politicians are expected to give social media a more prominent place in their campaign is intra-party competition. The Danish electoral system is proportional and not first past the post, as it is known from Great Britain and the United States. This means that parties compete to get as big a proportion of the public vote as possible in order to win seats in parliament. However, half of the votes during the 2011 parliamentary election were cast on a specific candidate and not merely a party (Danmarks statistik 2012) and the individual politician might very well benefit from voters ticking the box with their name on the ballot. Most Danish parties use open lists, meaning that the seats which the party wins in parliament are assigned to the candidates on the party list with the highest share of personal votes in their constituency. Consequently, less well-known candidates further down the party list can win a seat ahead of more well-known and experienced politicians if they organize an individualized campaign and mobilize supporters to vote for them personally.

Due to this intra-party competition, we expect that low-profile candidates on an open list will put more emphasis on the social media in their campaign mix than other candidates. For them, the social media offer an opportunity to compensate for the lack of access to the mainstream media and to reach out to party supporters and mobilize them to cast a preferential vote. Candidates of parties with a closed list miss a similar incentive to organize an individualized campaign through the social media. High-profile candidates such as experienced incumbents are likely to prioritize mainstream media over social media. Not only do they have easier access to the mainstream media, but also they are more certain to be elected than low-profile candidates. For these high-profile candidates, the main objective is to gain as many votes as possible for the party in order to maximize the party's influence in parliament. Mainstream media are a more useful channel for this than social media, since a wide audience including both undecided voters and voters leaning towards other parties can be reached, especially through television.[3]

Nursing supporters or winning over voters?

Newsworthiness and campaign incentives are not only likely to influence the importance of social media, but also the purpose of using social media. The different reasons to include social media in the campaign mix can be divided into two rough categories. One is to win over undecided voters or voters leaning towards other candidates/parties, which can be labeled as conquest communication. The other is to mobilize and strengthen the bond with the ones who already support them, which can be labeled as maintenance communication (Maarek 2011, p. 45).

Considering the high internet penetration and the more than three million Facebook profiles in Denmark, this can be an interesting channel for conquest communication, aiming to reach as many voters as possible. Connected to this is the politicians' aim to make themselves and their political views visible to the public and for this purpose, social media can supplement already well-known channels such as mainstream media, canvassing, election posters and political debates. Our expectations are that high-profile candidates more engaged in inter-party competition than intra-party competition are preoccupied with reaching a broad audience and winning over voters to their party.

Social media can also be used for conquest communication in another way: as a means to gain visibility in the mainstream media. Messages on the social media have become an important source of information for mainstream media (Broersma & Graham 2012) and journalists are also often in politicians' network (Verweij 2012). This means that if politicians deliver newsworthy information on their social media profiles, they might very well spark a news story.

Low-profile candidates engaged in intra-party competition can be expected to use social media more for the purpose of maintenance communication rather than for conquest communication. Social media offer a platform to have personal contact with their supporters. In the American context, social media have been highlighted as an efficient means of organizing local campaigns and the volunteers involved (Karlsen 2011). The unique distinguishing feature of social media as communication channel is the potential to interact with voters without having to meet them face to face. Politicians can react to wallposts by followers (Duvander Højholt & Kosiara-Pedersen 2011) and thereby strengthen their bond with these potential voters (Jackson & Lilleker 2011). This is particularly interesting for candidates who want to mobilize their supporters to vote for them personally.

For some politicians, the reason to be on Facebook or Twitter might not be the strategic use of the new campaigning possibilities, but rather the perception that it is the thing to do in a modern campaign. They might only have 'joined a bandwagon around the latest must-have fad' (Jackson & Lilleker 2011, p. 92).

Design, method and data

To answer our research questions and study the relation between newsworthiness and campaign incentives on the one hand and the place of social media in the overall mix of communication channels on the other, we analyze the results of a survey of the candidates for the 2011 parliamentary election in Denmark. We find this method suitable to study the campaign mix of candidates. Most studies on the use of Facebook and Social media are based on an analysis of volume or content of social media updates, but we want to study the relative importance that candidates attach to social media in the campaign in comparison with other communication channels. Our survey allows us to compare the significance of different communication channels.

The survey was conducted in October and November 2011 shortly after the election in September as the Danish part of the Comparative Candidate Survey.[4] In total, 805 candidates ran for office and the whole population was surveyed apart from 20 candidates not affiliated with a party. Twenty additional candidates were not reachable due to insufficient contact information. We circulated a self-administered questionnaire including questions on the campaign strategy, media, political beliefs as well as individual background characteristics to 765 candidates. After two reminders, 325 had responded. To increase the response rate, we sent a paper version of the questionnaire to the ones who had not answered. This resulted in 50 additional responses adding up to a total of 375.[5] The overall response rate is 49 percent. We compared the composition of group of respondents to the population of candidates to check for representativeness on age, gender, party affiliation and constituency. None of the variables show statistically significant differences between our sample and the population. However, the response rate among elected candidates was lower than among the whole population (27 percent). This is probably due to the fact that members of parliament in general are busy and that they receive quite a few requests to participate in surveys.

Results

Three types of campaign mixes

This article set out to distinguish different types of campaign mixes among the candidates in the Danish parliamentary election 2011. We did this by conducting a cluster analysis on a battery of questions concerning the importance of different communication channels during the election campaign. The candidates were asked 'On a scale ranging from 1 to 5, 1 meaning "not important" and 5 meaning "very important", how important were the following communication channels in your campaign?'(See Table 1 for the mentioned communication channels). The cluster analysis can be used to identify patterns in respondents' answers and group the respondents according to these patterns. In the case of this analysis, it means that we were able to identify three different types of campaign mixes and group candidates according to the type of campaign mix they apply in their election campaign. We retracted the three groups in a two-step procedure. First step was a hierarchical cluster analysis using Ward's method. The results indicated that three distinct types of campaign mixes should be identified. Next step was a *k*-means clustering procedure where we based on the results from the first step calculated three clusters. In this manner, the candidates were sorted into three clusters assigning the candidate to the cluster with the shortest distance to the mean (see Hanitzsch 2011 for a similar approach).

Table 1 shows how the relative importance of the different channels is for the three groups. As indicated by the plusses, the first group of candidates attaches great importance to the classic mainstream media with particular emphasis on national television, national newspapers, national radio and regional television. This group we label as the traditional media group. The second group emphasizes

TABLE 1 Profiles of three types of campaigners.

	Traditional media group	New media group	Low media group
National television	++++	− − −	− − −
Regional television	+++		− − − −
National newspapers	++++	− −	− − −
Regional newspapers	++		− − −
Local newspapers	+	+	− − −
National radio	++++	− −	− − −
Local radio	++		− − − −
Own website		++	− − −
Social media	+	++	− − − −
(e.g. Facebook/Twitter)			
N	96	103	79

Note: The cells indicate the clusters' mean deviation from the overall mean in standard deviations: ++++/− − − −   .80 SD; +++/− − −   .60 SD; ++/− − .40 SD; +/− .20 SD.

social media and their own website, while national mainstream media are relatively less important to them. This group we label as the new media group. The third group attaches less significance to all the communication channels in their campaign than the other two groups. This last group we label as the low media group. These three groups with distinct campaign mixes can now be utilized for further analysis of who campaigns how.

Social media in the campaign mix

The results in Table 1 show the relative importance of different communication channels in the three groups, i.e. how they prioritize the individual channels in their mix. However, this does not necessarily mean that candidates who give high priority to mainstream media find social media not important at all. To gain a more detailed understanding of the place of social media among candidates with different types of campaign mixes, we look at how much importance the candidates with different campaign mixes attach to each channel in absolute terms (Table 2).

Overall, 30 percent of Danish politicians find social media a very important campaign channel. This makes it the fourth most important channel, after regional television and regional and local newspapers. Not surprisingly, the candidates in the new media group are the ones finding social media most important as a communication channel. Candidates in the traditional media group also find social media rather important as a supplement to the mainstream media, which

TABLE 2 The importance of different channels for three types of campaigners (per cent answering 'very important').

	National television	National newspapers	National radio	Regional television	Regional newspapers	Local newspapers	Local radio	Own website	Social media (Facebook/ Twitter)
Traditional media group (N = 96)	69	40	41	73	47	55	37	26	35
New media group (N = 103)	0	2	1	37	41	57	25	37	44
Low media group (N = 79)	0	3	1	0	11	22	3	4	6
All groups (N = 278)	24	15	15	40	35	46	23	24	30

they find even more important. This means that social media also have a place in their campaign mix, though not as prominent as for the candidates in the new media group. Candidates in the new media group do not focus exclusively on social media. They also find regional and local media important, which is in line with our argument that newsworthiness is connected to campaign style. The threshold for newsworthiness of local candidates is bound to be lower in the regional and especially local media than in the national media. It is rational for candidates who find it difficult to get into the national media to focus on regional and local mainstream media as well as the social media.

To get more insight into how social media are integrated in the different campaign mixes, Table 3 shows how much the candidates in the different campaign groups used social media and internet. Facebook is by far the most popular tool among all candidates. Seventy-eight percent used Facebook during the election campaign, while 27 percent used blogs and 16 percent used Twitter. There are differences between the groups. Ninety-three percent of candidates in the new media group used Facebook compared to 81 percent and 54 percent in the traditional media group and the low media group, respectively. For the use of Twitter and blogs, there are only minor differences between the new media group and the traditional media group, while the low media group is significantly lower. This underlines that the new media are an integral part of the campaign for candidates in the traditional media group, though they put relatively less emphasis on them in the total campaign mix.

TABLE 3 Use of social media and internet among politicians with different campaign styles.

	% who used Facebook actively in campaign	% who used Twitter actively in campaign	% who used a blog in their campaign
Traditional media group (N = 96)	81	17	33
New media group (N = 103)	93	22	32
Low media group (N = 79)	54	6	14
All groups (N = 278)	78	16	27

Campaign style, newsworthiness and competitive incentives

The distribution between the three groups for each political party (Figure 1) supports our argument that the place of social media in the campaign mix is related to newsworthiness and campaign incentives. As expected, the three opposition parties Social Democrats, the Social Liberals and the Socialist People's Party, have the highest proportion of candidates in the new media group. Since challengers are generally covered less in the mass media than incumbents, this increases the incentive of these parties to utilize new media. In line with this argument, candidates of the incumbent parties (The Liberal Party and Conservative People's Party) more often belong to the traditional media group than to the new media group.

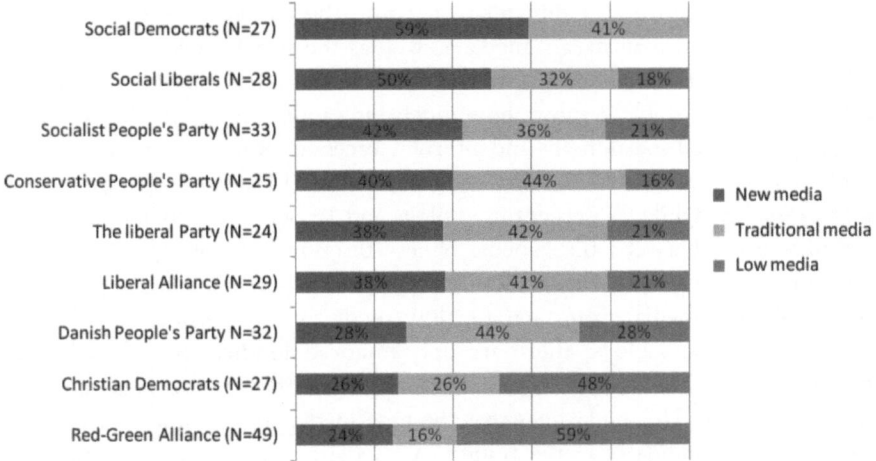

FIGURE 1 Share of politicians with different campaign styles per party.

Two parties (Red-Green Alliance and the Christian Democrats) had a larger share of candidates in the low media group than in the new media group. For candidates in these parties, the incentives to campaign individually were low. In 9 out of 10 constituencies, the Red-Green Alliance unlike the other parties organizes its list of candidates as a closed list with a prioritized order of candidates on the ballot.[6] Even though the Red-Green Alliance was doing well in the polls, it was more difficult for a member further down the list to be elected ahead of a candidate further up the list than was the case for the open lists applied by other parties. The reduced incentive to campaign individually can explain the high proportion of candidates in the low media group. The Christian Democrats only had one seat in parliament before the election. In the 2011 election, the party was constantly below 1 percent in the polls during the three weeks of campaigning, and they were never predicted to reach the threshold of 2 percent. In line with our argument that campaign incentives matter for the place of social media in the campaign mix, their share of candidates in the new media group is low. Campaigning seems pointless in a situation where it would take a small miracle to win any seats in parliament.

Table 4 presents the background characteristics of the candidates in the three groups. This shows that the relation between newsworthiness and campaign incentives and the place of social media in the campaign mix, which was present at the party level, can also be found at the candidate level.

In line with the newsworthiness argument, candidates in the new media group are less experienced and more often challengers than candidates in the traditional media group. One in four candidates in the traditional media group has been elected for parliament before, while this only goes for one in seven in the new media group. The candidates in the new media group are also younger than the candidates in the traditional media group. These candidates are in general considered less newsworthy by mainstream media and therefore are more inclined to prioritize social media higher.

The mainstream media in general find candidates who are likely to gain political influence more newsworthy (Hopmann et al. 2011). This allows us to use candidates' self-reported measure of the likelihood of winning a seat in parliament as a proxy for newsworthiness. Candidates in the traditional media group were at the start of the campaign more inclined to believe that they would be elected than the candidates in the new media group and the low media group.[7]

The candidates in the new media group were more optimistic about their chances of being elected than candidates in the low media group, but more skeptical than the ones in the traditional media group. This means that the most newsworthy candidates and the ones feeling certain or almost certain to win a seat in parliament are more likely to emphasize the mainstream media in their campaign mix, while the candidates who are less newsworthy and under more

TABLE 4 Characteristics of politicians with different campaign styles.

	Mean age[a]	Experience (% elected for parliament at least once before)	% of challengers (not member of parliament)	% who at start of the campaign did not believe that they stood a chance of being elected	% who at start of the campaign believed that they were likely or certain to be elected	% of candidates on a closed list	Mean hours spent on campaign per week[a]	% elected in the 2011 election
Traditional media group (N = 90)[b]	47 (12)	26	81	22	37	12	62 (48)	20
New media group (N = 100)[b]	43 (13)	14	96	38	19	17	60 (34)	12
Low media group (N = 74)[b]	46 (15)	5	96	61	5	38	35 (27)	5
All groups (N = 277)[b]	45 (13)	15	91	39	21	21	54 (39)	13

Notes: [a]Standard deviation in brackets.
[b]Lowest N.

competitive pressure are more likely to give priority to the social media, probably due to their limited access to the mainstream media.

The five-point scale for likelihood of being elected can be used for a more
detailed look at the relation between likelihood of being elected and the use
of social media. In Figure 2, we illustrate how much importance candidates
attach to national media, regional/local media and social media in their campaign
mix when this is combined with the likelihood of being elected. This shows that
while the importance of the mainstream media increases with the candidate's
likelihood of being elected, most pronounced so for the national mass media,
this is not the case for the social media. The candidates finding themselves in
an open race for a seat in parliament are the ones emphasizing social media
the most. This supports the argument that candidates who are less newsworthy
for the mainstream media and who have strong incentives to compete for their
own seat in parliament place social media more prominently in their campaign
mix. Candidates who are more certain to be elected can focus more on
winning over undecided voters. This is best done through the mainstream
media, where they also have better access.

The percentage of candidates on a closed list in the three groups further supports the argument that intra-party competition is of importance to the campaign mix (Table 4). This becomes clear when we compare the low media and
the new media group. While low media users do not differ from social media
users in terms of challenger status, they are more likely to belong to a closed
list. Candidates on a closed list have fewer incentives to use social media and

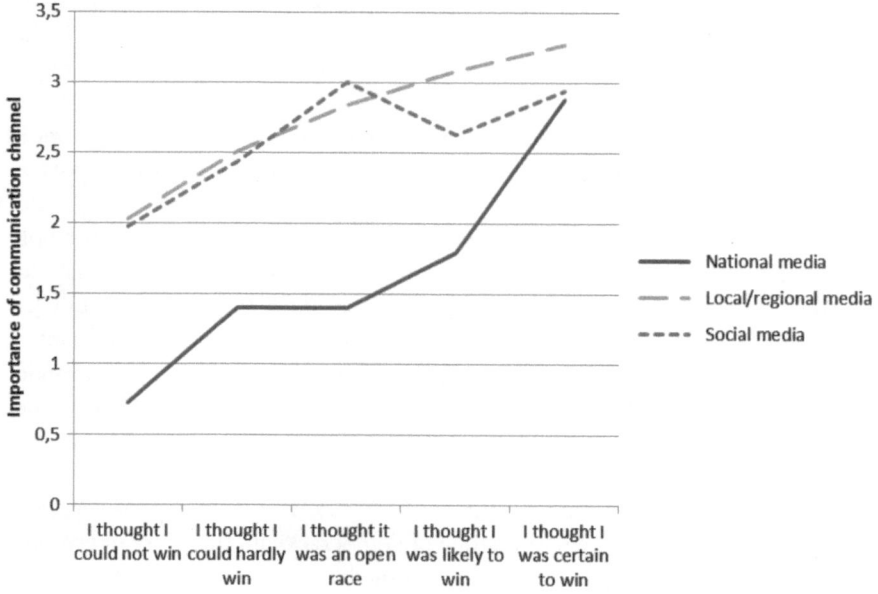

FIGURE 2 The importance of communication channel by the likelihood of winning a seat.

mobilize their supporters, since it is highly unlikely to influence their personal chance of being elected. Therefore, they also spent less time on the campaign. Where the new media group spent 60 hours a week on average, comparable to the traditional media group, the candidates in the low media group spent on average half that time. At the end of the campaign, 20 percent of the traditional media group, 12 percent of the new media group and 5 percent of the low media group were elected for parliament.

The purpose of using social media

Table 5 shows the reasons for including social media in the campaign mix. Across all groups, gaining visibility and reaching as many voters as possible are the main reasons for using social media. This is central to any campaign and considering the internet penetration and amount of Facebook profiles in Denmark, it seems that social media are considered a useful means to that end. It could be a way to reach younger voters and the ones with the least political interest, because they could be introduced to political messages and candidates when browsing the profiles of their friends (Utz 2009, p. 223).

On the other hand, it can be questioned how successful this strategy is. People who see social media as most valuable for political participation are often already politically active offline (Gustaffson 2012, p. 1111). Most Danish Facebook users who became friends with political candidates during the 2007 campaign were already in the network of these candidates before they became friends on Facebook (Normann Andersen & Medaglia 2009, p. 110). This implies that politicians preach to the already converted on the social media (Karlsen 2011). Nevertheless, gaining visibility is rated highly among Danish candidates when they give reasons for using social media in their campaign.

Danish candidates indicate that communicating directly with voters is equally important as making their own political views visible and more important than reaching as many voters as possible. This is somewhat surprising, since research in the United States, Australia and the UK has shown that most politicians use social media for self-promotion and broadcasting rather than dialogue and conversation (Goldbeck et al. 2010; Grant et al. 2010; Jackson & Lilleker 2011). In Denmark, Members of Parliament only dedicate a small amount of their Facebook communication to dialogue with constituents (Duvander Højholt & Kosiara-Pedersen 2011), while the majority of messages were one-way communication. One possible explanation is that responsiveness is particularly important during election campaigns where voters have to decide on a candidate to vote for. Another is that candidates realize that responsiveness to the electorate is a normative cornerstone of democracy and therefore overreport the significance to this aspect of their social media use compared to their actual practice online.

TABLE 5 Goals of social media use for politicians with different campaign styles (percentage answering 'very important').

	Reaching as many voters as possible	Communicating directly with voters	Appearing modern	Gaining visibility in the traditional media	Making yourself and your political views visible	Organizing the campaign in your constituency
Traditional media group (N = 83)[a]	51	51	18	28	53	27
New media group (N = 93)[a]	40	51	19	16	53	23
Low media group (N = 47)[a]	17	19	17	9	13	15
All groups (N = 223)[a]	39	44	18	19	45	23

Notes: Question: If you used social media – such as Facebook or Twitter – how important were these in your campaign when it comes to …?
[a]Lowest N.

In the American context, social media have successfully been used by politicians to organize the campaign (Karlsen 2011). Danish candidates also to some extent find this aspect of the social media important, but less so than reaching and communicating with voters. Some candidates find it important to use the social media to appear modern or maybe rather not to appear unmodern. As described earlier, it has been claimed several times that social media are the future in election campaign, and this seems to lead to politicians jumping the bandwagon.

We now turn to the different goals of the three groups. The candidates in the low media group attach less importance to the different functions of the social media than the other two groups apart from appearing modern. The candidates in the traditional media group and the new media group are remarkably similar. There are, however, interesting differences between the two groups. Candidates in the traditional media group find it more important to reach as many voters as possible and to use the social media as a means to gain visibility in the mainstream media than candidates in the new media group. This is in line with our expectation that candidates in the traditional media group are more focused on conquest communication, i.e. winning over undecided voters or voters leaning towards other parties, than the candidates in the new media group. As argued above, the mainstream media are still the most efficient communication channel for conquest communication, since communicating on the social media might be to preach to the already converted (Karlsen 2011). Therefore, it makes sense that the ones most focused on conquest communication also find it more important to utilize social media as a means to break through the gates of the mainstream media. Due to the higher newsworthiness of these candidates, they will probably also find it easier to do so than the candidates in the new media group. In this sense, candidates in the traditional media group integrate social media in their campaign mix in accordance with an overall strategy which focuses on the mainstream media and conquest communication.

The findings do not show that candidates in the new media group emphasize maintenance communication more, which would be expected due to the intra-party competition they face and the need to strengthen their bond with supporters. Contrary to this expectation, the traditional media group finds it equally important to communicate directly with voters and to use social media to organize the campaign in their constituency as the new media group. It could be that candidates in the traditional media group also use maintenance communication to hold on to party supporters, who can serve as ambassadors for their party. It could also be that they see direct interaction with social media users as an opportunity to win over new voters, i.e. as a form of conquest communication.

Discussion

This article studied how Danish candidates for the 2011 parliamentary elections used social media. Based on the observation that most previous studies have studied the use of social media in isolation, we analyzed the place of social media in the campaign mix. Results show that the candidates have embraced social media. But rather than replacing other communication channels, the social media are integrated into the overall mix of communication channels in the campaign. This integration appears to be rational in the sense that the place of social media in the campaign mix to a large extent seems to be conditioned by the newsworthiness of the candidate – and consequently access to the mainstream media – and his or her position in the competition for a seat in parliament. In general, candidates who best fit the news values of the mainstream media will also emphasize these more in their campaign mix and use the social media more for conquest communication. Less newsworthy low-profile candidates who are in competition with other candidates from their own party for a seat in parliament tend to emphasize the social media more in their campaign mix, because they are able to communicate with voters without having to pass the critical gatekeepers in the mainstream media. Contrary to our expectation, candidates who place most emphasis on social media are not more likely to use Facebook and Twitter for maintenance communication than candidates who see traditional media as their main channel.

Broersma and Graham (2012) have argued that social media are tipping the power balance between politicians and journalists more in the favor of politicians, who are better able to control their message. However, our results indicate that the mainstream media are still candidates' first pick if they can get access. So even if social media provide a communication channel where candidates control their own message, the power still very much resides with the mainstream media. Nevertheless, the less newsworthy candidates can still benefit from using the social media given that the alternative is unsuccessfully banging the gates of the mainstream media. This does not mean that the power is necessarily moving away from the mainstream media, but that candidates now have a tool that in some sense helps them dodge the reluctant mainstream media.

This study only focused on how candidates integrate the social media in their campaign. The impact of the social media might very well reach further than the candidates' use of them. Independent of how politicians employ the social media, the voters might share political information, discuss issues related to the election or link to interesting information, be it news from the mainstream media or other political information available on the internet. In this sense, social media might still be influential as an alternative way for voters to gain information that does not emerge from politicians own strategic information.

The particular characteristics of the Danish parliamentary election campaign (such as high turn-out and low capital intensity) should be taken into account when generalizing these findings to other countries and elections. In other contexts, social media may play a more important role in fundraising or mobilizing the electorate. As we have argued in this paper, studies in different contexts will benefit from studying the place of social media in the overall campaign mix, rather than in isolation.

Notes

1   https://www.retsinformation.dk/Forms/R0710.aspx?id=131197&exp=1.

2   Data from the Danish national election study 2007, available at: SurveyBanken under the heading 'valgundersøgelser' (http://bank1.surveybank.aau.dk/webview/).

3   See data from Danish national election study 2007 (note 2).

4   The data collection in Denmark was headed by Christian Elmelund-Præstekær, Associate Professor, Department of Political Science, University of Southern Denmark.

5   Not all respondents answered the battery of questions which is central to our further analysis. This means that the analysis will be based on 278 respondents.

6   The Socialist People's Party is the only other party to use this way of organizing the list – and this is only in 3 out of 10 constituencies.

7   A logistic regression including the candidates from the traditional media group and the new media group with membership of the new media group as the dependent variable allowed us to enter control variables. This shows that the perceived likelihood of winning a seat in parliament and being a challenger are significant when controlling for party affiliation, age and gender. This means that these differences between the two groups are not caused by party, age and gender.

References

Albrecht, J. (2011) 'Fire forklaringer på hvorfor Facebook vil praege valget' [For explanations for why Facebook will dominate the elections], [Online] Available at: http://www.journalisten.dk/fire-forklaringer-pa-hvorfor-facebook-vil-praege-valget (1 November 2012).

Atcore.dk (2012) 'Infograhic om Twitter', [Online] Available at: http://atcore.dk/infographic-om-twitter/ (1 November 2012).

Bode, L., Lassen, D., Kim, Y. M., Shah, D., Fowler, E. F., Ridout, T. N. & Franz, M. (2011) 'Social and broadcast media in 2010 midterms: the expanding repertoire of senate candidates' campaign strategies', working paper, [Online] Available at: http://users.polisci.wisc.edu/behavior/Papers/BodeEtAl2011.pdf (1 October 2012).

Broersma, M. & Graham, T. (2012) 'Social media as beat. Tweets as news sources during the 2010 British and Dutch elections', *Journalism Practice*, vol. 6, no. 3, pp. 403–419.

Danmarks Statistik (2012), 'Folketingsvalget den 15. September 2011' [The Parliamentary Election September 15th 2011], [Online] Available at: http://www.dst.dk/pukora/epub/upload/17989/ftvalg.pdf (1 November 2012).

Duvander Højholt, L. & Kosiara-Pedersen, K. (2011) 'Forandrer Facebook partiernes forhold til vælgerne?' [Does Facebook change parties' relation to voters?], *Tidskrift Politik*, vol. 14, no. 3, pp. 57–66.

Eurobarometer (2012) 'Media use in the European Union', [Online] Available at: http://ec.europa.eu/public_opinion/archives/eb/eb76/eb76_media_en.pdf (1 November 2012).

Goldbeck, J., Grimes, J. M. & Rogers, A. (2010) 'Twitter use by the US Congress', *Journal of the American Society for Information Science and Technology*, vol. 61, no. 8, pp. 1612–1621.

Grant, W. J., Moon, B. & Busby Grant, J. (2010) 'Digital dialogue? Australian politicians' use of the social network tool Twitter', *Australian Journal of Political Science*, vol. 45, no. 4, pp. 579–604.

Gustaffson, N. (2012) 'The subtle nature of Facebook politics: Swedish social network site users and political participation', *New media & Society*, vol. 14, no. 7, pp. 1111–1127.

Hanitzsch, T. (2011) 'Populist disseminators, detached watchdogs, critical change agents and opportunist facilitators: professional milieus, the journalistic field and autonomy in 18 countries', *The International Communication Gazette*, vol. 73, no. 6, pp. 477–494.

Hoejgaard Nielsen, S. (2011) 'sådan vil sociale medier påvirke folketingvalget' [This is how social media will influence the parliamentary elections], [Online] Available at: http://www.journalisten.dk/node/19119 (1 November 2012).

Hopmann, D. N., de Vreese, C. H. & Albæk, E. (2011) 'Incumbency bonus in election coverage explained: the logics of political power and the media market', *Journal of Communication*, vol. 61, no. 2, pp. 264–282.

Internet World Stats (2012) [Online] Available at: http://www.internetworldstats.com/stats4.htm (1 November 2012).

Jackson, N. & Lilleker, D. (2011) 'Microblogging, constituency service and impression management: UK MPs and the use of Twitter', *The Journal of Legislative Studies*, vol. 17, no. 1, pp. 86–105.

Jønsson, R. (2006) 'Den professionelle politiske kommunikation kræver nye journalistiske perspektiver' [Professional political communication demands new journalistic perspectives] in *Politisk Journalistik og kommunikation*, eds P. Bro, R. Jønsson & O. Larsen, Samfundslitteratur, Frederiksberg, pp. 43–66.

Karlsen, R. (2011) 'A Platform for individualized campaigning? Social media and parliamentary candidates in the 2009 Norwegian election campaign', *Policy & Internet*, vol. 3, no. 4, Article 4.

Kleis Nielsen, R. (2012) *Ground Wars: Personalized Communication in Political Campaigns*, Princeton University Press, Princeton.

Lassen, D. S. & Brown, A. R. (2011) 'Twitter: the electoral connection?' *Social Science Computer Review*, vol. 29, no. 4, pp. 419–436.

Maarek, P. J. (2011) *Campaign Communication & Political Marketing*, Wiley-Blackwell, Oxford.

Mazzoleni, G. & Schulz, W. (1999) 'Mediatization of politics: a challenge for democracy?' *Political Communication*, vol. 16, no. 3, pp. 247–261.

Normann Andersen, K. & Medaglia, R. (2009) 'The use of Facebook in national election campaigns: politics as usual?' *Electronic Participation*, vol. LNCS 5694, pp. 101–111.

Plasser, F. & Plasser, G. (2002) *Global Political Campaigning: A Worldwide Analysis of Campaign Professionals and their Practices*, Praeger, Westport, CT.

Socialbakers (2012a) 'Denmark. Facebook statistics', [Online] Available at: http://www.socialbakers.com/facebook-statistics/denmark (19 October 2012).

Strömbäck, J. (2008) 'Four phases of mediatization: an analysis of the mediatization of politics', *The International Journal of Press/Politics*, vol. 13, no. 3, pp. 228–246.

Utz, S. (2009) 'The (potential) benefits of campaigning via social network sites', *Journal of Computer-Mediated Communication*, vol. 14, pp. 221–243.

Van Dalen, A. (2012) 'Structural bias in cross-national perspective. How political systems and journalism cultures influence government dominance in the news', *International Journal of Press/Politics*, vol. 17, no. 1, pp. 32–55.

Vergeer, M. & Hermans, L. (in press) 'Campaigning on Twitter. Micro-blogging and online social networking as campaign tools in the 2010 general elections in the Netherlands', *Journal of Computer-Mediated Communication*.

Verweij, P. (2012) 'Twitter links between politicians and journalists', *Journalism Practice*, vol. 6, nos 5–6, pp. 680–691.

Gunn Sara Enli & Eli Skogerbø

PERSONALIZED CAMPAIGNS IN PARTY-CENTRED POLITICS
Twitter and Facebook as arenas for political communication

Social media like Facebook and Twitter place the focus on the individual politician rather than the political party, thereby expanding the political arena for increased for personalized campaigning. The need to use social media to communicate a personal image as a politician and to post personalized messages online seems less obvious in a party-centred system such as the Norwegian. Within this framework, the personalized and dialogical aspects of social media may be contradicted by the political parties' structural communication strategies. The article uses data from interviews and status updates from two Norwegian election campaigns and asks for what purposes Norwegian politicians use social media as a tool for political communication. The findings show that politicians' report both marketing and dialogue with voters as motives for their social media use and their practices varied, too. Politicians' reported motive to use social media for marketing purposes was reflected in their actual use. The preferred social media platform for marketing purposes was Facebook. Twitter was more used for continuous dialogue compared to Facebook. Social media marketing was personalized and involved private exposure and individual initiatives. The article concludes by indicating hypotheses and need for further research.

Social media have over the past few years become integrated into election campaigning and other forms of political communication (Skogerbø 2011). As such they provide new impetus to the *personalization of politics*, a returning theme in political communication (Thompson 1995; van Zoonen & Holtz-Bacha 2000). Our hypothesis is that social media, as a result of their design, affordances, their interplay with other media and the opportunities for creating intimate relations to voters, add to processes of personalization. Social media such as Facebook and Twitter place the focus on the individual politician rather than on the political party, thereby expanding the political arena for increased personalized campaigning.

Consequently, social media may also contribute to the levelling out of differences between different party systems. In candidate-centred political systems such as the American, the candidate and not the party organization is the main focus of election campaigns. Unlike proportional systems, the candidates individually compete for seats in the Congress, state legislatures and for the presidency. In this system, Twitter and Facebook fit well in with candidates' need to communicate directly with voters and election workers as well as for building their political image.

In party-centred systems, such as the Norwegian, the political party plays the main role for originating and spelling out politics, and the need for candidates to build a personal image is less obvious. Here, the parties are in charge of the overall communication strategies in the election campaign. Within this framework, the *personalized* and dialogical aspects of social media may be contradicted by the political parties' *structural* communication strategies. Yet, politics have become increasingly personified also in party-centred system and it is in this context that social media should be analysed (Karlsen 2011a; Larsson & Moe 2012).

This article will investigate to what extent and purpose Norwegian politicians use social media to communicate politics. Simply put, *how and why do Norwegian politicians, who compete for votes in a party-centred system, use social media as a campaign tool?* We discuss the relationship between the political parties' strategies for social media and the individual politicians' personal motivations for social media presence. The key aim is to shed light on how social media impact on and possibly change both content and structures of political communication.

Personalization of politics and social media

We started out by asserting that social media add to the personalization of politics. This is not to say that personalization is a product of politicians' social media presence. Rather, we argue that social media fit into long-term ongoing processes where political communication has become increasingly focused on personalities and personal traits of politicians. In line with, e.g. Hjarvard (2008) and Strömbäck (2008), we see this as an aspect of the mediatization of politics that characterize most Western societies, and which implies, among other traits, that politicians have to meet demands not only to share their public image but also their personal and private sides. Unavoidably, these processes are also tied to the popularization of politics, the blurring of border between the political and the private, the public and the personal. Personalization is pivotal if not the only characteristic of popularization of politics. Parallel to the personalization of political, the politicization of popular culture, in particular entertainment, have become increasingly common, both in terms of TV-drama, game and talk shows (Thompson 1995; van Zoonen & Holtz-Bacha 2000; van Zoonen et al. 2007).

For some theorists, such as Habermas (1989, 1992), Sennett (1976) and Postman (1985), personalization of politics have been described as lamentable, for others, they signal a democratization of the relationship between elites and citizens (van Zoonen 2005). However, personalization may also be regarded as an intrinsic characteristic of social and media developments over the past century. The claims on political candidates to present themselves as multidimensional persons with personal and private sides as well as public images has increased (Lilleker 2010), partly because of increasing media competition where different news rooms compete for the most exciting and attracting political news. In campaign periods, this is particularly noticeable: Politicians compete for attention by, for instance, inviting journalists, and thereby voters, home, offering a personal meeting in a public space. Political campaigning has always been about personal encounters between politicians and voters, and traditional campaigning such as knocking-on-doors and town-hall meetings involve personalization of politics, too.

Social media such as Facebook and Twitter fit well into this setting. They represent semi-public, semi-private spaces for self-representation where borders between offline personal and online mediated relations are blurred (Enli & Thumin 2012). They allow politicians (and voters) to stage their public *and* private roles, and to shift between them seamlessly and more or less consciously and strategically. For campaign purposes, social media thus add to the spaces where candidates may involve voters in personal encounters. These encounters may serve several purposes, e.g. market their candidacies, mobilize voters for the upcoming election, discuss politics or a combination.

Personal traits as well as structural constraints may affect how candidates apply social media in their campaigns. The competitive position of candidates is likely to be important. Studies from the United States documented that politicians' use of social media correlated with their competitive position: challengers were more likely to be early adopters of social media, while incumbents adopted slower but more steadily. Transferred and translated to the Scandinavian setting, these findings indicate that a candidate's competitive position, i.e. both the position, the party list and the party's chances of taking a mandate is important. Whether a candidate has secured a seat, occupies an insecure position or has no chance of being elected, might be of more relevance for the politicians' social media practices than the structural communication strategies within each political party. In turn, a candidate's social media profiling might signal a more personalized campaign strategy within the framework of the party-centred system.

In the following study, we first address the motives of individual candidates for using social media. By looking at how candidates actually used them, we seek to uncover different patterns of use between candidates.

Data material and methods

The research design can be described as explorative, qualitative and longitudinal, aiming to identify development and emerging practices of social media strategies and user patterns practice in Norwegian politics. The analysis draws on two sets of data, research interviews with 29 Norwegian politicians conducted in the aftermath of the parliamentary election in 2009 and content analyses of Facebook and Twitter profiles of 35 Norwegian politicians during and after the local elections in 2011. The interview sample was non-random and included the two top candidates of each of the seven parties represented in parliament in the previous period in four different constituencies. The interviews were collected and analysed by employing a grounded theory approach (Corbin & Strauss 2008). The candidates were asked about how they conducted their election campaigns and their motives and experiences with social media during the preceding election campaign.

The sample of social media profiles was non-random and strategic, too. The profiles selected belonged to the top candidates of the same seven parties in five large- and medium-sized Norwegian municipalities in the local elections in 2011. We included all their updates on Facebook and Twitter in three different periods before and after Election Day, 12 September 2011. Norwegian election campaigns comprise two distinct phases: the 'long campaign' starts about a year before election day, and the 'short campaign' includes the intensive last four weeks (Aardal et al. 2004). The material included a two-week period in the 'long campaign'-period, the entire 'short campaign'-period[1] and a two-week post-election campaign-period.[2] The updates were analysed by quantitative content analysis. The coding manual was worked out by the research team and done manually by several coders. The design of the study does not allow for generalization of findings to the universe of candidates or of social media messages. Instead, the findings indicate concepts and hypotheses that may help develop empirical insights as well as theory building.

Norwegian politics, parties and election campaigns

Politically, Norway can be described as a stable democracy with a parliamentary government, a multiparty system and well-organized membership parties. The political parties have over time been weakened by declining membership, reduced party identification, and similar processes, yet the party organizations have remained strong and influential (Heidar & Saglie 2003). The Left–Right conflict has remained significant and the parties place themselves according to this continuum (Figure 1) (Aardal 2011).

The Norwegian electoral system consists of direct elections and proportional representation. The country is geographically and administratively divided into 19 counties which for parliamentary and county elections make up the

Left   Right

Socialist	Labour	Centre	Christian	Liberal	Conservative	Progress
Left Party	Party	Party	Peoples'	Party (V)	Party	Party (Frp)
(SV)	(Ap)	(Sp)	Party		(H)	
			(KrF)			

FIGURE 1 The Norwegian Party System. The seven parties represented in Parliament 2005–2013, positioned from Left to Right.

constituencies. Below the national level, the 429 municipalities make up the political and administrative level of local government as well as the constituencies for local elections. Elections are held every two years at fixed dates, interchangeably between parliamentary and local and county elections.

As noted, the party organizations draw up the central campaign strategies. These strategies guide although do not determine the local and regional campaigns that are usually run by local and regional party branches. Within the confines of the parties' central campaigns, local candidates may front their individual candidacies and issues (Karlsen and Skogerbø, forthcoming).

Further, the parties dominate the process for nomination of candidates. The nominations are made by representative conventions organized by the constituency branches of the party organizations. They decide on lists of candidates in a ranked order. In local elections, voters may change the ranking order or cumulate candidates, i.e. give candidate their personal votes, whereas in parliamentary elections the influence of the voters on the party lists is only theoretical. In local election campaigns, the importance of the established parties and the central campaigns vary somewhat with the size of the constituency and the strength of the local party organizations. In most constituencies, however, the composition and conflict structure of the municipality council is quite equal to the composition of the parliament and the parties will normally be more important than the individual candidates when the voters make up their minds (Narud & Valen 2007). These characteristics make up institutional constraints for the candidates' campaigning communication.

The characteristics of the Norwegian political system highlight the differences between campaigning communication in different political systems (Strömbäck & Dimitrova 2006; Strömbäck & Aalberg 2008; Karlsen 2010a). Scandinavian party systems are rooted in a welfare state tradition that carries certain regulatory and cultural constraints. One aspect is highly regulated media markets, including subsidization of newspapers, public broadcasters, and restrictions on political TV-advertising (Mjøs et al., forthcoming). One characteristic of Scandinavian political campaigning is the low degree of professionalization (Karlsen 2010b). Political parties are financially supported by the state according to the size of their membership and provided with resources to run campaigns. Another is the diversity of arenas for political communication on the local, regional and national level. These are important elements of the political public sphere into which the social media have entered. A likely consequence of the ban on political TV-advertisements is, e.g. the fact that *YouTube* is less used in Norwegian election campaigns. *YouTube* is particularly well-suited for disseminating campaign communication produced by or for television (Gulati & Williams 2010), less of an option in the Norwegian setting.

Norwegian election campaigns accordingly take place on a variety of media platforms. For party leaders and other 'celebrity politicians' (van Zoonen 2005), nationwide television has been all important, whereas for regional and local candidates local and regional newspapers (printed and online) were the main media stages (Skogerbø 2011). Online and social media have become increasingly important as complementary campaign arenas. Facebook, Twitter, and YouTube may be regarded as global media that emerge in contrast to the structure of public and welfare state media. The social media are, nevertheless, central to the Norwegian public sphere. In 2011, 75 per cent of the Norwegian population used Facebook and 9 per cent used Twitter on a weekly basis.[3] Both Twitter and Facebook were to some extent integrated into mainstream media as sources and as spaces for debates.

Politicians' appearances on social media not only result from their own efforts to reach voters, but also they are part of the parties' central campaign strategies. Candidates may have personal Facebook and Twitter accounts, however, they have increasingly been equipped with online tools by the parties, too, starting with personal websites and blogs and more recently personal social media accounts directly linked from party websites. Many of the interviewed candidates in the 2009 election pointed to expectations from the party, the media and the voters as reasons for why they were or should have been active on social media.

There are differences between large and small parties concerning campaign budgets and the size of the party organization. In the 2009 and 2011 election campaigns between 2009 and 2011, all Norwegian party organizations encouraged their candidates to have social media presence, but to varying degrees offered assistance to the candidates in maintaining them, leading to varying degrees of use. Nevertheless, the rather low threshold and accessibility of Facebook and Twitter make them into tools that are likely to increase individual presence. The interview data provided information on motives for use as well as non-use. Below, we conceptualize different conditions, motives and practices of social media as means for political communication and place them in the context of strategic political communication.

Motives for using social media in election campaigns

We analysed the motives that political candidates gave when asked about their social media use in the 2009 general election campaign (Skogerbø 2011). They provided us with a picture of the conceptions of social media campaign tools in what was popularly termed 'the first Twitter election'.

The findings pointed towards three central motives for using social media. First, *marketing*, meaning that the candidates used them to increase the visibility of their candidacies and parties in the public sphere. In this respect, social media were yet another place to promote their politics and one in which they could reach other groups of voters, e.g. young people, than in traditional media, in line with what other studies have found (Karlsen 2011b). Although being active on many different arenas, most candidates reported that they should have a social media presence, too, in order to reach the young and be attractive to journalists.

Marketing in social media is more personal than in mainstream media. Some politicians experienced that sharing personal updates and pictures attracted considerably more attention from readers and voters than updates with political statements. Norwegian politicians distinguished clearly between Facebook and Twitter and were well aware that the semi-private sphere of Facebook constituted a different public than the public arena of Twitter:

> Facebook lies in the intersection between the private and the public sphere. If you get too political on Facebook, it loses its private function, namely to keep in touch with old friends. Nevertheless, my generation politicians use it both ways, because being an active politician is a large part of your identity. (Candidate in the Parliamentarian election 2009, 31 years old)

Among the interviewed candidates who used social media, the division between the intimate familiar Facebook and Twitter as a marketing arena was well established. More surprisingly, they were willing to promote their politics by communicating their 'private identity' as well as their political persona, for example by sharing photos from their private lives:

> It is more fun when there are personal feelings and less political statements. (...)When I post photos of my children I get immediate response, when I write about politics, it's quiet. (Candidate in the Parliamentarian election 2009, 36 years old)

The politicians cross-promoted their individual online presence by being visible both as a personal candidate and as party representatives. A candidate who was active on several social media, including Facebook and Twitter in 2009 referred to his cross-promotion of 'my blog' rather than 'the party site':

> I use Twitter to draw attention to my blog. I do that on Facebook, too. (Candidate in the Parliamentarian election 2009, 31 years old)

Second, the politicians mentioned *mobilization* as a key motive for being present on Facebook and Twitter, most often in tandem with use of 'mundane Internet tools' (Nielsen 2011) such as email, SMS and mobile telephone, and traditional media and offline campaigning. The effect of social media mobilization is not studied here, but Enjolras *et al.* (2012) found that Facebook was an efficient tool for mobilization for the so-called 'rose ceremonies' after the terror attacks in Norway on 22 July 2011, when several hundred thousands gathered in towns across the country to protest against terrorism and in memory of the dead. However, there have also been failed attempts to shift online engagement into offline political action. The challenge for political organizations is to translate online engagement into real action. Our findings indicate that social media enhanced the effect of other campaign strategies, online and offline. In 2009, several interviewed candidates reported that they personally often used Facebook to invite voters to events and, perhaps more unexpected, that people had contacted them on Facebook *after* a physical meeting, in order to express support, or ask for information or help.

A third motive mentioned by our interviewees was opportunities for *dialogue* with the voters. Several politicians claimed that social media represented new opportunities for connecting with the voters, getting feedback on political issues, discuss politics more continuously, and engaging more voters than previous media. Other studies have reported that dialogue was a central motive and expectation for other politicians, too (Johansen 2011). This motive may echo techno-optimistic visions about the emancipatory and democratic potential of communications, most recently appropriated to the Internet (Shirky 2008). However, they may also reflect experiences. A candidate who had many years of experience with online politics remarked:

> Over the past few years, I have used Facebook to talk politics with friends and people who know me. There is a lot of good political discussion there. (Candidate in 2009 parliamentary election, 32 years old)

This politician saw Facebook, in line with the network's own terminology, as a more 'friendly space' than Twitter. Twitter he described as populated with opponents and people who did not 'wish you well', thereby also contradicting predictions that social media were 'echo chambers' for users' own opinions (Sunstein 2007). The observation that this politician shared is, interestingly, in line with new findings on social media use in Norway: it is more common to be opposed than supported (Enjolras *et al.* 2013).

The politicians' social media presence and practices

In 2011, social media had increased in popularity among the voters, and Facebook had become commonplace media-related activities not only for young people but for Norwegian citizens in general. This development was reflected in the politicians' implementation of their strategies for social media presence and the way their profiles were updated.

Personalized political marketing

First, in terms of marketing, *Facebook* was the primary choice of our sampled politicians. We found diverging uses, yet the prevailing tendency was that the politicians' preferred social medium was unquestionably Facebook, both in terms of presence and in terms of activity. Only 2 of 31 politicians did not have Facebook accounts, and equally few did not have a public profile. The adoption of Twitter was somewhat lower. Seventeen of the 35 sampled candidates in 2011 had Twitter accounts in the long-election period, 21 in the short and post-election periods.

Measured in activity, *Facebook* was used far more than *Twitter*. In total, 31 of the sampled candidates in the 2011 election had Facebook and Twitter accounts. They posted altogether 1304 Facebook status updates and 754 tweets. In this respect, local politicians likened their voters. They preferred the medium that reached the largest number of people, or in other words, they chose to be where their voters were, thereby strengthening the conceptualization of social media as a strategy for political marketing.

Nearly half (45 per cent) of all updates on Facebook and Twitter contained a link. Linking was widespread on both, but more used on Facebook (54 per cent) than Twitter (36 per cent). Often the links from Twitter was to the candidate's own Facebook-profile, aiming at directing voters to specific online sites promoting their candidacies. The largest group was links to media coverage of the candidates' campaign, followed by linking to the politicians' blogs, the party's website, and other self-produced online material, including cross-promotion of various social media updates. These findings support what the candidates in 2009 said and confirm other studies that have pointed to the high degree of marketing, self-promotion and communication with one's own party in political social media communication.

Social media also enabled politicians to make personal comments on news stories and the agendas of traditional media. They often added an interpretation, a correction, or a comment contesting the mass media versions of their public images or promoting their own angle of a news story, thereby protesting against journalistic interpretations or correct quotations. This is a kind of *interpretative linking practice* that may be regarded as an adding of a personal angle to the public stories, another trait of personalization.

Campaign-sensitive mobilization

The second motive for social media presence was to mobilize and engage citizens in campaign-related activities. Mobilizing was a considerably more prominent practice in the Facebook-updates than the tweets, confirming the interviewees' statements.

Social media activity was naturally mainly focused at mobilizing voters to turn out at the polls, and was, accordingly, *campaign-sensitive*. Measured in terms of frequency, the politicians posted considerably more updates and comments on social media during the 'short election campaign', than in 'the long-election campaign', and 'the post-election campaign'. The content analysis showed that the sample collected within the 'long-election campaign' was characterized by relatively low social media activity. Over the two weeks, only 312 updates on Facebook were posted by 29 political candidates. It translates into an average of 22 updates per day or 1, 3 updates per politician per day. There were 103 Twitter updates by 17 candidates amounting to 0, 4 updates per candidate per day.

Figure 2 shows, however, that the intensity rose significantly in 'the short election campaign', with a total amount of 1,660 updates for both media, increasing to an average of 59 per day, or nearly two updates per politician per day. The activity, nevertheless, dropped like a rock in 'the post-election phase' with a total amount of 295 postings, less than in the 'long-election campaign'-period, clearly following the campaign cycle.

In the post-election period, the postings were more equally divided between Facebook (158) and Twitter (137) than in the two campaign periods. The number of Facebook-updates decreased considerably after the Election Day, whereas the number of tweets increased to about 30 per cent, indicating that Facebook functioned as a strategic campaign tool, while Twitter came out as less campaign-sensitive.

Politicians from larger parties had more campaign-sensitive user patterns than politicians from smaller parties. Large party-candidates were most active during 'the short election campaign', while small party-candidates were more consistent users throughout the three periods and thus dominated both the phase prior to and after the 'short election campaign'. The best examples of the campaign cycle sensitive use were the public Facebook accounts that were immediately shut down after the Election Day. In our sample, this *campaign and withdraw-strategy* was a trait of candidates representing the two

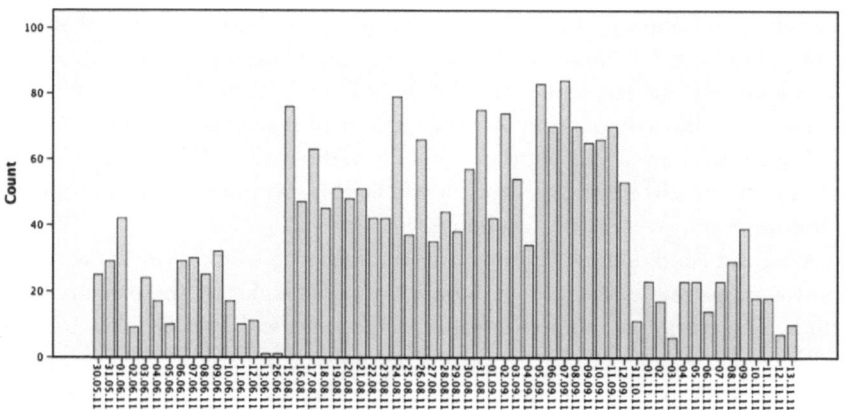

FIGURE 2 Facebook-updates in the three sampled periods. May–November 2011.

largest parties, the Labour Party and the Conservative party. They had the most resources and probably had the most professionalized campaigns (Karlsen 2010b). They were highly active during 'the short election campaign', but once the election ended, they reduced their social media activity significantly. Withdrawal seems part of the central campaign strategies to avoid post-election exhaustion or inactivity, investing less in establishing a dialogue with voters over time. This contradicts the motivations of individual candidates who emphasized continuous presence and dialogue both as ideals and valuable features of Facebook. Another explanation may be that the large parties also invite voters and members to their own sites and the candidates may have prioritized these over Facebook and Twitter in-between the campaigns (Følstad et al. 2011). This leads us to the third motivation for social media presence, dialogue with the voters. To what degree did the politicians actually engage in political discussions with the voters in social media?

Dialogue through Twitter

A precondition for dialogue is to be connected. On *Facebook*, the degree of connection was measured in numbers of fans. In our sample, the majority of politicians had between none and 2,500 fans, equally divided between the lower and the upper part of this category. Only three politicians had more than 2,500 followers in the periods of study, and these were all 'celebrity politicians' (van Zoonen 2005), meaning that they were well known among voters also outside their local constituencies.

On *Twitter*, politicians' connectedness was measured by a number of followers. Most politicians had between none and 250 followers during the 'short election campaign' in 2011. The next group had between 250 and 500 and the third between 500 and 750 followers. Three politicians had over 2,000 followers and only one had more than 5,000 followers in 2011.

The top-followed politician was the incumbent mayor in the capital, Oslo, a well-known Conservative politician. He followed between 250 and 500 Twitter users during the 2011 campaign and clearly had an asymmetric relationship with his followers on Twitter and Facebook.

A second condition for dialogue was maintenance of social media accounts. This was measured by the average number of updates during the three research periods. The average number of updates on Facebook and Twitter taken together was 25, which amounts to 0, 38 updates per politician per day. The average frequency of updates was thus quite low considering the fact that the politicians reported access to direct dialogue with voters as a main motive.

Still, it would be unfair to conclude that the politicians generally ignored the potential for interactivity in social media. There were large variations within our sample of local politicians. Based on these variations of activity, we defined four categories of social media presence that characterized the politicians:

1. *The invisible* (no official profiles). In our sample, they represented non-Socialist parties, i.e. the Progressive party (Frp) and the Christian People's party (KrF). These candidates did not run for top positions in their constituencies, neither were they equipped with resources for using social media by their party organizations.
2. *The silent* (between 0 and 10 updates). Representatives from all parties. Some of these politicians were competitors for top positions, yet they were fairly inactive on social media. One possible explanation is that their access to other platforms compensated for social media use.
3. *The moderate* (between 10 and 100 updates, mostly Facebook). This is the largest group and includes politicians from all political parties, and from all sampled municipalities.
4. *The active* (between 100 and 150 updates, mostly Twitter). Represented all parties, except KrF and Frp. Several were competing for the top positions in their constituencies, mayor and, in two cases, heads of the town councils. These were candidates from the Labour party (Ap) and the Conservative party (H). The active also includes *challengers* from minor parties, such as candidates from the Left Socialist party (SV) and the Liberal party (V) who had to campaign intensely to secure their seats.

The typology suggests the main patterns of activity among the Norwegian local politicians during the 2011 election campaign. The fact that most parties were represented in all categories indicates that the individual candidates' strategies were equally important as parties' campaign strategies. Other factors may explain activity, among them being economic resources, competitive position, size of the municipality, access to other media platforms, the structure of the local campaigns, as well as individual strategies and competence and preferences.

In terms of dialogue, the group defined as 'active' had the highest potential of maintaining a conversation with the voters. Still, even the active politicians might be mostly broadcasting messages on social media rather than engaging in dialogue with other users.

A third condition for the dialogue was found in politicians' actual use of the functions for interactivity and exchange of ideas available on social media. Previous studies have indicated that politicians tend to use social media as tools for broadcasting messages rather than for dialogue (Grant *et al.* 2010). Our findings to some extent contradict this as more than half (56 per cent) of all Tweets from the sampled politicians included features for dialogue such as *mentions*, i.e. replying to updates by using @username, or *retweets*, i.e. republishing tweets by other users.

The use of mentions (44 per cent) were more common in our sample than retweets (18 per cent), meaning that the politicians directed their dialogue at certain users whom they already knew or who had addressed them. These findings indicate that dialogue took place within established networks of politically engaged Twitter users. They might be ordinary voters but, just as likely, journalists or other politicians in opinion leader-positions. Our data are suggestive and further studies are needed here.

Likewise, retweets may suggest that politicians republish tweets from users who were well-informed about political issues. The retweets were posted with and without additional comments, either to signal agreement with statements in the original tweet, express disagreement, or take an oppositional perspective. This could mean that the politicians used Twitter to communicate with the political or cultural elite, more than with ordinary voters.

There was also a significant share of *broadcasting updates* in our sample tweets (38 per cent). These updates did not relate to other users or messages, but simply were posted as one-way messages to the politician's followers. They typically addressed all the politicians' followers, including their networks, and were formulated in order to market the politician and his/her political standpoints.

In sum, there were significant differences between how the politicians used social media. The ideals of democratic dialogue were only to a certain extent reflected in the actual social media activity. Rather, social media were tools for political communication used with different motivations and purposes.

Conclusions: marketing, mobilization, and dialogue in a party-centred system

We asked initially how and why Norwegian politicians used Facebook and Twitter as campaign communication. Drawing on theories on increased personalization of politics, we investigated whether the way politicians motivated and used social media reinforced these processes. We addressed this question by analysing the relationship between the politicians' reported motivations for using social media and their actual use of social media. Our findings are tentative, given the nature of the data material and the analyses and suggest areas where more research is needed.

A first key finding is that the politicians' report higher and more *idealistic motivations for democratic dialogue* for their social media use than they actually manage to manoeuvre in practice. The candidates who used social media in 2009 referred to marketing of their candidacies and contact with voters. These politicians had managed to add social media to their campaign repertoire without extensive support from the parties. The politicians whose profiles we analysed in 2011 divided themselves into quite different categories varying widely in activity, and with marketing as the most common use. When dialogue was sustained after the election, it was by politicians who seemed to have a personal interest in engaging in social media dialogue, not unlike their 2009 predecessors. Twitter was more used for continuous dialogue compared with Facebook. Perhaps surprising, the many retweets and mentions indicated that democratic dialogue with voters was a part of the Norwegian Twitter sphere, whereas Facebook-updates indicate more linking. Returning to personalization, we see that politicians have and are expected to have personal presence on social media. For some politicians, social media have become a new and welcome stage for discussing politics. In order to substantiate and confirm this finding, further research into the qualitative content of social media updates and structural conditions that favour communication between politicians and voters on social media should be undertaken.

For other politicians, social media represent yet another marketing tool. Our second finding is that politicians' reported motive to use social media for marketing purposes was reflected in their actual use. Still, social media *marketing was personalized* and involved private exposure and individual initiatives. Facebook was the preferred social media platform for marketing. The sharing of private and personal information may, however, be more 'fun' for voters and at the same time allow politicians to stage their own multidimensional personae on a continuous basis. The use of Facebook as a personalized marketing tool may make politics more inclusive, a conclusion echoing van Zoonen's (1998) findings that entertainment and TV-series portraying politics engage voters. The blurring of borders between the private and public spheres is a sign of the times and a process likely to last. Here, too, further research into the hybridization of public spheres and the claims that presence in these media place on politicians of all categories, is called for.

Social media marketing seemed to be mainly about *mobilizing for the election* and less about 'branding' candidates and parties in the minds of the voters. Politicians in disadvantaged competitive positions who needed the votes the most were among the most active on social media. They used social media fairly instrumentally in order to turn their followers and fans into voters and activate their networks for campaign purposes. This might imply that the politicians will strategically try to appeal to the interests of users who have many followers rather than trying to appeal to everybody, and thus become more targeted and perhaps also elitist. This tentative conclusion needs to be substantiated by further research into what kind of socio-cultural and economical segments the politicians relate to on social media. Network analysis and research interviews could provide useful empirical data.

Taken together, our findings from the study of the Norwegian politicians' social media strategies and practices on Facebook and Twitter suggest that the candidates' use of social media is of several kinds, but that the need for personal visibility and marketing of their candidacies is a major factor. Considered in the light of the party-centred system, i.e. the fact that people vote for parties more than for candidates, our findings suggest that social media had become a new tool for personal politics, but not a fully established part of campaign communication.

As such, we need to support our tentative findings with additional studies of how politicians manoeuvre in the intersection between the party organizations' campaign strategies and their own personal agenda for using social media, as both the invisible and active among Norwegian politicians has chosen an individual approach to the semi-private public sphere. Our findings cannot answer the questions of whether differences between candidate-centred and party-centred systems are levelled out, but they indicate that the competitive position of candidates and resources explain differences in the way social media were used. Challengers were often the active, in Norway as in the United States. I Norway, the resourceful withdrew from social media once the campaign was over. Comparative data on user patterns suggest whether such patterns pertain across more national settings.

Notes

1   In 2011, the 22 July terrorist attacks on the Norwegian Government and the massacre at the Labour Party's youth camp on Utøya lowered the intensity in the short campaign. The events may have influenced the social media presence.

2   The first period was 30 May–12 June; the second 15 August–12 September; and the third 31 October–14 November 2011.

3   *Source*: TNSGallup Norway, GallupInterbuss, 3. Quarter 2011.

References

Aardal, B. (2011) *Det politiske landskap. En studie av stortingsvalget 2009*, Cappelen-Damm, Oslo.

Aardal, B., Krogstad, A. & Narud, H. M. (2004) *I valgkampens hete: strategisk kommunikasjon og politisk usikkerhet*, Universitetsforl, Oslo.

Corbin, J. M. & Strauss, A. L. (2008) *Basics of Qualitative Research: Techniques and Procedures for Developing Grounded Theory*, Sage, Thousand Oaks, CA.

Enjolras, B., Steen-Johnsen, K. & Wollebæk, D. (2012) Social media and mobilization to offline demonstrations: transcending participatory divides? *New Media & Society*. Published online 26 November 2012, pp 1–19.

Enjolras, B., Karlsen, R., Steen-Johnsen, K. & Wollebæk, D. (2013) *Liker – liker ikke: sosiale medier, samfunnsengasjement og offentlighet*, Cappelen Damm akademisk, Oslo.

Enli, G. S. & Thumin, N. (2012) 'Socializing and self-representation online: exploring Facebook', *Observatorio (OBS*) Journal*, vol. 6, pp. 87–105.

Følstad, A., Lüders, M. & Johannessen, R. M. (2011) *Engasjement på Mitt Arbeiderparti*, SINTEF, Trondheim, Norway.

Grant, W. J., Moon, B. & Grant, J. B. (2010) 'Digital dialogue? Australian politicians' use of the social network tool Twitter', *Australian Journal of Political Science*, vol. 45, pp. 579–604.

Gulati, G. & Williams, C. (2010) 'Congressional candidates' use of YouTube in 2008: its frequency and rationale', *Journal of Information Technology & Politics*, vol. 7, pp. 93–109.

Habermas, J. (1989) *The Structural Transformation of the Public Sphere: An Inquiry into a Category of Bourgeois Society*, Polity, Cambridge.

Habermas, J. (1992) *Faktizität und Geltung: Beiträge zur Diskurstheorie des Rechts und des demokratischen Rechtsstaats*, Suhrkamp, Frankfurt am Main.

Heidar, K. & Saglie, J. (2003) 'Predestined parties?: organizational change in Norwegian political parties', *Party Politics*, vol. 9, pp. 219–239.

Hjarvard, S. (2008) 'The mediatization of society. A theory of the media as agents of social and cultural change', *Nordicom Review*, vol. 30, pp. 105–134.

Johansen, G. S. (2011) *Valg 2009: den siste TV-valgkampen?: en studie av norske politikeres bruk av sosiale medier*, G.S. Johansen, Oslo.

Karlsen, R. (2010a) 'Candidates and social media in party centred campaigns. Empirical evidence from the 2009 Norwegian campaign', paper presented at the workshop 'Elections, Campaigning and Citizens Online' Oxford Internet Institute, 15–16 September.

Karlsen, R. (2010b) 'Fear of the political consultant', *Party Politics*, vol. 16, pp. 193–214.

Karlsen, R. (2011a) 'A platform for individualized campaigning? Social media and parliamentary candidates in the 2009 Norwegian election campaign', *Policy and the Internet*, vol. 3, pp. 1–25.

Karlsen, R. (2011b) 'Still broadcasting the campaign: on the internet and the fragmentation of political communication with evidence from Norwegian electoral politics', *Journal of Information Technology & Politics*, vol. 8, pp. 146–162.

Karlsen, R. & Skogerbø, E. (forthcoming) "Candidate campaigning in parliamentary systems individualized vs. localized campaigning", *Party Politics*, Accepted for publication.

Larsson, A. O. & Moe, H. (2012) 'Studying political microblogging: Twitter users in the 2010 Swedish election campaign', *New Media & Society*, vol. 14, pp. 729–747.

Lilleker, D.G. N. A. J. (2010) 'Towards a more participatory style of election campaigning: the impact of Web 2.0 on the UK 2010 general election', *Policy and Internet*, vol. 2, pp. 67–96.

Mjøs, O., Enli, G., Moe, H. & Syvertsen, T. (forthcoming) *The Nordic Welfare State Media*, Michigan University Press.

Narud, H. M. & Valen, H. (2007) *Demokrati og ansvar: politisk representasjon i et flerpartisystem*, Damm, Oslo.

Nielsen, R. K. (2011) 'Mundane internet tools, mobilizing practices, and the coproduction of citizenship in political campaigns', *New Media & Society*, vol. 13, pp. 755–771.

Postman, N. (1985) *Amusing Ourselves to Death: Public Discourse in the Age of Show Business*, Heinemann, London.

Sennett, R. (1976) *The Fall of Public Man*, Cambridge University Press, Cambridge.

Shirky, C. (2008) *Here Comes Everybody: The Power of Organizing Without Organizations*, Penguin, New York.

Skogerbø, E. (2011) 'Everybody reads the newspaper': local newspapers in the digital age', in *Local and Regional Media – Democracy and Civil Society Shaping Processes*, eds I. Biernacka-Ligięza & L. Koćwin, Wydawnictwo MARIA, Nowa Ruda – Wrocław, pp. 357–373.

Strömbäck, J. (2008) 'Four phases of mediatization: an analysis of the mediatization of politics', *International Journal of Press-Politics*, vol. 13, pp. 228–246.

Strömbäck, J. & Aalberg, T. (2008) 'Election news coverage in democratic corporatist countries: a comparative study of Sweden and Norway', *Scandinavian Political Studies*, vol. 31, pp. 91–106.

Strömbäck, J. & Dimitrova, D. V. (2006) 'Political and media systems matter. A comparison of election news coverage in Sweden and the United States', *The Harvard International Journal of Press/Politics*, vol. 11, pp. 131–147.

Sunstein, C. R. (2007) *Republic.com 2.0*, Princeton University Press, Princeton, NJ.

Thompson, J. B. (1995) *The Media and Modernity. A Social Theory of the Media*, Polity Press, Cambridge.

van Zoonen, L. (1998) 'A day at the zoo: political communication, pigs and popular culture', *Media Culture & Society*, vol. 20, pp. 183–200.

van Zoonen, L. (2005) *Entertaining the Citizen: When Politics and Popular Culture Converge*, Rowman & Littlefield, Lanham, MD.

van Zoonen, L. & Holtz-Bacha, C. (2000) 'Personalisation in Dutch and German politics: the case of talk show', *Javnost – The Public*, vol. 7, pp. 45–56.

van Zoonen, L., Muller, F., Alinejad, D., Dekker, M., Duits, L., Vis, P. V. & Wittenberg, W. (2007) 'Dr. Phil meets the candidates: how family life and personal experience produce political discussions', *Critical Studies in Media Communication*, vol. 24, pp. 322–338.

Hallvard Moe & Anders Olof Larsson

UNTANGLING A COMPLEX MEDIA SYSTEM
A comparative study of Twitter-linking practices during three Scandinavian election campaigns

This article provides empirical insights into how one online service — Twitter — was used for political purposes during three separate election campaigns in Sweden, Denmark and Norway, specifically how Twitter users, with hyperlinks, connect with other channels for political communication. Methodologically, the study employs three large sets of data on Twitter use tagged as relevant for each of the election campaigns, covering a one-month period. The approach allows for an untangling of the complex interconnections between novel online services, mainstream media, official political party websites, public information, individual blogs and social network sites. By moving beyond a study merely of the type of websites linked to, to also include classification of the actors publishing the content linked to, the article provides insights into the actual use by politicians, interest groups as well as grassroots activists of diverse Web genres.

Introduction

Contemporary media and communication systems are complex. For information dissemination as well as for public debate, old and new modes of communication intersect on different technological platforms. Untangling this complexity, improving our understanding of the parts and their connections, is of key importance if we want to understand the ecology of new media. With this in mind, there is a need to study the Internet as an integral part of everyday life (e.g. Rogers 2009). As offline media actors offer Web services, as politicians host a range of online presences, and as other societal actors are similarly present online, simply mapping Web genres will not suffice. Merely establishing that linking between different services occurs provides limited insights unless we also analyze the providers of the content being linked to. Actors ranging from citizens to political parties use blogs as well as services like Facebook and YouTube. Therefore, how specific services relate to each other must be addressed on two levels: first, the technological level to assess how different services are connected to each other, and, second, the actor level to asses who uses these services.

This study focuses on the connections users of one online service – Twitter – make to other parts of the Web when communicating about politics. Preceded only by Facebook, Twitter is often pointed to as 'the world's second most important social media platform' (Bruns 2011, p. 2). For political communication, Twitter is heralded as a new channel for discussions among citizens and politicians (e.g. Bruns & Burgess 2011; Vergeer *et al.* 2011). Similarly, established actors such as public authorities have started to make use of the service (e.g. Crump 2011; Gilmore 2011; Klang & Nolin 2011). Twitter use is deeply entangled with other services and media forms, not least breaking news and televised events (e.g. Larsson & Moe 2012). Such use and connections merit untangling, in this paper expressed as follows: How does Twitter as an arena for political communication relate to the overall online media and communication environment?

To answer this question, we analyze and compare linking practices during election campaigns based on Twitter messages from the three Scandinavian countries: Sweden (2010, $N = 99,311$), Denmark (2011, $N = 28,739$) and Norway (2011, $N = 32,217$). We study links from all messages tagged by users as concerning the elections, mapping the genres or kinds of sites linked to ('Web 1.0' sites, news sites, sharing sites and 'Web 2.0' sites) and scrutinizing the actors providing the content on these sites (politicians, citizens, commercial actors, NGOs, etc.).

In the remainder of this article, we first relate the present study to existing research, reviewing research of politicians' Twitter use in relation to studies, like the one presented here, which includes political communication on Twitter by general users. The next part elaborates on our cases and the comparative set up. Then we introduce our rationale for data collection and analysis. Following this, we present and discuss the obtained results. While the targets of links emanating from political practices on Twitter were rather similar between the three Scandinavian countries, we could also discern differences, which we explain with references to the wider media systems as well as political and cultural features of the cases. The final section points to limitations as well as opportunities for further analysis, and offers overarching conclusions. Our findings provide nuance to often-repeated claims of the Internet's revolutionizing potential as we show how established offline actors are the same that attract attention on new media platforms. This has consequences for our understanding of today's complex media systems.

Political Twitter use and complex media systems

Twitter can be conceptualized as a microblog, allowing users to send messages containing up to 140 characters. With this basic limitation in mind, three common Twitter communication practices can be discerned as relevant for our present purposes. First, undirected messages are those sent to an undisclosed network of followers. Second, by utilizing the @ character immediately preceding a Twitter user handle, users can send so-called @ messages directed to specific users. Finally, the practice of retweeting involves the redistribution of a tweet sent by another user. Moreover, the contents of the tweets themselves carry specific functions. For example, hashtags are commonly used to signify keywords, or thematic connotations of messages sent.

Research on Twitter practices in a number of different contexts is on the rise – especially in political communication. As much focus has been given to contexts characterized by political turmoil (e.g. Gaffney 2010), there is also a need to study Twitter use in more stable political environments (e.g. Wojcieszak 2012). Much of the work performed studies politicians. In the United States, Golbeck *et al.* (2010) analyzed the use of Twitter by congress members. Findings indicated that while a small portion of congressional politicians made use of Twitter for communicating with constituencies, most tended to employ the service as a 'vecicle for self-promotion' (Golbeck *et al.* 2010, p. 1612), providing links to their blogs and to news articles about themselves.

The focus on politicians is also found outside the United States. Sæbø (2011) content analyzed tweets sent by members of Norwegian parliament, finding results akin to the aforementioned study by Golbeck: politicians used Twitter primarily for information dissemination and for discussion amongst themselves. Vergeer *et al.* (2011) focused on Twitter use by Dutch candidates up for election to the European Parliament, concluding that candidates from opposition parties used Twitter more frequently. Similar results, indicating mostly limited use of social media by politicians, have been reported from other European countries, including Italy (Mascheroni & Mattoni 2012) and Sweden (Larsson 2011; Larsson & Moe 2012) – while slightly different use patterns also can be discerned (e.g. Ausserhofer & Maireder 2013).

Beyond politicians, Bruns and Burgess (2011) studied Twitter use during the 2010 Australian election, providing large-scale analyses of Twitter use based on the #ausvotes hashtag. A similar approach was employed by Larsson and Moe (2012), who provided a structural analysis of Twitter use during the 2010

Swedish elections. Both studies showed that while Twitter activity increased throughout the respective election periods, the vast majority of tweets were sent on Election Day. Other events sparking Twitter use were televised debates or interviews with political leaders.

While studies like these have provided insights into political Twitter use, they have largely omitted relations between Twitter and other online services. Indeed, there is a need to study 'the extent of media diversity in the content [...] shared and discussed by the Twitter community' (Bruns & Burgess 2011, p. 53). In contemporary media systems, different on- and offline channels for mediated communication are consistently interlinked. Consider news organizations as an example. Combinations of paper and Web aside, the Web itself is growing increasingly complex. Such organizations are experimenting with services like Facebook and Twitter to promote their journalistic output and, presumably, to communicate with their readership. Similar developments also describe non-media actors, from NGO's to political parties. These developments are reminiscent of what media ecologists, following Innis and McLuhan, would call *the intermedia dimension* of media ecology' (Scolari 2012, p. 209, italics in original) – that is, the ways in which different media relate to and change each other. Analyzing this dimension of media ecology should strengthen our understanding of the Internet as a ubiquitous part of everyday life. Moreover, the study should yield insights into power relations, specifically the ways in which new actors are gaining entry into the main areas for public debate.

To look into these relations in the present case of political Twitter use, focus is placed on hyperlinks. Links constitute a direct and visible way to share information and connect to other sources online (Larsson 2012). As such, they allow for ease of use when users 'click on a word, phrase [...] in order to jump to another piece of information or website' (Dimitrova et al. 2003, p. 404). Therefore, links provide a suitable entry point for scrutiny of relations between online arenas for political communication (e.g. Himelboim et al. 2009). By studying Twitter-linking patterns during election campaigns, the present study provides an assessment of the role of Twitter in contemporary complex media systems.

Comparative design and case descriptions

The analytical setup follows a 'most similar cases' - strategy, geared toward studying a manageable number of comparable cases – cases that share some basic characteristics, but vary concerning dimensions we want to study (e.g. Lijphart 1975). The basic idea is that comparison provides context for understanding the individual cases, facilitating more nuanced understanding of the novel phenomena at hand. The design, then, is case-oriented, aimed at interpreting shared social processes, focusing on complexity and uniqueness rather than on generalizations (e.g. Ragin 1987).

The case countries are Sweden (9.4 million inhabitants), Denmark (5.6 million), and Norway (4.9 million). All represent what is often labeled the Nordic welfare state (e.g. Hilson 2008), and share a multi-party parliamentary system with universal voting privileges. In Sweden, parliamentary, regional and local elections are held on the third Sunday of September every four years, the one studied here taking place on 19 September 2010. In Denmark, local and regional elections are held every four years on a fixed date, while Parliamentary elections are called at least every four years, the one studied here on 15 September 2011. In Norway, parliamentary as well as local and regional elections are held on fixed, but separate, dates. The election analyzed here was the combined local and regional one on 12 September 2011. A Right–Center coalition has ruled Sweden since 2006, surviving the 2010 election, although as a minority government. The 2011 election in Denmark led to a change in government from a Right to a Left coalition. In Norway, a Left–Centre coalition has been in office since 2005. The 2011 election saw the Conservative party and Labour as overall winners, in addition to, on a smaller scale, the Green Party.

Sweden, Denmark and Norway have similar media policy regulations, including publicly funded broadcasters and press subsidies, based on the arm's-length principle (e.g. Moe & Mjøs, forthcoming). The cases also rank high on penetration of information technologies. As for Internet penetration, around 90 percent of citizens in all countries enjoy Internet access at home (Nordicom 2009).

As for Twitter use, a 2010 Swedish survey (Facht & Hellingwerf 2011) indicated that about one percent of online Swedes made use of Twitter every day. In Denmark, statistics from the same year showed that three percent of the online population were Twitter users (Statistics Denmark 2011), while nearly four percent of online Norwegians made use of Twitter on a weekly basis (NRK/Ipsos 2011). As such, while Twitter has enjoyed attention in the mass media as well as among researchers, it cannot be considered a frequently used service in any of the cases – despite the number of advanced Internet users. The lack of reliable statistics on the use of novel Internet services is a general challenge. When conducting comparisons, it is important to keep this in mind, and aim to use the findings to further hypothesize about differences among user groups.

Moreover, as two of the cases (Sweden and Denmark) concern parliamentary elections, while the third relates to local and regional elections, this should facilitate identification of interesting differences. Of course, such differences also entail that straightforward comparative efforts become difficult – while the events studied are indeed similar thematically, they differ in scope. By studying the use of emerging technology during different types of elections in similar countries, we make a contribution to the understanding of the use of these rapidly changing services.

Data and methodology

Data collection was performed by using the yourTwapperKeeper service (Twap-perKeeper 2010). yourTwapperKeeper utilizes various Twitter APIs, producing archives containing data and metadata regarding collected tweets. The archives are summarized in Table 1 and further outlined below.

Hashtags can be useful for delimiting Twitter searches and archiving (e.g. Bruns 2011; Larsson & Moe 2012).[1] As such, suitable hashtags, determined by close observation of the unfolding pre-campaign communication on Twitter, were chosen for each of the cases. Two hashtags covered both the Danish and the Norwegian cases: 'valg' means election in both languages, and #valg2011 and #valg11 served as hashtags in both cases. These two archives were filtered and manually checked to separate tweets relevant for each country. Moreover, all five archives were controlled for irrelevant content (e.g. where the hashtags referred to unrelated topics).[2] Concentrating on the final parts of the campaigns, the data covers a month (31 days) before Election Day and three days after in all cases.[3]

To bring out information on links, we utilized an array of different scripts for data-processing tool Gawk on each data set (see Bruns 2011). The data were then analyzed using descriptive statistics.

In addition, the two authors coded all links in the data sets according to two broader sets of categories. First, focus was placed on the level of genre or form of website, defined here as the type of Web services and sites users linked to. The coding scheme was derived iteratively, ultimately covering 11 categories of Web services (e.g. traditional media site, social network site). Second, links were assessed in a similar way at the level of actors, that is, who had published the linked-to content. Here, 17 categories of actors (e.g. commerce, citizens, inter-est groups or politicians) were included in the final coding scheme.

The lead author coded the Norwegian and Danish cases, while the second author coded the Swedish case. Intercoder reliability was assessed as each of the two authors recoded a random 20 percent sample of each other's coding,

TABLE 1 Summary of included archives used in the data collection.

Case country	Hashtag archives	No. of Tweets
Sweden	#val2010 (election2010)	99,311
Denmark	#fv11 (parliamentary election2011), #valg2011 (election2011), and #valg11 (election11)	28,739
Norway	#valg2011 (election2011), #valg11 (election11), and #kommunevalg (municipality election)	32,217

using Krippendorf's alpha (Hayes & Krippendorff 2007) to gage reliability. Alpha scores for each of the cases were reported above the often-suggested level of .70, indicating satisfactory levels of reliability (e.g. Lombard *et al.* 2002).

Findings and discussion

While far from all tweets include a URL, some include several. Links were found in 27 percent of tweets in the Swedish case, 35 percent in the Danish and 20 percent in the Norwegian case. The Danish data set, however, includes instances of spamming (see below): discounting these 2,500 spam tweets, the Danish case positions itself on level with the Swedish, with links in 27 percent of the tweets. The interesting question, then, is what the users linked to, both in terms of Web genres or types of services, and in terms of actors.

To facilitate presentation, we divide the analyzed links into four tentative groups based on genre or type of site: *'Web 1.0' sites, News sites, Sharing sites* and *'Web 2.0' sites.* The graphs presented below depict the overarching results for each category of genres, while we provide more detail in the text.[4] The graphs all compare categories to the total number of links derived from each case country.

'Web 1.0' sites

While recent years have seen a shift to a supposed 'Web 2.0' paradigm where users play important parts as content providers, traces of a precursory 'Web 1.0' are still present in the online realm. Such '1.0' sites, conceptualizing users as consumers (e.g. Cormode & Krishnamurthy 2008), can however also include functionalities for user activation. This first category deals with these types of staples of the Web. For the purposes of this study, 'Web 1.0' covers two categories in the coding scheme: traditional static sites such as portals and informational sites (signaling a lack of focus on user participation) and discussion forums. The results are presented in Figure 1.

Figure 1 shows the number of links to these two Web genres as a percentage of the total number of links in each case. At the outset, the first subcategory (traditional websites) sees Denmark stand out (with eight percent) compared to the other two, which has twice as many links (Sweden, 17 percent) or more (Norway, 21 percent). On a dynamic, even ephemeral, Web, traditional websites can constitute something stable and well known. Thus, findings indicate that the Twitter election activity in Sweden and Norway linked to 'stable', traditional sources to a larger extent than in Denmark. Looking closer at the kind of actors covered by the traditional website subcategory, results indicate that about 45 percent of links to such traditional websites connect to political parties in the Swedish and Norwegian cases, whereas about 30 percent of the

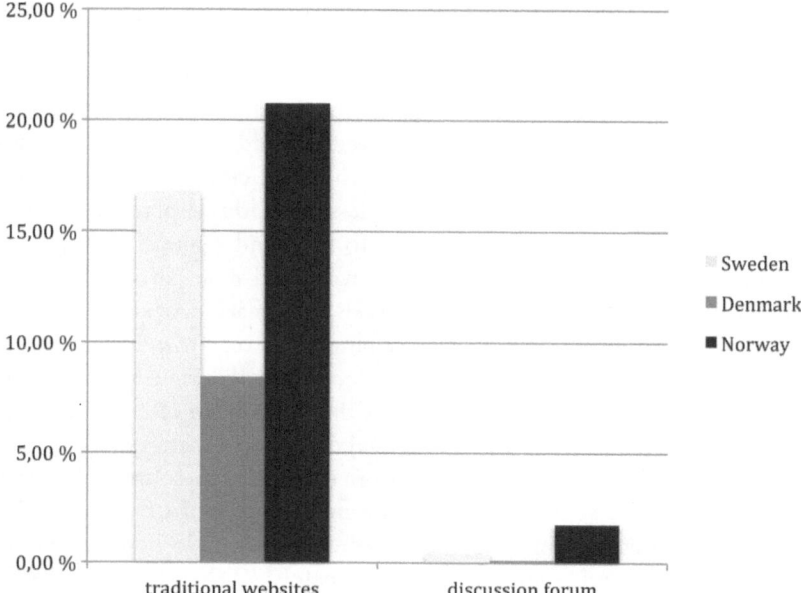

FIGURE 1   Links to 'Web 1.0' sites in the three cases, percentages of total number of links (Sweden $N = 26{,}876$, Denmark $N = 10{,}066$, Norway $N = 6{,}679$).

links derived from the Danish case has similar targets. For Denmark, a prevalence of political-satirical content was found. Moreover, the category of traditional websites tends to be the grouping in the data set where links to the sites of NGOs and interest groups are most frequently found – perhaps indicating that such actors have yet to adopt a succinct social media strategy.

For discussion forums, their limited presence indicates that perhaps the influx of blogs and social networking sites has overtaken their roles. The relative multitude of these links in Norway – the only case where this statistic surpasses one percent – can perhaps be explained by a considerable number of links to origo.no, a site that serves as collective discussion forums for several local newspapers.

News sites

The websites of media organizations have today 'grown in importance in the media systems of most countries' (Mitchelstein & Boczkowski 2009, p. 562). Additionally, various alternative news outlets have utilized the potential of the Internet (e.g. Platon & Deuze 2003). News publishers have also taken to the Internet without a coexisting offline version. These three types of actors – established offline media, explicitly alternative ones (and more institutionalized than, e.g. a group blog) and purely online-based – represent analytical categories of different news sites. On an actor level, we can also separate between domestic (local, regional and nationwide) and international sites.

First, as visible in Figure 2, traditional media outlets are the most popular among news sites. Constituting 39 percent of all links in Denmark, 38 percent in Norway and 36 percent in Sweden, traditional media dominate across the cases. This signals a tendency to favor established news actors. While international news sites make up less than three percent across all cases, variations are bigger when it comes to local and regional as opposed to nationwide actors. In the Norwegian case, we found nine percent local sites, 15 percent regional and 71 percent nationwide. Denmark provides a stark contrast, as only two percent of links to any news site were to a local actor, 0.9 percent regional and 92 percent nationwide. These differences are probably due to the scope of the campaigns: whereas the Norwegian election concerned local and regional politics, the Danish focused on national matters. For Norway, this could be expected to lead to a debate more dependent on sources close to the local candidates. It is also important to stress differences in the Danish and Norwegians media systems. While Norway is home to about 225 newspapers all in all, Denmark's comparable number is approximately 40 (Nordicom 2012). The Norwegian case, then, stands out especially from the Danish with a more diverse range of sources, leaning substantially on a 'long tail' of local and regional

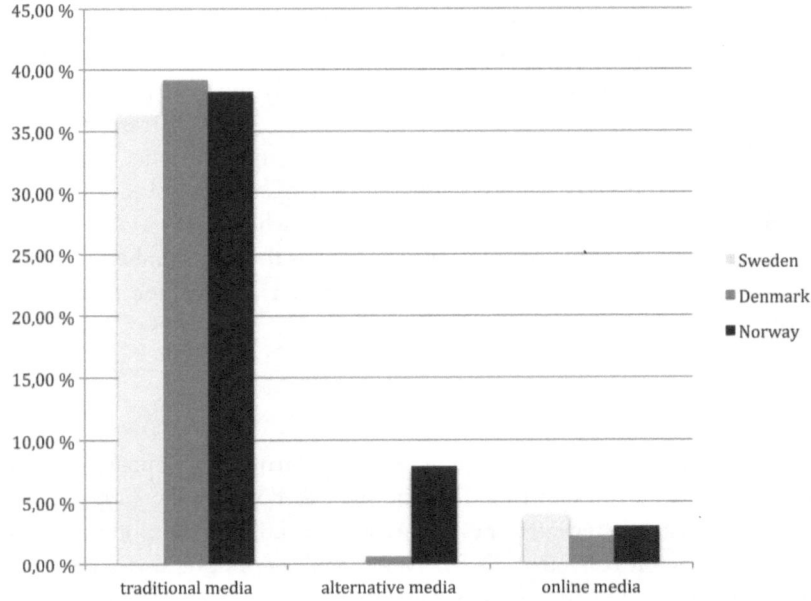

FIGURE 2 Links to different forms of media sites in the three cases, percentages of total number of links (Sweden $N = 26{,}876$, Denmark $N = 10{,}066$, Norway $N = 6{,}679$).

traditional news providers. The Swedish case positions itself in between the other two.

The Swedish market for news is larger than those in its neighboring nations, and the size difference is evident when focusing on the distribution of links among the top domains in the three data sets. The actors found here are similar across the cases (specifically, leading broadsheets, tabloids and broadcasters). But where the Norwegian and Danish cases exhibit a power-law distribution where the number of linked-to references decreases rapidly, the Swedish case exhibits a multitude of different news sites being linked to by Twitter users. This could signal a more diverse use of sources when people discuss politics in Sweden. This result is somewhat balanced if we introduce a simple measure of pluralism among traditional media sources based on the total number of domains divided by the number of links in the category. Here, the Norwegian case, much due to its sprinkling of local and regional sites, scores the highest (0.049), Sweden 0.026 and Denmark 0.018.

The second category shown in Figure 2, Alternative media, covers sites expressing a clear activist or political objective – indymedia.org could serve as an international example. Alternative media are interesting since they represent different perspectives, often discussed as an example of the supposed democratic potential of the Web. As Figure 2 shows, our findings in this category seem meager. In the Danish and Swedish cases, alternative media sources account for 0.6 and 0.2 percent, respectively. Links in the Norwegian context stand out with eight percent, but one site accounts for the vast majority: www.morsmal. no (morsmål is Norwegian for 'native language'). The site, a non-commercial initiative that collects and translates news into minority languages, featured a special election campaign section. On the one hand, its dominance in the data set can be seen as an example of how a truly new kind of news provider is able to spread its content with the aid of services like Twitter. On the other hand, since the links almost exclusively were sent by a user identifying himself as the initiator of the site, we should not overestimate any effect of the site's presence. Further analysis of this user's activity has revealed limited use of @ messages and retweets, both signaling little impact within the Norwegian debate (Moe & Larsson 2012). Moreover, the fact that one user can make such an impression seems to strengthen the observation based on the prevalence of discussion forums in the Norwegian case, pointing to the relatively small volume of tweets in the data set. It serves as a reminder that Twitter remains a minor platform for public communication in this instance.

The third category, Online news, covers news actors native to the Internet. Overall, the volume of links to such sites is low, below four percent in each case. Much like the previous subcategory, online media could provide novel perspectives, forms or services. For example, in the Danish case, sites covered by this subcategory include altinget.dk (focused on politics) and atlasmag.dk (discussing broader aspects of current affairs). The overall low impact of such sites in the data sets, however, could be a symptom of the general markets for Web news in Scandinavia: the growth of online news in general has been marked by established, print newspaper publishers, at the expense of new market entrants (e.g. Falkenberg 2010). The data presented here seem to confirm this tendency.

Sharing sites

Sites that allow users to share different types of content, such as videos, photos and music with each other, are a key part of recent online developments. For our purposes, we separate between services primarily geared at video sharing (e.g. YouTube), sites concentrating on photo sharing (Instagram, Flickr) and music-sharing sites (which here include general file-sharing sites like Piratebay). Figure 3 shows the distribution of links to sharing sites found in our data.

First, for the subcategory of video sharing, such links appear more than twice as often in Sweden than elsewhere. Upon examining the Swedish context closer, we see that political actors (i.e. persons affiliated with some political party) dominate the category (with 42 percent). This means videos linked to by Twitter users during the Swedish campaign were dominantly published by political actors. The finding suggests a professional campaigning approach to the

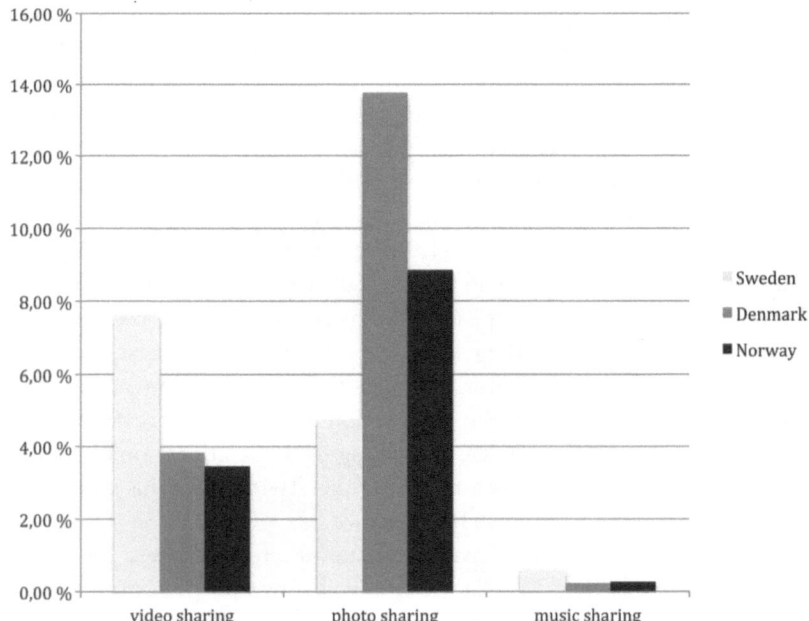

FIGURE 3 Links to sharing sites divided into three categories in the three cases, percentages of total number of links (Sweden *N* = 26,876, Denmark *N* = 10,066, Norway *N* = 6,679).

use of online video in Sweden. A similar trend is found in Norway, with 55 percent of the links to video-sharing sites pointing to content published by political actors. For Denmark, about 25 percent of video-sharing links points to political actors – arguably a large share, but still considerably smaller than in the other cases. By contrast, as much as 65 percent of the video content linked to in the Danish case was posted by individual citizens. These two categories – politicians and individual citizens – dominate the provision of videos across the cases.

Much like with previous categories, interest groups and NGOs did not to any substantial extent get their videos tweeted, nor did grassroots actors: only in the Swedish data did this group surpass one percent of the links to video-sharing sites. Moreover, the comparably larger degrees of linked-to videos found in the Swedish case could perhaps be explained by the fact that the 2010 election was the first that allowed for political advertisements on broadcast as well as Web television.

In contrast to the previous category, the Danish case emerges with comparably more links to photo-sharing sites than its Scandinavian counterparts – 14 percent, compared to 9 percent in Norway and 5 percent in Sweden. As for the photos linked to, we can discern similar tendencies to those described above: the Swedish and Norwegian cases are dominated by photos posted by political actors, while the Danish case mostly exhibits individual citizen posters. A substantial number of these individuals' photos were photos of 'adbusted', or in other ways tampered with, election campaign posters. In Denmark more so than in the other countries, cardboard posters typically portraying single candidates are in widespread use in the streets. On Twitter, individual users spread satirical and creatively altered versions of such posters. No similar practice was found in Sweden or Norway.

We should be careful not to overstate a pattern here: To a certain extent, the use of photo as well as video-sharing sites by politicians and political parties seem unsystematic, even incidental. In Denmark, Radikale Venstre, a minor Center–Left party, is the only one that comes through with a consistent use of such sites in our data set. The presence of politicians from other parties appears to be based on individual initiatives more than a common strategy. The other cases give a similar impression – for example, only the Socialist Left and a local branch of the Conservative party having specific profiles on photo-sharing sites present in our data sets during the Norwegian campaign.

The low volume of links to photo-sharing sites in the Swedish case, it should be noted, could perhaps be explained by the temporal factor: The year that passed between the elections saw the rise of trending picture-sharing services. As an example, Instagram, one of these services popular in 2011, only launched in October 2010, that is, after the Swedish election. This points to the dynamic nature of the phenomena at hand.

Third, and finally, while the online sharing of music as computer files has gained much attention in societal debate, music sharing appears here as the smallest in the category of sharing sites. This is not surprising, since the use of music in political campaigning is more seldom than photos and videos. Swedish users link marginally more (0.6 percent) than the Norwegian and Danish. Most of the Swedish links point to The Pirate Bay, a file-sharing site that gained much attention during the Swedish campaign.

In sum, political actors in Norway and Sweden were comparatively more successful in getting their videos distributed on Twitter than in Denmark. In the latter case, video, as well as photo sharing was first and foremost a channel for individuals to share content. As such, Danish politicians appear to be having a more difficult time than their Swedish and Norwegian colleagues in getting their message across in the Twittersphere.

Web 2.0 sites

The potential of user-generated content as part of the online experience has been highlighted in various contexts. Recent developments, giving rise to a supposed 'Web 2.0' (e.g. O'Reilly 2005), has further heightened this perceived importance. Figure 4 shows the distribution of links to various sites often pointed to as offering such content in the cases under consideration here. Specifically, three different types of sites were identified: blogs, social network sites (boyd & Ellison 2007) and microblogs (e.g. Jansen *et al.* 2009).

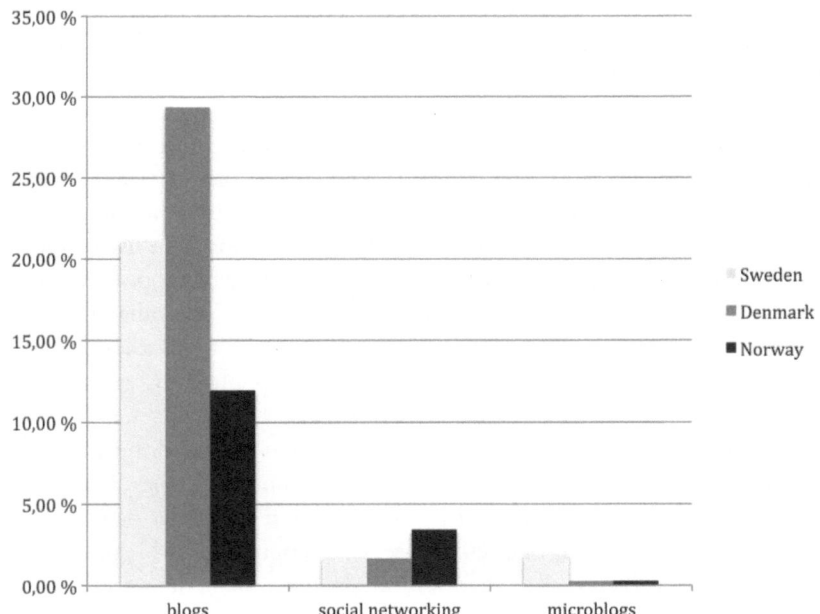

FIGURE 4 Links to different forms of 'Web 2.0' sites in the three cases, percentages of total number of links (Sweden *N* = 26,876, Denmark *N* = 10,066, Norway *N* = 6,679).

First, blogs emerge as the largest category for all three countries. However, as spamming marred the Danish case, this left traces in the results presented in Figure 4. The blogs linked to in Norway were mostly written by individuals (73 percent), while links to Swedish blogs mostly (53 percent) led to political professionals. This finding could be related to the often-discussed innovation hypothesis of online political communication, stating that politicians would adopt novel online practices of communication, such as blogging (e.g. Larsson & Hrastinski 2011). This could be interpreted as a result of online campaign strategies put to work during the Swedish election – strategies that were apparently not in place during the other two campaigns. For those two cases, we can discern a number of blogs whose main focus is political satire. The presence of such satirical content can perhaps be tied in with the popularity of televised political satire in the US context (e.g. Xenos & Becker 2009). Finally, the findings in the blog category need to be interpreted in light of the national blogospheres. Studies have shown the Norwegian blogosphere to be scarcely populated, and not densely networked (Moe 2011).

Second, for social network sites, the overall number of links seems quite low. One might expect communication on a platform like Twitter to be extensively interwoven with platforms like Facebook. However, with the volume of links to social network sites peaking in Norway (3.4 percent), the reliance on established genres like traditional 'Web 1.0' sites and traditional news providers is substantially more widespread across the cases studied here. Of the links to social networking sites, most were directed at political actors on Facebook, Foursquare, etc. Individual variations between the cases were also discerned: specifically, the presence of political actors accounted for approximately double the number in Sweden (39 percent of links) and Norway (44 percent of links) when compared to Denmark (21 percent of links). For Sweden, this result could stem from the prevalence of links to political blogs. For Norway, this result reminds us of the overall low volume of links: the prolific Facebook activity of a local group of the Conservative party in a wealthy part of a major city was the aim for the majority of these links. As discussed earlier regarding morsmal.org, this shows how a niche group can use social media to receive plenty of attention – at least within the realm of a localized hashtag.

Third, the links to microblogging sites in our data sets are chiefly links to Twitter itself. In most of the cases, such links point to a photo published via Twitter's Twitpic service. Otherwise, links to Twitter point to earlier tweets, typically by celebrities or leading politicians. So what on the surface could look like connections between Twitter and other similar Web services are by and large links with a purely technical rationale, revealing little about social connections.

Conclusion

While the results presented here provide insights into linking practices during three political elections in three similar countries, the activity studied cannot be said to represent a mass phenomenon. Twitter is used by a small minority of mostly savvy Scandinavian Internet users. What we are studying are essentially 'power users' (Orlikowski 2000, p. 406) or 'early adopters' (Rogers 2003). Therefore, the possibility for generalization based on the results is limited. However, by studying the communicative traces left by such advanced users, we can discern use patterns that might spread to the rest of the population in the future.

The practice of connecting to online actors using hyperlinks is clearly an act of recognition. As held by Rogers and Marres (2000), linking to a site suggests its importance for the one providing the link. Linking can also be assessed as a means to provide a context or frame for one's political statements or arguments (Foot & Schneider 2006, p. 105). As such, while this study cannot make extensive claims about the specific content being linked to, we can provide insights into what actors are being linked to. Such information should be useful in order to advance our understanding of the political practices on Twitter.

While the individual cases for Sweden, Norway and Denmark presented here were similar to large degrees, we have also discerned unique aspects for all three contexts. We have presented and discussed the findings related to four groups of websites ('Web 1.0', News, Sharing and 'Web 2.0'). Seen together, the findings bring out aspects across these groups and across the cases. These aspects allow us to suggest three tendencies in the connections between Twitter and the remaining Web in the case countries.

A first tendency is that established channels still matter on new platforms. Along with the 'Web 1.0'-sites particularly of political parties, media providers based offline (from national broadcasters to local newspapers) constitute the bulk of links across the cases. This impression is strengthened in our scrutiny of the actors linked to on more novel platforms, like sharing sites, blogs and social networking sites. Also here, established media and political parties constitute key content providers. This shows how a mere categorization of Web genres has limited value: by looking closer at who actually contributes the information discussed, linked to and criticized in political online communication, we get a better grasp of complex media systems.

A second tendency concerns professionalism. In Sweden and Norway, we see a consistently larger impact of official political sources in the linking practices. This is not the least clear in how political actors utilize what we have grouped together as 'Web 2.0' – services – the widespread linking to politicians' blogs as seen in Sweden and the somewhat random, but still marked, presence of political parties on social networking sites in the Norwegian data set. In contrast, the

Danish case could be described by the key terms humor and individual citizens. Satirical content, often posted by individual online users, makes this case stand out. We have pointed to some contextual factors that can help us understand these differences. The result is that political communication on Twitter links to what could be called a 'grassroots' or 'bottom-up' sphere in the Danish case, while it to a larger extent links to a 'professional' sphere in the Swedish and Norwegian cases.

The third and final tendency identified here concerns the scope of Twitter use. As the scale of use is rather limited, this creates opportunities for alternative actors or interests to gain online ground and possibly new followers. One example of this can be found in the Norwegian case, with a relatively large number of links pointing to the niche site morsmal.org. With this in mind, it is also worth noting that the lower total volume of tweets in the Danish and Norwegian cases make these two more exposed to fluctuations in Twitter trends – it takes relatively few tweets to create a peak, when compared to the Swedish case.

In sum, then, we conclude from the analyses presented here that Twitter does not exist in a vacuum, nor does it emerge from one in terms of use. Results indicate that Twitter users are mostly linking to sites hosted by a variety of established societal actors, providing counterpoint to the often-heard claims of the Internet's revolutionizing potential for unrecognized political pundits (e.g. Hindman 2009). Indeed, this speaks to Hargittai and Walejko's (2008) argument that uses of the Internet carry with them offline social connotations – our argument here being that if a social actor is established offline, they are indeed most likely to enjoy a similar amount of attention online. This is a key point for any attempt to untangle complex media systems. Be that as it may, the study presented here has also shown how niche actors managed to establish themselves by procuring a significant number of links. While the overall scale of use was admittedly limited, this result shows the potential of the Internet for political communication – a potential that, as we have seen, is perhaps not acted upon as often as one might be led to believe from popular as well as academic debates.

This analysis has contributed to the untangling of complex media systems through an analysis of links from Twitter during elections in three similar countries. Research is needed to further these untangling efforts. First, more dissimilar cases should be added to get at system-specific characteristics and to provide a better understanding of how political systems in combination with media systems matter for the connections between new arenas for political communication online and the remaining Web. Second, such analysis should also aim to interpret content. Through content analysis – qualitative or quantitative – we can try to get at the sentiments, what types of communicative context the links are disseminated within. Third, as argued, a focus on Twitter only provides us with a select group of Internet users. Consequently, we should strive to add other platforms, established as well as emerging, to compare how technological and cultural aspects impact on the connections between the parts that constitute our dynamic, complex media systems.

Notes

1   As hashtags were used to guide data collection in the present study, Twitter content not tagged accordingly was not included in our archiving processes. It should also be noted that yourTwapperKeeper only collects tweets with unique URLs, which excludes so-called automatic retweets (for further discussion of the method for data collection, see Bruns 2011; Larsson & Moe 2012).

2   Except for the #val2010 archive, collections of all archives were mirrored on two servers and then compared using a script-based tool to reveal potential discrepancies between them and to rule out technical glitches. Results showed no more than 0.25 percent deviation in any archive.

3   Periods for data collection: Sweden: 19 August to 22 September 2010, Norway 12 August to 15 September 2011 and Denmark 15 August to 18 September 2011.

4   A number of links in the data sets were not categorized for two reasons: they were either incomplete or pointed to webpages inaccessible at the time of coding (late 2011). In the Danish case, this concerned 0.37 percent of the links, in the Norwegian 0.26 percent and in the Swedish 4.5 percent. The reason for the considerably higher number in the latter case is most probably the longer time-lag from initial publication as tweets to coding, combined with the fact that some of these services (e.g. Twitter's use of default photo-sharing service as well as an in-house URL shortener) had matured and were more stable during the 2011 campaigns.

References

Ausserhofer, J. & Maireder, A. (2013) 'National politics on Twitter', *Information, Communication & Society*, pp. 1–24, [Online] Available at: http://www.tandfonline.com/doi/abs/10.1080/1369118X.2012.756050 (20 March 2013).

boyd, d. & Ellison, N. (2007) 'Social network sites: definition, history, and scholarship', *Journal of Computer-Mediated Communication*, vol. 13, no. 1, pp. 210–230.

Bruns, A. (2011) 'How long is a tweet? Mapping dynamic conversation networks on Twitter using Gawk and Gephi', *Information, Communication & Society*, vol. 15, no. 9, pp. 1323–1351.

Bruns, A. & Burgess, J. (2011) '#ausvotes – how Twitter covered the 2010 Australian federal election', *Communication, Politics & Culture*, vol. 44, no. 2, pp. 37–56.

Cormode, G. & Krishnamurthy, B. (2008) 'Key differences between Web 1.0 and Web 2.0', *First Monday*, vol. 13, no. 6, [Online] Available at: http://firstmonday.org/htbin/cgiwrap/bin/ojs/index.php/fm/rt/printerFriendly/2125/1972 (20 March 2013).

Crump, J. (2011) 'What are the police doing on Twitter? Social media, the police and the public', *Policy & Internet*, vol. 3, no. 4, pp. 1–29.

Dimitrova, D. V., Connolly-Ahern, C., Williams, A. P., Kaid, L. L. & Reid, A. (2003) 'Hyperlinking as gatekeeping: online newspaper coverage of the execution of an American terrorist', *Journalism Studies*, vol. 4, no. 3, pp. 403–414.

Facht, U. & Hellingwerf, K. (2011) *Nordicom-Sveriges Internetbarometer 2010*, Nordicom, Göteborg.

Falkenberg, V. (2010) '(R)evolution under construction: the dual history of online newspapers and newspapers online', in *Web History*, ed. N. Brügger, Peter Lang, New York, pp. 233–256.

Foot, K. A. & Schneider, S. M. (2006) *Web Campaigning*, MIT Press, Cambridge, MA.

Gaffney, D. (2010, April 26–27) '#iranElection: quantifying online activism', paper presented at the WebSci10: extending the Frontiers of Society On-Line, Raleigh, NC.

Gilmore, J. (2011) 'Ditching the pack: digital media in the 2010 Brazilian congressional campaigns', *New Media & Society*, vol. 14, no. 4, pp. 617–633.

Golbeck, J., Grimes, J. M. & Rogers, A. (2010) 'Twitter use by the US Congress', *Journal of the American Society for Information Science and Technology*, vol. 61, no. 8, pp. 1612–1621.

Hargittai, E. & Walejko, G. (2008) 'The participation divide: content creation and sharing in the digital age', *Information, Communication & Society*, vol. 11, no. 2, pp. 239–256.

Hayes, A. & Krippendorff, K. (2007) 'Answering the call for a standard reliability measure for coding data', *Communication Methods and Measures*, vol. 1, no. 1, pp. 77–89.

Hilson, M. (2008) *The Nordic Model. Scandinavia Since 1945*, Reaktion books, London.

Himelboim, I., Gleave, E. & Smith, M. (2009) 'Discussion catalysts in online political discussions: content importers and conversation starters', *Journal of Computer-Mediated Communication*, vol. 14, no. 4, pp. 771–789.

Hindman, M. (2009) *The Myth of Digital Democracy*, Princeton University Press, Princeton and Oxford.

Jansen, B. J., Zhang, M. M., Sobel, K. & Chowdury, A. (2009) 'Twitter power: Tweets as electronic word of mouth', *Journal of the American Society for Information Science and Technology*, vol. 60, no. 11, pp. 2169–2188.

Klang, M. & Nolin, J. (2011) 'Disciplining social media: an analysis of social media policies in 26 Swedish municipalities', *First Monday*, vol. 16, no. 8, [Online] Available at: http://firstmonday.org/htbin/cgiwrap/bin/ojs/index.php/fm/article/view/3490/3027 (20 March 2013).

Larsson, A. O. (2011) '"Extended infomercials" or "Politics 2.0"? A study of Swedish political party Web sites before, during and after the 2010 election', *First Monday*, vol. 16, no. 4, [Online] Available at: http://firstmonday.org/htbin/cgiwrap/bin/ojs/index.php/fm/article/view/3456/2858 (20 March 2013).

Larsson, A. O. (2012) 'Staying In or Going Out? Assessing the Linking Practices of Swedish Online Newspapers', published online before print at *Journalism Practice*, [Online] Available at: http://www.tandfonline.com/doi/abs/10.1080/17512786.2012.748514 (20 March 2013).

Larsson, A. O. & Hrastinski, S. (2011) 'Blogs and blogging: current trends and future directions', *First Monday*, vol. 16, no. 3, [Online] Available at: http://firstmonday.org/htbin/cgiwrap/bin/ojs/index.php/fm/article/view/3101/2836 (20 March 2013).

Larsson, A. O. & Moe, H. (2012) 'Studying political microblogging: Twitter users in the 2010 swedish election campaign', *New Media & Society*, vol. 14, no. 5, pp. 729–747.

Lijphart, A. (1975) 'The comparable-cases strategy in comparative research', *Comparative Political Studies*, vol. 8, no. 2, pp. 158–176.

Lombard, M., Snyder-Duch, J. & Bracken, C. C. (2002) 'Content analysis in mass communication: assessment and reporting of intercoder reliability', *Human Communication Research*, vol. 28, no. 4, pp. 587–604.

Mascheroni, G. & Mattoni, A. (2012) 'Electoral campaigning 2.0 – the case of 2010 Italian regional elections'. Published online before print at *Journal of Information Technology & Politics*, [Online] Available at: http://www.tandfonline.com/doi/abs/10.1080/19331681.2012.758073 (20 March 2013).

Mitchelstein, E. & Boczkowski, P. J. (2009) 'Between tradition and change: a review of recent research on online news production', *Journalism*, vol. 10, no. 5, pp. 562–586.

Moe, H. (2011) 'Mapping the norwegian blogosphere: methodological challenges in internationalizing Internet research', *Social Science Computer Review*, vol. 29, no. 3, pp. 313–326.

Moe, H. & Larsson, A. O. (2012) 'Twitterbruk under valgkampen 2011', *Norsk Medietidsskrift*, vol. 19, no. 2, pp. 151–162.

Moe, H. & Mjøs, O. J. (forthcoming) 'The arm's length principle in nordic public broadcasting regulation', in *Public Service Media in the Nordic Countries*, ed. U. Carlsson, Nordicom, Gøteborg.

Nordicom. (2009) *Access to Internet at home 1999–2009*, [Online] Available at: http://www.nordicom.gu.se/?portal=mt&main=showStatTranslate.php&me=1&media=PC%20and%20Internet&type=media&translation (20 March 2013).

Nordicom. (2012) *Number of newspapers 2010*, [Online] Available at: http://www.nordicom.gu.se/?portal=mt&main=showStatTranslate.php&me=1&media=Newspapers&type=media&translation=Dagspress (20 March 2013).

NRK/Ipsos MMI. (2011) *Nettbrukerundersøkelse 2011*, NRK, Oslo.

O'Reilly, T. (2005) 'What is Web 2.0? Design patterns and business models for the next generation of software', [Online] Available at: www.oreillynet.com/lpt/a/6228 (20 March 2013).

Orlikowski, W. J. (2000) 'Using technology and constituting structures: a practice lens for studying technology in organizations', *Organization Science*, vol. 11, no. 4, pp. 404–428.

Platon, S. & Deuze, M. (2003) 'Indymedia journalism: a radical way of making, selecting and sharing news?' *Journalism*, vol. 4, no. 3, pp. 336–355.

Ragin, C. C. (1987) *The Comparative Method: Moving Beyond Qualitative and Quantitative Strategies*, University of California Press, Berkeley.

Rogers, E. M. (2003) *Diffusion of Innovations*, 5th edn, Free Press, New York.

Rogers, R. (2009) *The End of the Virtual. Digital Methods*, University of Amsterdam Press, Amsterdam.

Rogers, R. & Marres, N. (2000) 'Landscaping climate change: a mapping technique for understanding science and technology debates on the World Wide Web', *Public Understanding of Science*, vol. 9, no. 2, pp. 141–163.

Sæbø, Ø. (29 August–1 September 2011) 'Understanding Twitter^{TM} use among parliament representatives: a genre analysis', paper presented at ePart 2011, Delft, The Netherlands.

Scolari, C. A. (2012) 'Media ecology: exploring the metaphor to expand the theory', *Communication Theory*, vol. 22, no. 2, pp. 204–225.

Statistics Denmark. (2011) 'Befolkningens brug af internet 2010', [Online] Available at: http://www.dst.dk/pukora/epub/upload/15239/it.pdf (12 April 2012).

TwapperKeeper. (2010) 'yourTwapperKeeper – archive your own tweets', [Online] Available at: http://your.twapperkeeper.com/ (1 March 2010).

Vergeer, M., Hermans, L. & Sams, S. (2011) 'Is the voter only a tweet away? Micro blogging during the 2009 European Parliament election campaign in the Netherlands', *First Monday*, vol. 16, no. 8, [Online] Available at: http://firstmonday.org/htbin/cgiwrap/bin/ojs/index.php/fm/article/view/3540/3026 (20 March 2013).

Wojcieszak, M. (2012) 'Transnational connections symposium: challenges and opportunities for political communication research', *International Journal of Communication*, vol. 6, pp. 255–265.

Xenos, M. A. & Becker, A. B. (2009) 'Moments of Zen: effects of *The Daily Show* on information seeking and political learning', *Political Communication*, vol. 26, no. 3, pp. 317–332.

Linh Dang-Xuan, Stefan Stieglitz, Jennifer Wladarsch & Christoph Neuberger

AN INVESTIGATION OF INFLUENTIALS AND THE ROLE OF SENTIMENT IN POLITICAL COMMUNICATION ON TWITTER DURING ELECTION PERIODS

In this paper, the authors investigate how Twitter is used for political communication during election periods with a specific focus on characteristics and communication behavior of influential accounts. Our analysis focuses on the state parliament election in Berlin (Germany) on 18 September 2011. Tweets of the top-30 most retweeted users are analyzed with respect to content-related features such as emotionality, appraisal of political parties or politicians, and topics. Furthermore, the authors test hypotheses regarding the relationship between sentiment in terms of emotionality and appraisals occurring in tweets and their quantity and speed of dissemination. Our work helps both researchers and politicians to better understand the nature of influentials in political communication and the role of sentiment in information diffusion on Twitter.

Introduction

In recent years, social media have experienced tremendous growth in user base and are said to have an impact on the public discourse and on communication. For example, there are about one billion active members per month of the Facebook network (Facebook 2013) while Twitter counts about 170 million active accounts in total (Techcrunch 2012). This mainstream adoption of social-media applications has changed the physics of information diffusion which is no longer controlled by a small number of 'gatekeepers'. Given their tremendous growth, social media are recently increasingly used in a political context. It has been observed that in a very short time, politicians in modern democracies across the world have eagerly adopted social-media platforms seeing powerful new media in them which can be used for engaging their constituents, especially during election campaigns (Hong & Nadler 2011; Thimm et al. 2012). In this regard, US politicians are said to have a leading role with the most prominent example of Barack Obama who has successfully employed social media within the election campaigns both in 2008 and 2012. Furthermore, Twitter has become a legitimate and frequently used communication channel in the political arena for citizens (Tumasjan et al. 2011). With the unique feature of 'retweeting' as a simple yet powerful mechanism for information diffusion, Twitter is an ideal platform for any user to spread political information and opinions. Nevertheless, so-called political 'influentials' or opinion-makers exist who are said to have an impact on the political opinion-making and agenda-setting processes as well as on communication behavior of other users. However, little research has been devoted to this group of influential users. Therefore, in this paper we seek to investigate how Twitter is used for political communication during election periods with specific focus on characteristics and communication behavior of influential accounts.

Given the rapid growth of social media, people are enabled to express their opinions, appraisals, attitudes, and emotions – which are generally termed as *sentiment* (Pang & Lee 2008; Liu 2011) – more than ever on almost anything in forums, weblogs, social networks, and reviews. This applies particularly to political communication which is assumed to be of polarizing controversial nature. Yet it is unclear how sentiment might impact the dynamics of information in a social-media setting. Therefore, as another contribution, we aim at examining whether sentiment of political tweets – both in terms of *emotionality* and *appraisal* – have an influence on retweet behavior as a key feature for promoting information diffusion on Twitter.

The remainder of this paper is organized as follows. The next section provides a review of literature on Twitter in the context of political communication. In the subsequent section, we discuss the concept and different measures of influence on Twitter. We then lay out the theoretical background for the development of our hypotheses regarding sentiment and information diffusion. The subsequent sections outline our methodology and the results of our study. Finally, we conclude with a discussion of our findings, research, and practical implications as well as potential future work.

Twitter and political communication

Social media have a growing importance in shaping political debates in the United States and around the world (e.g. Farrell & Drezner 2008; Wattal et al. 2010;

Tumasjan *et al.* 2011; Rainie *et al.* 2012). Recently, researchers have studied political microblogging (mostly Twitter) use, with studies focusing on either nonparliamentary or parliamentary uses of the service.

As for *parliamentary uses*, previous literature has mostly dealt with the United States by analyzing Twitter adoption and use by US Congress members (e.g. Golbeck *et al.* 2010; Lassen & Brown 2011) and US Senate candidates (e.g. Ammann 2010). Main findings indicate that while Congress members use Twitter to share information, especially referring to links to news articles about themselves and to their blog posts, Senate candidates use Twitter as a part of their political campaigns. However, the amount of use significantly varies by the level of resources a candidate possesses, state size, and the competitiveness of the congressional race. Other works on Twitter use by non-US politicians include, for example, the study by Thimm *et al.* (2012), which explores the strategic use of Twitter by German politicians in the context of election campaigns. They find that politicians use their account to announce their electoral campaign appearances, to mobilize supporters, for negative campaigning, as a tool for internal communication with party members, and for dialogs with citizens.

Other works focus on the *use of Twitter by citizens* in a political context (Rainie *et al.* 2012). Recent US-related studies, such as those by Conover *et al.* (2011) and Yardi and boyd (2010), demonstrate that the network of political retweets exhibits a highly polarized structure with extremely limited connectivity between left- and right-leaning users. However, this is not the case for the user-to-user mention network. Recently, the notion of 'Twitter revolutions' in totalitarian countries was introduced, although the exact contents and effects of these uprisings are disputed (e.g. Gaffney 2010). Other studies on Twitter-based political communication in other countries, such as those by Tumasjan *et al.* (2011) and Larsson and Moe (2012), show that Twitter serves as a channel for disseminating political contents. Furthermore, Twitter also serves as a new outlet for speakers already belonging to the elite or at least affiliated with prominent positions in mainstream media or the political debate in general.

Influence in social media

Meaning of influence

In its broadest sense, 'influence' in public communication means the ability of a media outlet or a single communicator as a node in the communication network to steer the diffusion of innovations, issues, information, and words (memes) or to achieve certain effects within the audience. These can be persuasive effects which change or reinforce the attitudes and opinions of the recipients (e.g.

according to the 'spiral of silence'), knowledge effects (such as agenda-setting or cultivation effects), or effects on behavior (such as decisions in consumption or votes in political elections) (Schenk 2007).

There are different views of influence. According to the traditional understanding, influence means the ability or qualities of someone to spread ideas to others (Rogers 1962) and change their opinions (Katz & Lazarsfeld 1955). Typical characteristics of 'influentials' are being informed, respected, and (strategically) well-connected (Schenk et al. 2009; Cha et al. 2010). There are more specific terms related to influence ranging from 'opinion leaders' (Lazarsfeld et al. 1948; Katz & Lazarsfeld 1955) over 'innovators' in the diffusion of innovations theory (Rogers 1962) to 'hubs' or 'connectors' in other works (Gladwell 2000). For example, the original concept of opinion leaders (Lazarsfeld et al. 1948) hypothesizes two different effects: the diffusion of information from mass media over opinion leaders to the population in a 'two-step flow' of communication and the influence of these opinion leaders on the opinions of the members of their reference groups. Overall, opinion leaders can be described by their social rather than personal characteristics; they influence people with similar socio-demographic characteristics in particular (Schenk et al. 2009).

However, it has been criticized that the traditional view of influence does not take into account the role of ordinary users besides the opinion leaders. A more modern view of influence focuses on different key factors behind influence which are the interpersonal relationship among ordinary users and their readiness to adopt an innovation (Domingos & Richardson 2001; Watts & Dodds 2007; Cha et al. 2010). It is argued that people make choices based on the opinions of their peers and friends rather than by a few influentials (Domingos & Richardson 2001).

Measuring influence on Twitter

The decentralized network structure of the Internet has changed the diffusion of information and effects of communication. While one-sided (from the media to the audience) and direct effects dominate in the context of mass media, indirect effects and multistep flow of communication in all directions are more common on the Internet. As a consequence, the methods of measuring influence are changing: whereas researchers used to identify opinion leaders by self-reporting and personal characteristics (e.g. strength of personality), they, especially since the rise of social media, have now much more (meta)data to empirically test different competing ideas about the notion of influence.

Several works have addressed the measurement of influence on Twitter (e.g. Cha et al. 2010; Kwak et al. 2010; Weng et al. 2010; Bakshy et al. 2011). Basically, there are three different approaches which the notion of influence is based upon: (1) followership influence, (2) retweet influence, and (3) mention influence. The first approach refers to the quantity of followers of a user indicating the size of audience of that user, which represents his/her popularity to a certain extent. Beyond the mere number of followers, recent studies have proposed other followership-based measurements based on PageRank and TwitterRank algorithms which take into account both the topical similarity between users and the followership structure (see Kwak *et al.* 2010; Weng *et al.* 2010). The second approach of measuring influence is based on retweeting which indicates the ability of that user to generate content with pass-along value. One can measure influence through the sheer number of retweets a user receives. Alternatively, other works have proposed influence in terms of the size of the entire diffusion tree associated with each event which is more directly associated with the diffusion and dissemination of information (e.g. Kwak *et al.* 2010; Bakshy *et al.* 2011). The final approach for influence emphasizes mentioning as an indicator the ability of a user to engage others in a conversation. Here, the number of mentions a user receives may serve as measure of influence.

Kwak *et al.* (2010) compared three different measures of influence – number of followers, PageRank, and number of retweets – and found that the ranking of the most influential users differed depending on the measure. Cha *et al.* (2010) also compared three different measures of influence: number of followers, number of retweets, and number of mentions. Their results showed that the most followed users did not necessarily score highest on the other measures. Finally, Weng *et al.* (2010) compared the number of followers and PageRank with a modified PageRank measure that accounted for the topic, again finding that ranking depended on the influence measure.

Sentiment and information diffusion on Twitter

As part of human communication, social-media content also often contains expression of opinions, appraisals, attitudes, and emotions toward entities, events, and their attributes. For example, a message may convey information about the author's emotional state (emotionality) or his/her judgment or evaluation of a certain person or topic (appraisal). These somewhat different concepts[1] are mostly subsumed under the generic notion 'sentiment' (see Pang & Lee 2008; Liu 2011).

Given the controversial nature of political discourse, politically relevant social-media content is expected to exhibit a high level of sentiment (i.e. opinions, appraisals, or emotions) associated with political identities and views, especially in times of elections (Conover *et al.* 2011). Recent studies showed that this particularly holds for Twitter (e.g. Bollen *et al.* 2011; O'Connor *et al.* 2010; Conover *et al.* 2011; Tumasjan *et al.* 2011).

Besides network and user characteristics, previous literature has attempted to reveal content-related factors behind the diffusion of information by retweeting practice, such as topics (e.g. Nagarajan *et al.* 2010; Romero *et al.* 2011; Bruns

& Stieglitz 2012), hashtag, and URL inclusion (e.g. Suh *et al.* 2010). However, little research has drawn attention to sentiment as another potential driver of information diffusion in a social-media setting. Some previous works may have addressed the relationship between emotions and information diffusion, but in other contexts than social media (e.g. Heath 1996; Luminet *et al.* 2000; Peters *et al.* 2009; Berger & Milkman 2012). Therefore, as a contribution, we seek to examine whether sentiment of political tweets have an influence on retweet behavior as a key feature for promoting information diffusion and thus, to a certain extent, the political opinion-making and agenda-setting processes. We thereby distinguish between *emotionality* and *appraisal* as their meaning does not exactly coincide.

For our hypotheses development, we draw on theories and empirical findings from prior research on emotions, particularly in the domain of social psychology and computer-mediated communication (CMC). In the context of written verbal communication, previous research has indicated that emotional stimuli in terms of emotion words or emotional framing of messages may elicit extensive cognitive processes such as attention (e.g. Smith & Petty 1996; Kissler *et al.* 2007; Bayer *et al.* 2012). A higher level of cognitive involvement may, in turn, lead to a higher likelihood of behavioral response to emotional stimuli in terms information sharing (e.g. Heath 1996; Luminet *et al.* 2000; Peters *et al.* 2009; Rimé 2009). Besides a higher level of cognitive involvement, certain kinds of emotions, such as anger, anxiety, awe, or amusement, might also trigger a higher level of physiological arousal which is shown to be a driver of information sharing (Berger 2011; Berger & Milkman 2012).

Previous research has indicated the effectiveness of CMC in transferring emotion-related information (Harris & Paradice 2007). The CMC of emotions has been shown to have a significant impact on how the receiver processes and interprets the message (Walther & D'Addario 2001; Riordan & Kreuz 2010). More specifically, Harris and Paradice (2007) showed that in CMC, message receivers are able to detect the sender's emotions through verbal cues, such as emotion words and linguistic markers (e.g. lexical or syntactical encoding of emotions) as well as nonverbal paralinguistic cues (e.g. emoticons). In fact, a number of recent works have revealed the impact of emotions in CMC on feedback (e.g. Huffaker 2010; Stieglitz & Dang-Xuan 2012a), participation (e.g. Joyce & Kraut 2006), sentiment diffusion (e.g. Huffaker 2010; Stieglitz & Dang-Xuan 2012a), and information sharing (e.g. Berger & Milkman 2012). Therefore, we argue that the expression of sentiment in social-media-based textual contents – both in terms of emotionality and appraisal – might also lead to more attention and arousal which in turn may positively affect information-sharing behavior. This leads us to conjecture a positive relationship between emotionality and appraisal articulated in tweets and their likelihood to spread through the Twitter network. Moreover, we reason that an increased level of attention and arousal triggered by sentiment might go along with sharing behavior with respect to not only quantity but also speed (i.e. how quickly emotional content might spread through social networks) which represents another important aspect of information diffusion (Yang & Counts 2010). Until now, very little research has been devoted to speed of information diffusion, particularly in a social-media context. Therefore, we derive the following hypotheses:

H1a: The higher the level of emotionality (positive or negative) a political Twitter message exhibits, the more often it is retweeted.
H1b: The more appraisals of politicians or political parties (positive or negative) a political Twitter message contains, the more often it is retweeted.
H2a: The higher the level of emotionality (positive or negative) a political Twitter message exhibits, the shorter is the time lag to the first retweet.
H2b: The more appraisals of politicians or political parties (positive or negative) a political Twitter message contains, the shorter is the time lag to the first retweet.

Data and methodology

Data collection

For our empirical analysis, we employed a data set of politically relevant tweets published on Twitter's public message board. The data set contains German-language tweets collected around the state parliament election in Berlin, Germany, on 18 September 2011 covering a period of four weeks beginning from 29 August to 25 September 2011. As there are usually also post-election Twitter activities, such as discussions about election results, data collection was continued seven days after the election (18–25 September 2011). We chose to collect data during times of elections since they are characterized by a higher level of user participation in the political communication and discourse on Twitter.

We developed a Java-based software tool which uses the application programming interface 'Search API' provided by Twitter to gather data (see Stieglitz & Kaufhold 2011). We collected all tweets (including retweets) that contained either one of the mostly used hashtags related to the election (#berlin, #ahw, #ltwbe, #berlinwahl, #agh, #abgeordnetenhaus, #abgeordnetenhauswahl) or one of the names of the candidates of the six biggest parties in Germany (CDU (Christian Democratic Union), SPD (Social Democratic Party), FDP (Free Democratic Party), Green Party, Left Party, and Pirate Party) including 'wowereit', 'henkel', 'künast', 'wolf', 'meyer', and 'baum' as keywords. As tweets that contain the hashtag #berlin may also refer to other irrelevant (none-lection) contexts, we only considered those tweets that, in addition, involve either one of the names of the six parties or one of the names of the candidates. In total, we obtained a sample of 17,788 tweets for our analysis.

Methodology

Measuring influence. In this study, we used the sheer number of retweets a user receives to identify and rank influentials. We chose that measure of influence for the following reasons. First, the unique feature of retweeting as a simple yet powerful mechanism for information diffusion makes it much easier for users to disseminate political information and opinions. Followership may represent a user's popularity, but is not related to other important notions of influence such as engaging audience which can be achieved by retweeting (Cha *et al.* 2010). Second, we employed the sheer number of retweets instead of normalized measure because normalizing retweet quantity by the total number of tweets would yield only local opinion leaders as the most influentials (see Cha *et al.* 2010). Based on retweet quantity, we identified the top-30 influentials for our analysis. From the rest of the sample (i.e. the top-30 identified influentials excluded), we randomly chose a subsample of other 30 users (named 'noninfluentials') for the purpose of comparison.

Text analysis. We applied different text analysis methods for detecting emotionality and appraisal as well as topics occurring in tweets of our sample. We thereby followed the triangulation approach by combining automated and manual analysis methods. On the one hand, given the massive amounts of social-media data, automated quantitative methods of text analysis are necessary. On the other hand, despite many advantages of automated approaches, manual text analysis is nevertheless needed to back up findings by automated analysis and to get a more fine-grained picture as it defines a set of practices that enable human coders to define reproducible categories for qualitative features of text more reliably (Krippendorff 2004).

For the full sample, we conducted automated sentiment analysis to detect emotionality articulated in tweets. For a subsample consisting of the top-30 influentials and the other 30 noninfluentials, we applied manual content analysis to thoroughly explore emotionality, appraisal of political parties or politicians, and political topics occurring around the election.

Automated sentiment analysis. Recent sentiment analysis algorithms are able to detect positive and negative emotion strength in short informal texts with a reasonable degree of success (Akkaya *et al.* 2009; Paltoglou & Thelwall 2010). In our analyses, we use the tool 'SentiStrength' (Thelwall *et al.* 2010, 2011) to analyze the level of emotionality in tweets. It has been proven useful to classify emotions in short informal messages from Myspace and Twitter taking additional linguistic rules for negations (e.g. 'not happy'), booster words (e.g. 'very nice'), amplification (e.g. 'haaaaaaaappy'), emoticons, spelling correction, and other factors, such as word weighting (Thelwall *et al.* 2011) into account. SentiStrength classifies texts for positive and negative emotion on a scale of 1 (neutral) to 5 (strongly positive) and -1 (neutral) to -5 (strongly negative), respectively. Each classified text is given *both* positive and negative scores.

We are interested in the level of emotionality of tweets regardless of their valence (i.e. positive or negative). Therefore, we adapted the following measure accounting for the level of emotionality in each tweet:

$$\text{emotion\_auto} = \text{positive} - \text{negative} - 2,$$

where positive denotes the SentiStrength positive-emotion score $(1-5)$ and negative the negative-emotion score $(-1$ to $-5)$. Note that we subtracted 2 (positive $-$ negative) to normalize the definition range from [2, 10] to [0, 8] to avoid confusion when $-$ in case of [2, 10] $-$ a positive number (i.e. 2) would indicate no emotion.

Manual quantitative content analysis. We manually analyzed all tweets posted by the top-30 influentials as well as noninfluential accounts for the purpose of comparison. In total, 1,495 tweets were analyzed, of which 1,420 tweets belong to top-30 accounts and 75 to the residual accounts. The average number of posted tweets per account among the top-30 influentials is 47 tweets, whereas the average for noninfluentials is only 2.5. However, the variation in posting activity among influentials is high, ranging from 1 to 604 tweets. In contrast, noninfluential users seem to be less active in general. Besides formal variables (e.g. date, name), 14 variables regarding the content were examined. Among them, the most important variables included main topic, emotionality, and appraisal of frontrunners and parties. The Holsti's coefficient of 0.961 shows a high reliability of the manual coding (Holsti 1969).

Regression analysis

Variables. From our automated and manual analysis, we constructed the following variables for each tweet:

- number of times the tweet has been retweeted: rt_no
- time lag between the tweet and the first retweet: rt_speed (in minutes)
- level of emotionality (automated analysis): emotion_auto (with a scale from 0 to 8)
- dummy variable for emotionality (manual analysis): emotion_manual
- number of appraised political parties or politicians (positive or negative): appraisal_no
- dummy variable for whether the tweet contains statement about public opinion regarding the election or about election forecasts: statement

- set of dummy variables for manually identified topics: topic_x (x denotes coding number of a topic)

Furthermore, studies have shown that there are a number of other factors that also have an impact on retweet behavior on Twitter such as the quantity of hashtags, the inclusion of URL, posting activity, as well as user's number of followers (e.g. Suh *et al.* 2010). In particular, a user's number of followers in part represents the degree of homophily (Aral *et al.* 2009) which means it is likely that the followers of the user will have similar interests and so – in terms of Twitter – are more likely to retweet contents of that user. Therefore, we also included the following variables as controls:

- number of hashtags a tweet contains: hashtag_no
- dummy variable for whether or not a URL was included in the tweet: url
- user's number of followers: follower_no
- number of tweets the user has posted during the sample period: tweet_no

Estimation. We performed regression analysis for both the full sample and the subsample consisting of the top-30 influentials. While regression on the full sample takes into account variables constructed from automated quantitative analysis (e.g. emotion_auto), regression on the small sample included all variables compiled from manual quantitative content analysis (e.g. emotion_manual, appraisal_no).

Regression analysis on the full sample allowed us to test H1a and H2a, i.e. to examine whether the level of emotionality of a tweet is associated with how often and how fast it is retweeted. Regarding H1a, the dependent variable rt_no represents true-event count data, i.e. non-negative and integer-based. As the standard deviation (and hence the variance) of the dependent variable (rt_no) is larger than its mean in both samples (see Table 6), the analysis needs to be adjusted for overdispersion. Therefore, we applied the negative binomial regression model assuming the dependent variable to follow the negative binomial distribution (Cameron & Trivedi 1998). The resulting regression model is as follows:

$$\log(E(\text{rt\_no}|^*)) = \beta_0 + \beta_1 \text{ emotion\_auto} + \beta_2 \text{ hashtag\_no}$$
$$+ \beta_3 \text{ url} + \beta_4 \log(\text{follower\_no}) \quad (1)$$
$$+ \beta_5 \log(\text{tweet\_no}),$$

where $E(\text{rt\_no}|^*)$ is the expectation of rt_no conditional on the set of the explanatory variables on the right-hand side of the equation.

Regarding H2a, we hypothesize that emotionally charged tweets would induce retweets more quickly. Since the dependent variable rt_speed represents a continuous time unit, we applied regression analysis using ordinary least square (OLS) estimation to test H2a. To account for non-normality, we log-transformed the dependent variables before employing OLS regression.[2] The regression model is as follows:

$$\log(\text{rt\_speed}) = \beta_0 + \beta_1 \text{ emotion\_auto} + \beta_2 \text{ hashtag\_no}$$
$$+ \beta_3 \text{ url} + \beta_4 \log(\text{follower\_no}) \quad \quad (2)$$
$$+ \beta_5 \log(\text{tweet\_no}) + \varepsilon.$$

Regression analysis on the small sample was conducted to test H1a, H1b, H2a, and H2b. Note that a set of topic dummy variables and statement were included to identify potential significant effects of different topics and statements about public opinion regarding the election or about election forecasts. The (negative binomial) regression model for testing H1a and H1b is as follows:

$$\log(E(\text{rt\_no}|^*)) = \beta_0 + \beta_1 \text{ emotion\_manual} + \beta_2 \text{ appraisal\_no}$$
$$+ \beta_3 \text{ statement} + \beta_4 \text{ hashtag\_no} + \beta_5 \text{ url}$$
$$+ \beta_6 \log(\text{follower\_no}) + \beta_7 \log(\text{tweet\_no}) \quad \quad (3)$$
$$+ \beta \text{ [set of topic dummies]}.$$

The OLS regression model for testing H2a and H2b is as follows:[3]

$$\log(\text{rt\_speed}) = \beta_0 + \beta_1 \text{ emotion\_manual} + \beta_2 \text{ appraisal\_no}$$
$$+ \beta_3 \text{ statement} + \beta_4 \text{ hashtag\_no} + \beta_5 \text{ url}$$
$$+ \beta_6 \log(\text{follower\_no}) + \beta_7 \log(\text{tweet\_no}) \quad \quad (4)$$
$$+ \beta \text{ [set of topic dummies]} + \varepsilon.$$

Empirical results

Sample statistics

Table 1 shows the distribution of different formats of communication on Twitter for the full sample. About 10 percent of all tweets contain an @-sign, which is in line with previous research that has also suggested that a large fraction of @-signs are used to direct a tweet to a specific addressee (Honeycutt & Herring 2009).[4] A more conservative measure of direct communication is direct

TABLE 1 Formats of communication (full sample).

Format	# Tweets (percent)
Mention (tweet containing @-sign)	1,683 (9.5 percent)
Direct message (tweet starting with @-sign)	395 (2.2 percent)
Retweet	8,510 (47.8 percent)
URL	10,680 (60.0 percent)
Singleton	2,506 (14.1 percent)
Total	17,788

Notes: The numbers might not add up to exactly 100 percent as a tweet can be of different formats at the same time (e.g. a retweet can also contain a URL). Furthermore, retweets which also contain an @-sign are excluded from the statistics of mention and direct message.

messaging from one user to another by posting tweets that start with an @-sign. About 2 percent of the messages in our sample are direct messages indicating that some people use Twitter not only to post their opinions but also engage in interactive discussions. The share of retweets is relatively high with roughly one half of all tweets. In addition, more than half of the tweets contain a link to a website (60 percent). These numbers indicate that people tend to share content with their network of followers.

The categorization of users according to their Twitter activity is illustrated in Table 2. It shows that a few highly active users (i.e. lead users) account for a large fraction of tweets. The top 2 percent lead users contribute to almost 30 percent of all posted tweets. This is consistent with findings by Jansen and Koop (2005) and Tumasjan *et al.* (2011) who also found a large inequality of participation in political communication on Twitter.

Analysis of influentials

Figure 1 and Table 3 present the top-30 influentials identified and ranked by the sheer number of retweets triggered. It is a quite heterogeneous group of actors

TABLE 2 User activity (full sample).

User group (# tweets during sample period)	# Users (percent)	# Tweets (percent)
Infrequent (1)	3,573 (61.8 percent)	3,573 (20.1 percent)
Light (2–5)	1,619 (28.0 percent)	4,485 (25.2 percent)
Moderate (6–20)	486 (8.4 percent)	4,826 (27.1 percent)
Active (21–50)	83 (1.4 percent)	2,603 (14.6 percent)
Power (50+)	18 (0.3 percent)	2,301 (12.9 percent)
Total	5,779	17,788

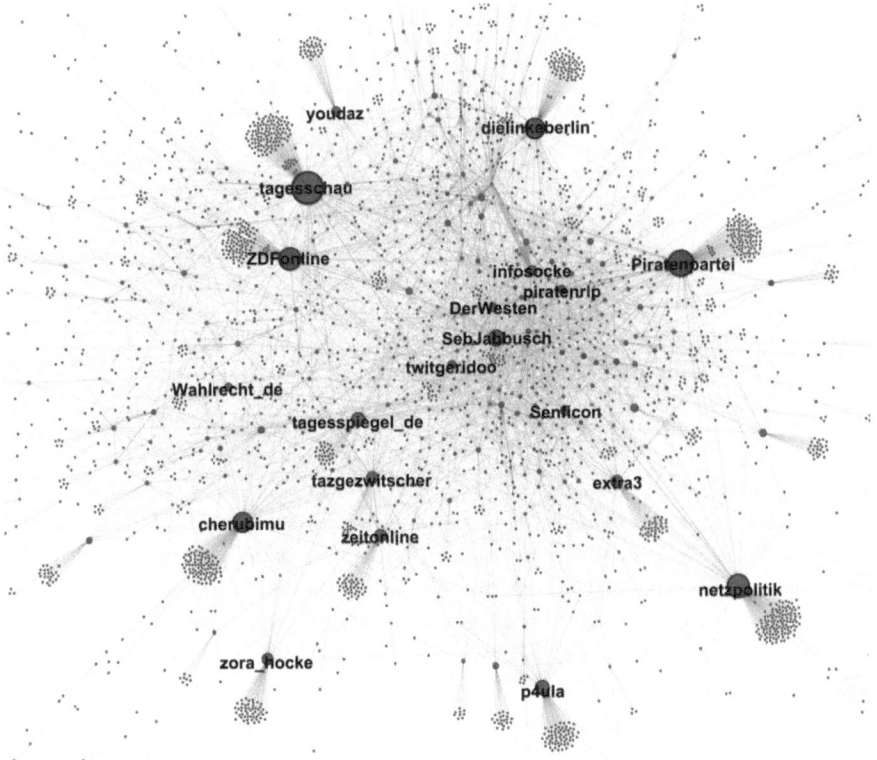

FIGURE 1   Retweet network (total sample).

regarding their background with four categories identified deductively. The first category *professional journalism* consists of 10 verified and official accounts of traditional media as well as individual professional journalists. The second category covers six accounts that have a connection to *political parties*, e.g. official party accounts or individual members of parties. Most accounts belong to the Pirate Party which, due to the fact that one of their strongest political arguments concerns open source informational politics, is not very surprising. Three citizens' groups and individual activists were assigned to the third category *civil society*. Finally, the fourth category contains *individual citizens*.

Most of the retweets were triggered by *tagesschau* (official account of the most important German newscast) with 315 retweets, followed by the official account of the Pirate Party (275 retweets). For the first time in political history, the Pirate Party actually played an important role in the election and was also active within, and relevant to, the communication flows on Twitter. The topics most occupied by them, such as Internet policy, privacy, and new opportunities of political participation, which became highly relevant during the election campaigns, soon even assumed a crucial role within Twitter communication.

TABLE 3 Top-30 influentials.

Username	Background	# Retweets triggered	# Berlin-related tweets	# Retweets per tweet (average)	# Topics	Percent emotional tweets
tagesschau	Professional journalism	315	49	6	3	–
Piratenpartei	Political party (Pirate)	275	32	9	3	9
ZDFonline	Individual citizen	218	15	15	3	–
dielinkeberlin	Political party (Left)	210	201	1	10	6
netzpolitik	Civil society	193	4	48	2	25
cherubimu	Individual citizen	169	105	2	5	60
SebJabbusch	Individual citizen	160	57	3	9	14
tagesspiegel_de	Professional journalism	120	40	3	7	–
p4ula	Individual citizen	105	1	105	1	100
infosocke	Individual citizen	100	14	7	2	7
tazgezwitscher	Professional journalism	91	11	8	2	18
zeitonline	Professional journalism	90	9	10	3	22
extra3	Professional journalism	88	1	88	1	–
zora_hocke	Political party	77	5	15	3	–
PiratenBerlin	Political party (Pirate)	69	95	1	4	–
piratig	Political party (Pirate)	69	35	2	4	11
Senficon	Individual citizen	66	5	13	2	40

Continued

TABLE 3 Continued

Username	Background	# Retweets triggered	# Berlin-related tweets	# Retweets per tweet (average)	# Topics	Percent emotional tweets
piratenrlp	Political party (Pirate)	65	15	4	3	20
youdaz	Professional journalism	64	1	64	1	100
berlinschaf	Individual citizen	62	604	0	13	10
DerWesten	Professional journalism	61	9	7	2	11
haraldmeyer	Individual citizen	59	1	59	1	100
twitgeridoo	Individual citizen	53	22	2	3	18
Wahlrecht_de	Civil society	50	4	13	1	–
flexi_bell	Individual citizen	49	15	3	3	33
dennishorn	Professional journalism	46	4	12	2	25
Linksdings	Professional journalism	45	12	4	1	–
p0litix	Individual citizen	45	35	1	6	46
A100stoppen	Civil society	43	14	3	2	7
N24_de	Professional journalism	42	5	8	1	–
Total		3,147	1,495	2	15	14
Individual citizen	Normal user	1,086	874	1	15	18
Professional journalism	Traditional media, individual professional journalists	962	141	7	8	5

Continued

TABLE 3 Continued

Username	Background	# Retweets triggered	# Berlin-related tweets	# Retweets per tweet (average)	# Topics	Percent emotional tweets
Political party	Official party accounts, individual members	765	383	2	11	6
Civil society	Citizens' groups, individual activists	286	22	13	3	9
Top-30-influentials	Top-30-accounts aggregated	3,099	1,420	2	15	13
30 non-influentials	30 non-influential accounts aggregated	48	75	1	6	15

Regarding the style of writing, in particular the emotionality of the tweet, a rather factual nonemotional way of writing by professional journalists can be observed through the quantitative content analysis. The contents of a few journalistic influential accounts, such as *tazgezwitscher* and *zeitonline*, are slightly more emotionally charged. Results show that political accounts do not have a large

TABLE 4 Distributions of appraisal-containing Twitter messages.

	Top-30 influentials	30 non-influentials
Tweets with appraisal...	770 (54.2 percent)	37 (49.3 percent)
of politicians	114 (8.0 percent)	10 (13.3 percent)
of parties	711 (50.1 percent)	31 (41.3 percent)
Appraisal direction		
more positive-appraisal tweets	274 (19.3 percent)	19 (25.3 percent)
more negative-appraisal tweets	358 (25.2 percent)	10 (13.3 percent)
mixed and unclear-appraisal tweets	138 (9.7 percent)	8 (10.7 percent)
Total	1,420	75

TABLE 5 Distribution of topics (in percent).

	Top-30 influentials (n = 1,420)	30 non-influentials (n = 75)	Civil society (n = 22)	Individual citizen (n = 874)	Political party (n = 383)	Professional journalism (n = 141)	Total (n = 1,495)
16: Election campaign (general) and political parties	61	72	27	59	62	75	62
00: Other	26	19	14	29	23	16	26
09: Social (e.g. social justice, housing, minimum wage)	4	3	–	3	7	4	4
15: Other election campaign issues	3	4	–	4	4	1	3
03: Urban highway A100	2	–	59	1	1	–	1
13: New political participation	1	–	–	0.3	2	1	1
05: Education (e.g. school reform, shortage of teachers, renovation of schools)	1	–	–	1	1	1	1
07: Internal security	0.5	–	–	0.3	1	1	0.5
10: Local traffic (Berlin)	0.4	–	–	1	0.3	–	0.4
12: Freedom of information	0.4	–	–	0.3	1	1	0.4
04: New airport in Schönefeld	0.3	1	–	0.3	0.3	–	0.3
11: Privacy	0.3	–	–	0.5	–	–	0.3
01: Privatization of municipal properties	0.2	–	–	0.3	–	–	0.2
14: Other issues of Internet policy	0.1	–	–	0.2	–	–	0.1

Continued

TABLE 5 Continued

	Top-30 influentials (n = 1,420)	30 non-influentials (n = 75)	Civil society (n = 22)	Individual citizen (n = 874)	Political party (n = 383)	Professional journalism (n = 141)	Total (n = 1,495)
02: Tempelhof Park	0.1	1	–	0.1	–	–	0.1
06: Right to vote (for not-EU-foreigners who live in Berlin permanently)	–	–	–	–	–	–	–
08: Speed limit of 30 km/h in Berlin city	–	–	–	–	–	–	–
Total	100	100	100	100	100	100	100

Note: N = 1,495.

amount of emotional tweets (0−20 percent), suggesting that professional politicians use Twitter as a channel for diffusion of information. Individual citizens, however, use Twitter as a platform to spread subjective and emotionally charged content, which also is the case for *netzpolitik* − an account of the blogger and Internet activist *Markus Beckedahl* (25 percent emotional tweets).

Results presented in Table 4 show that more than half of the tweets posted by the top-30 influentials contain appraisals of political parties or politicians (54 percent). Interestingly, the majority of the appraisals are related to political parties − more than six times more often, compared to politicians. Similar patterns can be observed when looking at the noninfluentials. However, the influentials tend to post more tweets containing negative appraisals while the opposite is the case for the noninfluentials.

We identified 16 topics in total which were regarded by the quantitative content analysis (see Table 5). Fifteen of these topics are specific election-campaign-related topics while the remaining one refers to the election campaign in general or political parties as organizations (which accounts for up to 62 percent of all tweets). The category 'other' covers all tweets that do not contain any election-campaign-related issue or information about the election in general (e.g. tweets that contain appraisals of a political party or politician).

Our analysis reveals that tweets posted by citizens' groups and individual activists (*civil society* group) mostly deal with three topics indicating a low level of thematic variety while *individual citizens* discussed up to 15 topics. Accounts of *political parties* and *individual citizens* had the highest average

TABLE 6 Summary statistics of relevant variables for regression analyses.

	Full sample		Top-30 sample	
	Mean	SD	Mean	SD
Dependent variables				
rt_no	0.73	4.63	2.73	12.13
rt_speed (in minutes)	100	613	83	463
Independent variables				
emotion_auto (scale from 0 to 8)	0.49	0.85		
emotion_manual (dummy)			0.14	0.34
appraisal_no			0.71	0.82
statement (dummy)			0.10	0.30
hashtag_no	2.29	2.24	3.11	1.91
url (dummy)	0.65	0.48	0.77	0.43
follower_no	1,361	6,730	21,124	32,164
tweet_no	4.24	14.10	48.17	116.91

numbers of topics with 4.5 and 4.4, respectively. Furthermore, *professional journalists* tweeted the most general topics and gave an overview of the election itself, whereas the other groups — as the number of topics indicated — also posted about more specific issues like the controversial discussion on the urban highway A100.

Content-related features and retweet behavior

Descriptive statistics of variables relevant for regression analysis are presented for the full and top-30 sample in Table 6.

Content-related features and retweet quantity. In H1a, we hypothesize that the higher the level of emotionality a political Twitter message exhibits, the more often it is retweeted. We estimate Equation (1) for the full sample and Equation (3) for the top-30 sample with rt_no as dependent variable and report the results in Tables 7 and 8. We find that the coefficients of emotion_auto and emotion_manual are each positive and statistically significant ($b_{\text{emotion\_auto}} = 0.11$, $p < 0.01$ and $b_{\text{emotion\_manual}} = 0.28$, $p < 0.05$).[5] This indicates that Twitter messages that feature a higher degree of emotionality indeed tend to trigger more retweets. H1a is therefore supported by our data.

TABLE 7 Negative binomial regression results (H1a – full sample).

Independent variables	Dependent variable: rt_no	
	Equation (1)	
	b	exp(b)
emotionality_auto	0.11*** (0.04)	1.12
hashtag_no	0.24*** (0.02)	1.27
url	−0.61** (0.06)	0.54
log(follower_no)	0.53*** (0.02)	—
log(tweet_no)	−0.10*** (0.02)	—
constant	−4.05*** (0.14)	0.02
Pseudo R^2	0.08	
# Observations	8,817	

Notes: *b* denotes estimated coefficient and exp(*b*) exponentiated estimated coefficient. Estimated robust standard errors are shown in parentheses.

*Significance level at 10 percent.

**Significance level at 5 percent.

***Significance level at 1 percent.

TABLE 8 Negative binomial regression results (H1a, H1b – top-30 sample).

Independent variables	Dependent variable: rt_no	
	Equation (3)	
	b	exp(b)
emotion_manual	0.28** (0.21)	1.32
appraisal_no	0.20** (0.08)	1.22
statement	0.43** (0.21)	1.54
set of topic dummies		
topic_15	1.48*** (0.34)	4.39
topic_16	−0.29* (0.17)	0.75
hashtag_no	0.10*** (0.04)	1.11
url	−0.53** (0.16)	0.59
log(follower_no)	0.17*** (0.04)	−
log(tweet_no)	−0.94*** (0.06)	−
constant	3.21*** (0.56)	24.78
Pseudo R^2	0.16	
# Observations	1,126	

Notes: b denotes estimated coefficient and exp(b) exponentiated estimated coefficient. Estimated robust standard errors are shown in parentheses. Among the set of topic dummies, only results with statistical significance are reported due to space constraints.
*Significance level at 10 percent.
**Significance level at 5 percent.
***Significance level at 1 percent.

H1b predicts a positive relationship between the number of appraisals of politicians or political parties in a political Twitter message and retweet quantity. We estimate Equation (3) for the top-30 sample and find that the coefficient of appraisal_no is positive and significant ($b = 0.20$, $p < 0.05$). This suggests that Twitter messages containing appraisal of political parties or politicians are also inclined to trigger more retweets which supports H1b.

Results regarding dummies for topics show that tweets containing other election campaign issues as their topic (topic_15) tend to trigger significantly more retweets compared to tweets with other topics while the opposite holds for tweets referring to the election campaign in general or political parties as organizations (topic_16). Furthermore, tweets containing statement on public opinion regarding the election or about election forecasts (statement) also are more likely to trigger significantly more retweets.

For both the full and the top-30 samples, the control variables hashtag_no and follower_no are each related to the quantity of retweets in a significantly

TABLE 9 OLS regression results (H2a – full sample).

Independent variables	Dependent variable: rt_speed Equation (2)
emotion_auto	−0.11 (0.06)
hashtag_no	−0.05* (0.03)
url	0.46* (0.10)
log(follower_no)	−0.11*** (0.03)
log(tweet_no)	0.05 (0.03)
constant	2.19*** (0.22)
Adjusted R^2	0.05
# Observations	1,677

Notes: The reduced sample contains only tweets which have triggered at least one retweet. Estimated robust standard errors are shown in parentheses.
*Significance level at 10 percent.
**Significance level at 5 percent.
***Significance level at 1 percent.

positive way which is in line with findings from the literature (e.g. Suh *et al.* 2010). On the other hand, there is a significant negative relationship between user activity (tweet_no) and URL inclusion (url), respectively, and retweet count. This indicates that posting activity and hyperlink inclusion does not necessarily result in a higher likelihood of being retweeted. In fact, the opposite might even hold, for example, in the light of information overload problems in social media.

Content-related features and retweet speed. H2a predicts that the higher the level of emotionality a political Twitter message exhibits, the shorter the time lag to the first retweet is. We estimate Equation (2) for the full sample and Equation (4) for the top-30 sample with rt_speed as the dependent variable (see Tables 9 and 10). Results reveal that the coefficients of emotion_auto and emotion_manual are both statistically insignificant providing no support for H2a. However, we find the coefficient of appraisal_no to be negative and significant ($b = −0.14$, $p < 0.05$) implying that tweets containing appraisals of political parties and politicians – in case they have been retweeted at least once – not only tend to be retweeted more often but also tend to be retweeted more quickly. This finding supports H2b. Results regarding dummies for topics show that tweets associated with the new airport in Schönefeld (topic_11) and privacy (topic_4) are more likely to trigger retweets more quickly. In addition, tweets containing statements on the public opinion regarding the election or about election forecasts (statement)

TABLE 10 OLS regression results (H2a, H2b – top-30 sample).

Independent variables	Dependent variable: rt_speed Equation (4)
emotion_manual	−0.03 (0.08)
appraisal_no	−0.14* (0.10)
statement	−0.65*** (0.25)
set of topic dummies	
topic_4	−1.00*** (0.31)
topic_11	−1.28*** (0.32)
hashtag_no	−0.02 (0.05)
url	0.47* (0.21)
log(follower_no)	−0.08 (0.06)
log(tweet_no)	0.30** (0.09)
constant	0.75 (0.81)
Pseudo R^2	0.14
# Observations	372

Notes: The reduced sample contains only tweets which have triggered at least one retweet. Estimated robust standard errors are shown in parentheses. Among the set of topic dummies, only results with statistical significance are reported due to space constraints.
*Significance level at 10 percent.
**Significance level at 5 percent.
***Significance level at 1 percent.

TABLE 11 Summary of findings.

Hypothesis	Description	Support?
H1a	The higher the level of emotionality (positive or negative) a political Twitter message exhibits, the more often it is retweeted	Yes
H1b	The more appraisals of politicians or political parties (positive or negative) a political Twitter message contains, the more often it is retweeted	Yes
H2a	The higher the level of emotionality (positive or negative) a political Twitter message exhibits, the shorter is the time lag to the first retweet	No
H2b	The more appraisals of politicians or political parties (positive or negative) a political Twitter message contains, the shorter is the time lag to the first retweet	Yes

also tend to be retweeted more quickly. A summary of the results of all hypotheses tests is provided in Table 11.

Conclusion

Findings

Several insights emerge from the results of this study. First, we find that the most influential accounts on Twitter in political communication can be referred to four groups: professional journalists (33 percent), political parties (20 percent), individual citizens (37 percent), and civil society groups or individual activists (10 percent). These four groups of influentials differ in expression of emotionality, appraisals, and topic variety. Compared to noninfluentials, they tend to post more tweets containing appraisals of political parties and politicians and their appraisals tend to be more negative.

Second, our results show that both emotionality and appraisals of political parties or politicians in Twitter messages are correlated with a larger retweet quantity, whereas appraisals additionally even correlate with higher retweet speed. This implies that expression of sentiment in a user's message might be another driver of information diffusion in addition to his/her potential sphere of influence in terms of the size of his/her followership network. Even if we considered only the top-30 influentials, the effect of sentiment was still significant (see Tables 8 and 10).

Research contribution and practical implications

Our study makes several research contributions. First, we shed light on how Twitter is used for political communication during election periods with specific focus on characteristics and communication behavior of influential accounts on Twitter. Second, we extend existing literature by examining the role of sentiment in terms of emotionality as well as appraisal in information diffusion in the context of Twitter. Moreover, we address the impact of sentiment on information sharing not only with respect to quantity but also to speed.

Our study has several implications. First, it is important for politicians and political parties to identify influential users, in particular individual citizens and groups related to civil society since they might be able to have an influence on political opinion-making and agenda-setting processes. More specifically, for the purpose of reputation management, political institutions are advised to analyze opinion leaders, follow the discussions among their peers, and especially detect sentiment in their content as sentiments might have viral effects in social-media communication as our study suggests. For these tasks, political parties and politicians might follow the approach of social-media analytics (Stieglitz &

179

Dang-Xuan 2012b), which has already been adopted, though to a limited degree, in a corporate context to systematically monitor and analyze user-generated content in social media for specific business purposes. Second, given the increased relevance of political communication in social media, it is also important for politicians and parties to use social media more proactively to enter into dialogs and discussions with citizens. Provided that sentiment could play an important role in information dissemination, they are encouraged to use more language that articulates emotionality or appraisals to better propagate their political issues.

Limitations and future work

It is a limitation of our study that our analysis is based on data samples restricted to a single regional political event, which might raise issues of generalizability. Future research might extend our analysis to a larger scale (e.g. longer time periods of data collection as well as other countries and languages). Furthermore, it might be interesting to see whether our findings regarding influentials and the relationship between sentiment and information sharing would also hold for other social-media platforms beyond Twitter such as social network sites or weblogs which differ in terms of design and platform concept. Finally, future works might investigate whether there is also a relationship between the sentiment of Twitter messages and the likelihood of being mentioned or directly replied to, i.e. whether sentiment might also spark more feedback or even conversations, and not only information dissemination.

Notes

1   For example, an appraisal sentence may express no emotion (e.g. 'His position in this issue is clear') and an emotionally charged sentence may express no appraisal (e.g. 'I am so happy to meet her') (see Pang & Lee 2008; Liu 2011).

2   Note that since not every tweet has been retweeted, our full sample – when it comes to testing H2a – was reduced to tweets which have triggered at least one retweet.

3   Again, note that since not every tweet has been retweeted, our small sample – when it comes to testing H2a and H2b – was reduced to tweets which have triggered at least one retweet.

4   Note that retweets which also contain an @-sign are excluded from these statistics.

5   The magnitude of the effects of the independent variables on the dependent variable can be inferred from the coefficients. However, as negative binomial regression was applied, the interpretation requires an exponential transformation of the coefficients (Cameron

& Trivedi 1998). For example, the coefficient of emotion_auto of 0.11 means that a one-unit increase in the total amount of sentiments, holding all other predictors constant, is expected to trigger 1.12 times as many or 12% more retweets ($\exp(0.11) = 1.12$).

References

Akkaya, C., Wiebe, J. & Mihalcea, R. (2009) 'Subjectivity word sense disambiguation', in *Proceedings of the 2009 Conference on Empirical Methods in Natural Language Processing*, Singapore, 6–7 August 2009, pp. 190–199.

Ammann, S. L. (2010) *Why Do They Tweet? The Use of Twitter by U.S. Senate Candidates in 2010*, [Online] Available at: http://ssrn.com/abstract=1725477 (1 December 2012).

Aral, S., Muchnik, L. & Sundararajan, A. (2009) 'Distinguishing influence-based contagion from homophily-driven diffusion in dynamic networks', *Proceedings of the National Academy of Sciences*, vol. 106, pp. 21544–21549.

Bakshy, E., Hofman, J., Mason, W. & Watts, D. (2011) 'Everyone's an influencer: quantifying influence on twitter', in *Proceedings of the Fourth ACM International Conference on Web Search and Data Mining*, 2011, Hong Kong, China, 9–12 February 2011.

Bayer, M., Sommer, W. & Schacht, A. (2012) 'Font size matters – emotion and attention in cortical responses to written words', *PLOS ONE*, vol. 7, no. 5, e36042.

Berger, J. (2011) 'Arousal increases social transmission of information', *Psychological Science*, vol. 22, no. 7, pp. 891–893.

Berger, J. & Milkman, K. (2012) 'What makes online content viral?' *Journal of Marketing Research*, vol. 49, pp. 192–205.

Bollen, J., Pepe, A. & Mao, H. (2011) 'Modeling public mood and emotion: Twitter sentiment and socio-economic phenomena', in *Proceedings of the 5th International AAAI Conference on Weblogs and Social Media*, Washington, DC, 17–21 July 2011, AAAI Press, Menlo Park, CA, pp. 450–453.

Bruns, A. & Stieglitz, S. (2012) 'Quantitative approaches to comparing communication patterns on twitter', *Journal of Technology in Human Services*, vol. 30, no. 3 & 4, pp. 160–185.

Cameron, A. C. & Trivedi, P. K. (1998) *Regression Analysis of Count Data*, Cambridge University Press, New York, NY.

Cha, M., Haddadi, H., Benevenuto, F. & Gummad, K. P. (2010) 'Measuring user influence on Twitter: the million follower fallacy', in *Proceedings of the 4th International AAAI Conference on Weblogs and Social Media*, Washington, DC, 23–26 May 2010, AAAI Press, Menlo Park, CA, pp. 10–17.

Conover, M. D., Ratkiewicz, J., Francisco, M., Gonalves, B., Flammini, A. & Menczer, F. (2011) 'Political polarization on twitter', in *Proceedings of the*

5th International AAAI Conference on Weblogs and Social Media, Washington, DC, 17–21 July 2011, AAAI Press, Menlo Park, CA, pp. 89–96.

Domingos, P. & Richardson, M. (2001) 'Mining the network value of customers', in *Proceedings of the 7th ACM SIGKDD International Conference on Knowledge Discovery and Data Mining*, San Francisco, CA, 26–29 August 2001, pp. 57–66.

Facebook (2013) *Facebook Key Facts*, [Online] Available at: http://newsroom.fb.com/Key-Facts (13 February 2013).

Farrell, H. & Drezner, D. (2008) 'The power and politics of blogs', *Public Choice*, vol. 134, no. 1, pp. 15–30.

Gaffney, D. (2010) '#iranElection: quantifying online activism', Paper presented at the 2nd WebScience Conference, Raleigh, NC, USA, 2010.

Gladwell, M. (2000) *The Tipping Point: How Little Things Can Make a Big Difference*, Little Brown, New York.

Golbeck, J., Grimes, J. M. & Rogers, A. (2010) 'Twitter use by the U.S. congress', *Journal of the American Society for Information and Technology*, vol. 61, no. 8, pp. 1612–1621.

Harris, R. B. & Paradice, D. (2007) 'An investigation of the computer-mediated communication of emotion', *Journal of Applied Sciences Research*, vol. 3, pp. 2081–2090.

Heath, C. (1996) 'Do people prefer to pass along good news or bad news? Valence and relevance of news as a predictor of transmission propensity', *Organizational Behavior and Human Decision Processes*, vol. 68, pp. 79–94.

Holsti, O. R. (1969) *Content Analysis for the Social Sciences and Humanities*, Addison-Wesley, Reading, MA.

Honeycutt, C. & Herring, S. C. (2009) 'Beyond microblogging: conversation and collaboration via twitter', in *Proceedings of the 42nd Hawaii International Conference on System Sciences*, Hawaii, 5–8 January 2009, pp. 1–10.

Hong, S. & Nadler, D. (2011) 'Does the early bird move the polls? The use of the social media tool "Twitter" by U.S. politicians and its impact on public opinion', in *Proceedings of the 12th International Conference on Digital Government Research*, College Park, MD, 12–15 June 2011, pp. 182–186.

Huffaker, D. (2010) 'Dimensions of leadership and social influence in online communities', *Human Communication Research*, vol. 36, no. 4, pp. 593–617.

Jansen, H. J. & Koop, R. (2005) 'Pundits, ideologues, and ranters: the British Columbia election online', *Canadian Journal of Communication*, vol. 30, pp. 613–632.

Joyce, E. & Kraut, R. (2006) 'Predicting continued participation in newsgroups', *Journal of Computer-mediated Communication*, vol. 11, no. 3, pp. 723–747.

Katz, E. & Lazarsfeld, P. (1955) *Personal Influence: The Part Played by People in the Flow of Mass Communications*, The Free Press, New York.

Kissler, J., Herbert, C., Peyk, P. & Junghöfer, M. (2007) 'Buzzwords: early cortical responses to emotional words during reading', *Psychological Science*, vol. 18, pp. 475–480.

Krippendorff, K. (2004) *Content Analysis: An Introduction to Its Methodology*, Sage Publications, Thousand Oaks, CA.

Kwak, H., Lee, C., Park, H. & Moon, S. (2010) 'What is Twitter, a social network or a news media?', in *Proceedings of the 19th International Conference on World Wide Web*, Raleigh, NC, 26–30 April 2010, pp. 591–600.

Larsson, A. & Moe, H. (2012) 'Studying political microblogging. Twitter users in the 2010 Swedish election campaign', *New Media & Society*, vol. 14, no. 5, pp. 729–747.

Lassen, D. S. & Brown, A. R. (2011) 'Twitter: the electoral connection?' *Social Science Computer Review*, vol. 29, no. 4, pp. 419–436.

Lazarsfeld, P. F., Berelson, H. & Gaudet, H. (1948) *The People's Choice. How the Voter Makes Up His Mind in a Presidential Campaign*, Columbia University Press, New York.

Liu, B. (2011) *Web Data Mining: Exploring Hyperlinks, Contents, and Usage Data*, Springer, Heidelberg.

Luminet, O., Bouts, P., Delie, F., Manstead, A. S. R. & Rimé, B. (2000) 'Social sharing of emotion following exposure to a negatively valenced situation', *Cognition & Emotion*, vol. 14, pp. 661–688.

Nagarajan, M., Purohit, H. & Sheth, A. (2010) 'A qualitative examination of topical tweet and retweet practices', in *Proceedings of the 4th International AAAI Conference on Weblogs and Social Media*, Washington, DC, 23–26 May 2010, AAAI Press, Menlo Park, CA, pp. 295–298.

O'Connor, B., Balasubbramanyan, R., Routledge, B. & Smith, N. (2010) 'From tweets to polls: linking text sentiment to public opinion time series', in *Proceedings of the 4th International AAAI Conference on Weblogs and Social Media*, Washington, DC, 23–26 May 2010, AAAI Press, Menlo Park, CA, pp. 122–129.

Paltoglou, G. & Thelwall, M. (2010) 'A study of information retrieval weighting schemes for sentiment analysis', in *Proceedings of the 48th Annual Meeting of the Association for Computational Linguistics*, Uppsala, Sweden, 11–16 July 2010, pp. 1386–1395.

Pang, B. & Lee, L. (2008) 'Opinion mining and sentiment analysis', *Foundations and Trends in Information Retrieval*, vol. 1, nos. 1–2, pp. 1–135.

Peters, K., Kashima, Y. & Clark, A. (2009) 'Talking about others: emotionality and the dissemination of social information', *European Journal of Social Psychology*, vol. 39, pp. 207–222.

Rainie, L., Smith, A., Lehman Schlozman, K., Brady, H. & Verba, S. (2012) 'Social media and political engagement', *Pew Internet & American Life Project*, Washington DC. [Online] Available at: http://pewinternet.org/~/media//Files/Reports/2012/PIP_SocialMediaAndPoliticalEngagement_PDF.pdf (20 January 2013).

Rimé, B. (2009) 'Emotion elicits the social sharing of emotion: theory and empirical review', *Emotion Review*, vol. 1, pp. 60–85.

Riordan, M. & Kreuz, R. (2010) 'Emotion encoding and interpretation in computer-mediated commu-nication: reasons for use', *Computers in Human Behavior*, vol. 26, pp. 1667–1673.

Rogers, E. M. (1962) *Diffusion of Innovations*, The Free Press, New York.

Romero, D., Meeder, B. & Kleinbeg, J. (2011) 'Differences in the mechanics of information diffusion across topics: idioms, political hashtags, and complex contagion on Twitter', in *Proceedings of the 20th International Conference on World Wide Web*, Hyderabad, India, 28 March–1 April, 2011, pp. 695–704.

Schenk, M. (2007) *Medienwirkungsforschung*, Mohr Siebeck, Tübingen.

Schenk, M., Jers, C. & Tschörtner, A. (2009) 'Wer ist Meinungsführer? – zur Differenzierung des Meinungsführerkonzeptes', in *Kommunikationswissenschaft. Medienrealitäten*, eds U. Dahinden & D. Süss, UVK, Konstanz, pp. 187–200.

Smith, S. M. & Petty, R. E. (1996) 'Message framing and persuasion: a message processing analysis', *Personality and Social Psychology Bulletin*, vol. 22, no. 3, pp. 257–268.

Stieglitz, S. & Dang-Xuan, L. (2012a) 'Impact and Diffusion of Sentiment in Public Communication on Facebook', in *Proceedings of 20th European Conference on Information Systems*, Barcelona, Spain, 10–13 June 2012, Paper 98.

Stieglitz, S. & Dang-Xuan, L. (2012b) 'Social media and political communication – a social media analytics framework', *Social Network Analysis and Mining*, Online First, doi: 10.1007/s13278-012-0079-3.

Stieglitz, S. & Kaufhold, C. (2011) 'Automatic full text analysis in public social media – adoption of a software prototype to investigate political communication', *Procedia Computer Science*, vol. 5, pp. 776–781.

Suh, B., Hong, L., Pirolli, P. & Chi, E. (2010) 'Want to be retweeted? Large scale analytics on factors impacting retweet in twitter network', in *Proceedings of the IEEE International Conference on Social Computing*, pp. 177–184.

Techcrunch (2012) *Twitter May Have 500M+ Users But Only 170M Are Active, 75% On Twitter's Own Clients.* [Online] Available at: http://techcrunch.com/2012/07/31/twitter-may-have-500m-users-but-only-170m-are-active-75-on-twittersown-Clients (15 January 2013).

Thelwall, M., Buckley, K., Paltoglou, G., Cai, D. & Kappas, A. (2010) 'Sentiment strength detection in short informal text', *Journal of the American Society for Information Science and Technology*, vol. 6, no. 12, pp. 2544–2558.

Thelwall, M., Buckley, K. & Paltoglou, G. (2011) 'Sentiment in Twitter events', *Journal of the American Society for Information Science and Technology*, vol. 62, no. 2, pp. 406–418.

Thimm, C., Einspänner, J. & Dang-Anh, M. (2012) 'Twitter als Wahlkampfmedium. Modellierung und Analyse politischer Social-Media-Nutzung', *Publizistik*, vol. 57, no. 3, pp. 293–313.

Tumasjan, A., Sprenger, T., Sandner, P. & Welpe, L. (2011) 'Election forecasts with Twitter: how 140 characters reflect the political landscape', *Social Science Computer Review*, vol. 29, no. 4, pp. 402–418.

Walther, J. B. & D'Addario, K. P. (2001) 'The impacts of emotions on message interpretation in com-puter-mediated communication', *Social Science Computer Review*, vol. 19, pp. 324–347.

Wattal, S., Schuff, D., Mandviwalla, M. & Williams, C. (2010) 'Web 2.0 and politics: the 2008 U.S. presidential election and an e-politics research agenda', *Management Information Systems Quarterly*, vol. 34, no. 4, pp. 669–688.

Watts, D. & Dodds, P. (2007) 'Influentials, networks, and public opinion formation', *Journal of Consumer Research*, vol. 34, no. 4, pp. 441–458.

Weng, J., Lim, E. P., Jiang, J. & He, Q. (2010) 'TwitterRank: finding topic-sensitive influential twitterers', in *Proceedings of the Third ACM International Conference on Web Search and Data Mining*, New York City, NY, 3–6 February 2010, pp. 261–270.

Yang, J. & Counts, S. (2010) 'Predicting the speed, scale, and range of information diffusion in twitter', in *Proceedings of the 4th International AAAI Conference on Weblogs and Social Media*, Washington, DC, 23–26 May 2010, AAAI Press, Menlo Park, CA, pp. 355–358.

Yardi, S. & boyd, d. (2010) 'Dynamic debates: an analysis of group polarization over time on twitter', *Bulletin of Science, Technology and Society*, vol. 20, pp. 1–8.

Index

Note: Page numbers in *italics* represent *tables*
       Page numbers in **bold** represent **figures**
       Page numbers followed by 'n' refer to notes